JEAN RACINE

RACINE IN HIS THIRTIES.
Musée de Versailles, School of Mignard. Portrait re-discovered in 1949.

JEAN
RACINE

A CRITICAL BIOGRAPHY BY
GEOFFREY BRERETON

with 8 pages of half-tone illustrations

LONDON
METHUEN & CO LTD
BARNES & NOBLE BOOKS
NEW YORK

First published by Cassell & Co Ltd in 1951
This edition reprinted in 1973 by
Methuen & Co Ltd
11 New Fetter Lane
London EC4P 4EE
and Barnes & Noble Books, New York
10 East 53rd Street
New York NY 10022
(a division of Harper & Row Inc.)
Printed in Great Britain by
Whitstable Litho, Straker Brothers Ltd

Methuen SBN 416 78400 3
Barnes & Noble SBN 06 470703 2

CONTENTS

CONTENTS

LIST OF ILLUSTRATIONS

[vi]

LIST OF PRINCIPAL DATES

1639. DECEMBER 22	Jean Racine baptized at La Ferté-Milon.
1649–58.	Pupil at Port-Royal.
1653–55.	Temporary Pupil at Beauvais.
1658–59.	At Collège d'Harcourt.
1660.	*La Nymphe de la Seine.*
1661. NOVEMBER– AUTUMN 1662(?)	At Uzès.
1663.	*Ode sur la convalescence du Roi.* *La Renommée aux muses.*
1664. JUNE 20	*La Thébaïde.* Produced by Molière.
1665. DECEMBER 4	*Alexandre.* Produced by Molière.
DECEMBER 18	Produced at Hôtel de Bourgogne.
1666. JANUARY or FEBRUARY	*Lettre à l'auteur des Hérésies imaginaires.*
1667. NOVEMBER 18	*Andromaque.* Produced at Hôtel de Bourgogne.
1668. NOVEMBER (?)	*Les Plaideurs.*
DECEMBER 11	Death of the Du Parc.
1669. DECEMBER 13	*Britannicus.*
1670. EASTER	The Champmeslé joins Hôtel de Bourgogne.
NOVEMBER 21	*Bérénice.*
1672. JANUARY 5	*Bajazet.*
1673. JANUARY 12	Enters Académie Française.
JANUARY 13 (?)	*Mithridate.*

1674.	AUGUST 18	*Iphigénie* produced at Versailles. Paris première January 1675 (?).
	OCTOBER	Becomes Trésorier de France à Moulins.
1677.	JANUARY 1	*Phèdre.*
	JUNE 1	Marriage to Catherine de Romanet.
	SEPTEMBER	Officially appointed Historiographer Royal with Boileau.
1678.	NOVEMBER 11	Birth of eldest child, Jean-Baptiste.
1679.	NOVEMBER 21	Accused by La Voisin of having poisoned the Du Parc.
1689.	JANUARY 26	*Esther* produced at Saint-Cyr.
1690.	DECEMBER	Appointed Gentilhomme Ordinaire du Roi.
1691.	JANUARY 5	*Athalie* produced at Saint-Cyr.
1692.	NOVEMBER 2	Birth of youngest child, Louis.
1696.	FEBRUARY	Appointed Conseiller Secrétaire du Roi.
1699.	APRIL 21	Death of Jean Racine.

INTRODUCTION
To The Library Reprints Edition

This book originated quite simply in a longstanding curiosity about the personality of the man who wrote plays for which I had a longstanding admiration, traceable back to undergraduate days. There was also the formidable figure of Racine's aunt, Agnès de Sainte-Thècle as she became, who seemed to me on the same simple level to represent all the frustrations and conflicts which complicated the dramatist's life. It was always obvious that there were other factors and other nuances, but that was the biographical foundation. Previous biographies, which were numerous in French, had depicted so many different and sometimes incompatible Racines that one began to wonder if any such person could really have existed. François Mauriac's *Vie de Racine*, still influential when this book was being meditated, presented a redeemed sinner and stressed the religious aspect. (It was in essence an updating of the earliest biography by Racine's son Louis, reflecting rather similar preoccupations.) In English Mr Turnell's *Classical Moment* made discreet use of the Freudian approach, to be practised later with great conviction and elaboration by the late Charles Mauron. Earlier biographies had offered a dissipated Racine, a calculating Racine and even, in the best Romantic tradition, a persecuted poet, too tender for the rough world around him. All these *personae* could be justified by actual evidence, but so selected and angled that the resulting portrait was a caricature. Meanwhile nearly all the elements of a balanced portrait were already there in Mesnard's great nineteenth-century edition of Racine's works, which contained most of the material necessary for an objective assessment. The relatively small amount of evidence and argument published since then expanded or corrected Mesnard on certain points.

My own interpretation of Racine—this book in its first edition—attempted to reconcile the creative artist with the religion-conditioned careerist who fought his way to distinction. It would be absurd to claim that the portrait was definitive (no biographical reconstruction ever can be) or that a certain number of unsolved problems did not remain. But the Racine who emerged seemed a credible personality in the context of his age, which included the theatre, the court, and the various social groupings which lay in or between them. This Racine is still the same man in all essentials that recent scholarship has recognised.

This book first appeared in March 1951; most of the writing of it was done in 1948. Around that time France saw a great renewal of studies on Racine with a strong biographical content. An early example was J. C. Orcibal's *Genèse d'Esther et d'Athalie*, whose main conclusions I feel bound to reject without undervaluing much of the incidental information it contains. At almost the exact date when my book was published M. Orcibal went on to produce in a review article virtual proof that Racine went to school at Port-Royal at the age of ten, not fifteen as had been hitherto supposed. This discovery greatly strengthens his early dependence on his aunt and the Jansenist community. Another book which appeared just before mine was Professor R. C. Knight's *Racine et la Grèce* (1950). Though not directly biographical, this thesis contains much that a biographer must ponder in assessing the influence of his formal education on the 'Hellenist' poet. Among native French scholars, some of them developing earlier research which had been delayed or obscured by the war years, M. Adam was soon to publish Volume IV (1954) of his *Histoire de la littérature française au XVIIe siècle*, which dealt extensively with Racine. M. Pommier gathered together his emendations to a number of accepted ideas in *Aspects de Racine* (1954), while in 1951-55 M. Vanuxem published articles throwing more light on Racine's association with opera. In 1955 came the late Lucien Goldmann's ambitious if questionable attempt to explain Racine's work in the light of Marxist class-theory (*Le Dieu caché*). In 1958 M. Jasinski offered various reinter-pretations in *Vers le vrai Racine*. Most important of all, M. Raymond Picard gave a new edition of Racine's works (1951-2) which now replaces Mesnard. He followed it in 1956 with *La Carrière de Racine*, the most thorough existing exposition of the material circumstances of Racine's life, backed by a solid documentation.

None of this for the most part deeply specialised scholar-ship seemed to invalidate my own general characterisation of Racine nor, on nearly all important points, my account of the facts of his life. I had already been puzzled by Racine's apparently late entry to Port-Royal (see p.4 below) and M. Orcibal's discovery confirmed my suspicions without affecting my general assessment of Racine's Jansenism. To say that the nature and effect of this in the later years of his life has become totally clear would, however, be an extravagant claim for anyone to put forward. There is also a feeling that the *Affaire des poisons* may have been overplayed by past biographers. Certainly it can be sensationalised in the manner of the *vie romancée*, but just as certainly it touched Racine in some way. Further light might be thrown by more detailed research, which to my knowledge has not yet been undertaken, into the activities of the Bouillon and Soissons groups and their relationships with Racine's patrons and associates.

Finally, there is Corneille. The idea of a rivalry, not only between two conceptions of drama, but between two clans of supporters and even between the two dramatists person-ally, has been confirmed rather than weakened by recent studies. My only doubt is whether it should be focused quite so strongly on *Bérénice* as has been done here. As for Corneille's own plays, they were described here from a strictly Racinian point of view, as partisan as that of some contemporaries. Having come to appreciate his qualities by a more careful reading of his entire work, not limited to the splendid but over-familiar Roman tragedies, I have tried to make some amends in the notes.

INTRODUCTION

In reproducing this book photographically my publishers
have allowed me to correct a number of misprints and minor
misstatements in the text. In addition, marginal asterisks
refer the reader to a new section of Notes at the end. These
correct or qualify other passages which seem in need of it
and update the book in the light of all the more significant
contributions of recent scholarship. The Bibliography, while
still highly selective, has been entirely renewed.

G.B.

1972

PART I

The Varied Prospect

CHAPTER I

BOYHOOD AND PORT-ROYAL

ON 22nd December 1639, Jean Racine was baptized in the church of Saint-Vaast at La Ferté-Milon, a small town some fifty miles north-east of Paris. From the custom of the time, it is probable that the date was very near his birthday.

He was the first child of young parents who both came of families long established in the district. His father, Jean Racine the elder, was a local official in the salt-tax office—a position which his grandfather (another Jean Racine) had also held. His mother, *née* Jeanne Sconin, was of a line which produced lawyers, small officials, and priests. On both sides, the ancestry of the future poet bound him to a provincial clan whose roots went firmly into the local earth and whose branches were more prolific than ornamental. His innumerable first and second cousins bore honest, solid-sounding names—Du Chesne, Passart, Parmentier, Chéron—and against this background of respectability the name of his distant connexion La Fontaine stands out as a rare exception. More typical of the young child's relatives were the Vitart family. Like the Sconins, they were a robust provincial stock fertile in lawyers and administrators. They were related to the future poet through his paternal grandmother, Marie (Desmoulins) Racine. One of them was to play a not inconsiderable part in his later life.

When Jean Racine was thirteen months old, his mother died in giving birth to his sister Marie. Two years later his father, after a brief second marriage, also died at the early

[2]

age of twenty-eight. The two young orphans were suc-
coured separately by the grandparents, Jean going to live
with the Racines and Marie with the Sconins. This separation in infancy might well have prevented the growth of
any intimacy between brother and sister, yet in spite of it
they remained surprisingly close. He always wrote to her
in a tone of fraternal protectiveness, had quarrelsome
meetings with her in his impatient youth, and came to
value her at last as a precious link with his uncomplicated
relatives at La Ferté. She spent the whole of her days
in her native town, uncursed by the restless fire which
descended upon her brother. Nor did she experience
the austere religious vocation which filled others of the clan.

One thing distinguished some of Racine's kin from the
generality of a middle class whose chief concern was with
material things. This was Jansenism, a Calvinistic doctrine
within the Catholic Church which taught that the wages
of sin is death and that, even without sin, a man might be
damned if he happened to miss the divine accident of grace.
At the date when Racine was orphaned the doctrine had
only recently been defined and the bitter theological dispute
which it provoked was in its opening stages. But Jansenist
theology was only the higher manifestation of an urge with
which these northern provincials were perfectly familiar:
the urge to live simply and strictly, to consider all costly
pleasures as corrupt, to fear and therefore condemn the
complications of worldliness. This philosophy of life was
embodied in concrete form in the twin religious houses of
Port-Royal, founded or reformed by the Arnaulds—a lusty
family of magistrates and theologians who enjoyed a higher
intellectual standing than the Racines and the Vitarts, but
who sprang from similar stock. Port-Royal de Paris was
primarily a convent, though at various times a school was
connected with it. Port-Royal des Champs, situated in the
Valley of Chevreuse south of Paris, formed a self-contained
community with its gardens, its fishponds, its bakery, and
its storehouses. It was peopled not only by nuns and
novices but by pious lay families, by scholars desirous of

living in retreat (among them was Pascal), and by the children of sympathizers for whom a special school was maintained. The existence of this community was continually threatened by its enemies, the Jesuits, and the history of Port-Royal through the seventeenth century is one of constant struggle against its more powerful, and finally triumphant, opponents.

The first persecution had struck Port-Royal in the year before Racine's birth. The scholars, or *solitaires*, had been obliged to flee. Three of them—Lancelot, Antoine Le Maître, and Le Maître de Séricourt—took refuge at La Ferté in the house of Racine's great-aunt, Madame Claude Vitart. The presence of the three refugees beneath her roof and, no doubt, the risk entailed in sheltering them, strengthened Madame Claude's convictions. When, after a year's exile, the *solitaires* were able to return to Port-Royal, she decided to follow them and to take her husband and five children with her.

As long as his grandfather was alive, Racine remained at La Ferté. But when he was nine, his family life was broken up a second time by his grandfather's death. His grandmother Marie Desmoulins, whom he had come to look upon as his mother, left La Ferté soon afterwards and followed her sister Claude to Port-Royal. In so doing she rejoined her own daughter Agnès, who had entered the convent as a novice some ten years before (she may have gone with the Vitarts). Now, as a young nun of twenty-three, she displayed the purest vocation of the whole family. Strangely enough, Marie Desmoulins did not take her grandson with her when she removed to Port-Royal, although the school for boys was then open and he was at an age when the *solitaires* liked to begin forming their pupils. He was sent instead as a boarder to the grammar school at Beauvais, an establishment in contact with the
* Jansenists but not controlled by them.

2

The *petites écoles* of Port-Royal had been open for some fifteen years when Racine arrived there. They represented * a bold experiment in progressive education, and as such were at the opposite pole to the traditional schools gathered under the wing of the University of Paris. These still conducted their teaching in Latin and clung as narrowly to the doctrine of Aristotle as the schoolmen of the Middle Ages. The most active and fashionable educators of the seventeenth century were the Jesuits, through whose schools passed the majority of the great men of the age, but here again the basis was Latin and the primary aim was to produce good classical scholars with a certain social polish. In contrast to both their rivals, the Jansenists taught in French and encouraged their pupils to use their own language fluently. They also found a place for Italian and Spanish and, without neglecting Latin, attached much greater importance than any of their contemporaries to Greek. This last element was decisive in Racine's intellectual formation. Had Port-Royal done nothing more than introduce him to Greek literature, it would have placed him permanently in its debt. It did, however, much more than this since it aimed at educating the whole man. By its system, under which not more than five or six pupils were grouped in the personal charge of each tutor, it developed the individual to a degree going beyond anything which even the Jesuits attempted.

The relationship between the enlightened teachers of Port-Royal and their pupils would in any case have been close. It became all the more so when the masters were dependent in times of persecution on the very families of the children they taught. Of the three *solitaires* who had been harboured by the Vitarts in the persecution of 1638, two became Racine's masters seventeen years later. One * of them, Lancelot, was a distinguished Hellenist, author of a quaintly-styled and revolutionary school-book, *The Garden of Greek Roots*, as well as of books designed to teach Latin and modern languages. The title of his Italian Course has a curiously modern ring. He called it *The New Method of Learning Italian Easily and Rapidly*. Both this and a Spanish Course were published in 1660, so it is likely enough that Lancelot was working out his " new methods " at the time when he was instructing Racine.

The second of the refugees was a man of more worldly background. In order to share in the trials and austerities of the community of Port-Royal, Antoine Le Maître had given up a brilliant career at the Paris bar. His portrait by Philippe de Champaigne shows an elegantly-dressed young man whose lively, intelligent face sports the small moustache and patch-beard of the pre-Fronde courtier. According to Louis Racine—though he is an uncertain guide on the facts of his father's life—Le Maître took a particular interest in the orphan and, noticing his quick intelligence, wished to train him for the legal career which he himself had abandoned. If the story is exact, it shows a shrewd appreciation of Racine's character. Not for this young man, Le Maître may have reflected, a life of cloistered study or obscure service. The same judgment is implicit in a letter to "le petit Racine", his "son", which Le Maître wrote when he was forced temporarily to leave Port-Royal. After asking him to send certain books from his library and to take good care of the others, he sees fit to add:

"Give my regards to Madame Racine (Marie Desmoulins) and to your good aunt, and follow their counsels in everything. Youth should always let itself be guided and endeavour not to be emancipated. Perhaps God will bring us back to the place where you are. Meanwhile, we must try to profit by this persecution and use it to detach ourselves from the world, which is so manifestly the enemy of piety."

No doubt the man who had himself felt the pull of the world had recognized the same tendency working in his pupil.

It is, however, significant that the man whom Racine remembered with most affection in later life was not Le Maître; nor was it the linguist Lancelot, nor the subtle and erudite Nicole whose strictures on the theatre were to sting the rising young dramatist into such bitter retort, nor even the Great Arnauld, the thundering theologian, who was Jansen's unbending champion for half a century. His sympathies were caught and fixed by a more humble, more human and more practical personality. When, forty years later, Racine came to make his will, he asked that he should be buried at the foot of M. Hamon, the medical officer of Port-Royal.

The traditional picture of Jean Hamon has been a little over-charged to stress his simplicity. He is shown riding round on his donkey to visit his patients, reading a book or knitting as he goes. For regular meals he never stops, but takes a crust of bread from the larder when hunger and opportunity coincide. His abnegation is proved by the fact that, on entering Port-Royal at the age of thirty-two, he sold all his possessions and gave the money to the poor. If unassuming, however, he was by no means unlearned. Before entering Port-Royal, he had been a private tutor in the eminent De Harlay family. While at Port-Royal he wrote a number of works of devotion (including a commentary on *The Song of Songs*) for the edification of the nuns whom he tended. In the gallery of Port-Royal portraits he is represented sitting book in hand against a background of other books. But for all that, he was not one of Port-Royal's major theorists on religion or education. It is likely that Racine loved him for his charity and good sense and especially for the positive view of life which his profession engendered in him.

To a young man as sensitive to environment as Racine was, and as filled with nervous vitality, there must have been something subtly repellent in the atmosphere of Port-Royal. First, the abstract theological disputes. But, much more, the odour of mortality of which he was aware as he stood in the Abbey courtyard and watched the nuns mounting the steps into the chapel. These women, dedicated to sterility in this life, were already half-engaged in the next, not only by their meditations and their continual talk of the vanity of the world, but in a more concrete, more horrible fashion. When they declared that they were of one community with their dead "saints" they did not mean it entirely in a spiritual sense, for religious minds in the seventeenth century had not yet shaken off the medieval obsession with the charnel-house. The proximity of the living to the dead had for them more literal implications than it would have for a modern, or, perhaps, for a Greek. In the three years he spent at Port-Royal Racine could hardly have avoided being present at the vigil round some member of the community who had died, or filing past the bier with the others to salute the departed sister or brother. Lancelot may have told his pupil—if not, others would do so, for it was a pious memory in the Abbey—how on the death of the Abbé de Saint-Cyran, the first Spiritual Director and implanter of Jansenism, he had dissected this body too precious to be left in a single resting-place. The entrails had gone to be interred at Port-Royal de Paris, "to satisfy the devotion of Mother Angélique". The heart was for Arnauld d'Andilly. The hands—"those pure and saintly hands which he had so often raised to God"—had been cut off and given to Antoine Le Maître, the once worldly Le Maître who was now so anxious to guard his pupil against worldliness.

Such a mental atmosphere could be equably accepted by slow, matter-of-fact minds like his great-aunt Vitart or his grandmother Marie Desmoulins, who had lived a long and full life, had given birth to eight children, had buried her husband and so many other relatives. To her the dead and the living might easily appear as one large, not uncomfortable, family. In quicker intellects and keener spirits, such as the leaders of the community or his aunt Agnès, the same traditions fed a flame of faith which purified their grossness and constantly pointed to a higher world than this. But in the mind of a sensitive adolescent they were most likely to inspire disgust. Not only the physical disgust which a modern youth would feel, but the impatience felt in any age by talent and vitality at the restraining hand of the dead and their partisans. Let his "aunt the nun" keep her

counsels for herself. Let her prate of abnegation with the
other nuns grouped like sheep round their director
Singlin. For his part, he would not renounce his right to
the world revealed through the senses.

3

Every influence in Racine's early life seemed hostile to
his development as an artist. His whole childhood was
coloured by the leaning of his relatives towards Port-Royal.
This leaning was reinforced in the most impressionable
years of his adolescence by the purposive teaching of his
masters. Even if he possessed no religious vocation, he
should at least have become a serious young pedant under
such guidance. And if he rejected Port-Royal entirely, his
only other refuge would appear to be in the stolid materialism of the rest of his family. From where did he draw the
imaginative qualities and the aesthetic sense which were
to make him one of the greatest artists of his age, and of
which his heredity and early environment were equally
barren? An obscure tendency in the mind, feeding on
every favourable accident or attracting them for its own
purpose, somehow won out in the end and ensured that
Racine should be neither a saint, a pedant, nor a lawyer—
though traces of each persisted in his character. But it was
not an easy victory. The emergence of the artist remained
in doubt for several years. At least once circumstances
almost thwarted it. It would certainly never have come
about if it had not happened to accord with Racine's over-
riding material ambition, which can be traced back to the
early death of his parents and hence to his hatred of dependence on others less close to him.

At Port-Royal, the embryo artist in him had two resources: the classical authors which his instructors unsus-
pectingly put into his hands in order to perfect his linguistic
knowledge of Greek and Latin; and then the place itself.
Not the Abbey buildings, but the woods and slopes of the
delightful valley in which the Abbey lay.

[9]

* Six months after he had arrived at Port-Royal, a victory of the Jesuit theologians in the Sorbonne had led to a temporary closing of the *petites écoles* by Royal Order (March 1656). Most of the *solitaires* were again forced into hiding, and it was during this exile that Le Maître's letter warning Racine against "emancipation" was written. Unlike most of the fifty-odd pupils, Racine had remained at Port-Royal because his kin were living there and it was the only home he had. The accident broadened his freedom at an age when no gift appears more precious. Left to his own devices, he could spend hours wandering alone about the gardens and fields of the estate. It was no doubt during this summer—in the year which had opened so memorably with Pascal's *Provinciales*—that Racine composed his first poems: the seven odes describing Port-Royal and the surrounding landscape.

The odes are usually dismissed as juvenile exercises and only noticed for a few strophes which dimly fore-shadow the choruses in *Esther* and *Athalie*. Their real interest, however, lies elsewhere. They reveal an appren-tice poet working in an idiom quite different from the idiom which he afterwards made his own. They help to show that, while at Port-Royal, Racine was not captured by Jansenism and that, surrounded though he was by examples of asceticism, his imagination remained obstinately sensuous. If a sensuous imagination is one which is most strongly stirred by outward phenomena and which meditates those phenomena for their own sake and not for their value as symbols, then Racine was first of all a sensuous writer.

The few passages in the *Promenades de Port-Royal* which have a pious context are either manifestly conventional or are given, as though instinctively, a concrete twist whenever the poet is able to introduce it. In the introductory ode Racine describes, as a good Port-Royalist must, the vanity of earthly palaces, "cemented with the blood of peoples". These will one day crumble and the grass grow over their ruins. But the contrast which he opposes is not the indes-tructible spirit, not the immortality of the simple and upright heart, but the natural beauty of the woods and fields. Long after the high towers and their masters have fallen, the gold of the harvests will remain. The poem, which opened with a tribute to the "holy dwellings of silence" of the Abbey, ends with an enthusiastic hymn to Free Nature—and without mention of a Creator.

Perhaps it was an accident. Perhaps having set out, or been instructed, to describe the landscape of Port-Royal in seven odes, Le Maître's pupil took his task literally and described the landscape. The fact remains that he had evident opportunities to include some considerations on the spiritual life at the heart of this landscape and that he neglected them, or turned from them as rapidly as possible. The nuns and novices worshipping in the chapel are *mille anges mortels*—a pure cliché; but birds building nests, or bringing insects to their young, are things to be curiously watched by the hour. The antlered stags, the enamelled flowers, the swallow skimming low over the pool "to kiss its image newly-born", are the subjects on which Racine expends his ingenuity. Over the fish-pond he takes particular pains. There are few sights more fascinating to the half-contemplative, half-observant eye than water. The changing glints and tones, the elusive movements of weeds, fish, and bubbles as they become gradually visible beneath the surface—all these delight the watcher and tempt the inexperienced artist. In paint, the result is thin and unsatisfying—precisely, watery. In words, it is even more unrealizable, but young Racine makes a serious attempt.

> *Je les vois, en troupes légères,*
> *S'élancer de leur lit natal;*
> *Puis tombant, peindre en ce cristal*
> *Mille couronnes passagères.*

A summer storm blows up and alters in a flash the whole carefully-sketched disposition of lights, bubbles, and colours:

> *Mais quelle soudaine tourmente,*
> *Comme de beaux songes trompeurs,*

[11]

Dissipant toutes les couleurs,
Vient réveiller l'onde dormante?
Déjà ses flots entre-poussés
Roulent cent monceaux empressés
    De perles ondoyantes,
Et n'étalent pas moins d'attraits
        Sur leurs vagues bruyantes
Que dans leurs tranquilles portraits.

While the epithets are often conventional and the rhyme tyrannical, it is evident that the young poet is observing with a sharp and eager eye and striving, with the imperfect instrument at his command, to render accurately what he sees. A no less striking feature of the Port-Royal odes is their richly-embroidered language. Before a sensual impression of luxuriance he responds with luxuriant words.

I come to you, fruitful trees,
Pear-trees of pomp and of pleasure,

he writes recklessly.

Je viens à vous, arbres fertiles,
Poiriers de pompe et de plaisirs,
Pour qui nos vœux et nos désirs
Jamais ne se sont vus stériles.

And having rendered the flowers and fruits of the garden with all the gusto, if not the skill, of a Bonnard painting a still-life, he writes magnificently:

Ils ont eu le lis pour berceau,
    L'émeraude est leur trône,
L'or et la poupre leur manteau.

Perhaps it is only the similarity of subject which makes us detect in Racine's immature odes on nature a faint reminiscence of Marvell. Perhaps there is only one manner of perceiving fruit, whether the perceiver is a Yorkshire metaphysical, a French classicist, or even a Cockney Romantic. They all see it, smell it, and taste it. The

[12]

luscious clusters of the vine crush their wine on the mouth of the Northern poet—a sensualist thinly disguised as a moralist. The more sentimentally sensuous Keats sees the mossed cottage-trees bending with apples and the late flowers budding for the bees to visit. Racine, incapable of this last blend of sentiment (it had not yet been born) and heir to a subtler because securer tradition of sensuality than Marvell knew, is not afraid to translate his impressions in the language of exuberant conceits.

It may not be surprising that a schoolboy with an ardent temperament should become a little intoxicated with words and should write verses in which opulent images are mixed with thin conventional phrases and occasional felicities of direct observation. But it becomes interesting when we remember that this schoolboy was Racine, then undergoing the guidance of his Jansenist tutors, and destined later to illustrate by his own poetry the theory that verse should not be highly coloured, that its images should be inconspicuous and its content rational.

Whilst at Port-Royal, Racine wrote Latin verses, either as exercises or as part of a mock-learned correspondence with his cousin Antoine Vitart who was a year older than himself and had preceded him to the Collège d'Harcourt in Paris. He may also have begun his French translation of the *Hymns from the Roman Breviary*. But if so, it was a first draft which he revised and completed many years later.

CHAPTER II

PARIS AND THE VITARTS

RACINE left Port-Royal in the autumn of 1658 and went to Paris to study at the Collège d'Harcourt. Here he spent the greater part of his twentieth year as a member of the *classe de philosophie*, which at that time constituted the Arts Course of the University. The brilliant but slightly rustic youth who had wandered among the woods of Port-Royal quickly adapted himself to the new surroundings. The Collège d'Harcourt was not Jansenist, though some members of the staff had Jansenist sympathies. It was ruled by the Latinizing tradition of the University and could not offer an intellectual equivalent to the progressive and slightly eccentric education of Port-Royal. It performed, however, the essential service of introducing Racine to the prevailing cultural tone of the day and of bringing him into contact with more polished if less pious companions. It was no inconsiderable part of his education to walk observantly through the streets of the Latin Quarter and to visit the taverns with his new friends and school-fellows. Except that his cousin Antoine Vitart was among them, their names are quite unknown and it hardly matters. Others, however, who were not students, joined them from time to time. One was the Bohemian La Fontaine who knew Racine through his La Ferté-Milon connexion and who, though nearly forty, felt perfectly at home with these young men. Another was Antoine Poignant, a soldier who conceived a great liking for Racine, his second cousin. Being about to leave for the wars, he made a will in which he named him as his heir. In the upshot, he survived cheerfully for another thirty years and died so short of cash that the heir was moved to pay off his benefactor's debts.

Others of Racine's kin took a more responsible interest in him and he was fortunate to find in Paris the Nicolas Vitart household, with which, having finished his year at the Collège d'Harcourt, he went to live. Nicolas was the elder brother of Antoine and the eldest son of Madame Claude Vitart who, now that her family had been educated and her three daughters married, had moved from Port-Royal to Paris. Here she was able to exercise her profession of midwife and to keep a sternly benevolent eye on her children and her great-nephew. Racine always referred to her as "my aunt Vitart" or "my holy aunt" in distinction to his real aunt, Agnès, who was "my aunt the nun". He found the company of Madame Claude's son more congenial and the world in which he lived incomparably more interesting than hers. Nicolas Vitart had become the intendant of the Jansenizing Duc de Luynes and occupied quarters in the Hôtel de Luynes on the Quai des Grands Augustins. With the young wife whom he had recently married, and the officials, servants, and clients who came and went in the great household, he provided a warm human background for Racine's serious introduction to the world.

The Nicolas Vitart whom we see in Racine's letters is a thoroughly sympathetic character. He is a robust and businesslike man in the middle thirties, constantly occupied with the administration of his master's estate, riding to Chevreuse to supervise work on the Duke's country house, to La Ferté to visit his relations. Indeed, he is often on horseback—except on the day when he discovers too late that he has lent his riding-boots and allows his wife to dissuade him from setting off without them through eight leagues of December mud. He is loyal to Port-Royal, to which he owes his position, but without bigotry, and certainly without puritanism. He has connexions with the Court and with men of letters and takes an interest in the

scandalous world of the theatre. He supports enthusiastic-
ally his young cousin's literary ambitions and is cultivated
enough to have Latin quoted to him, although, on the
negative evidence of Racine's letters, he does not possess
the more fashionable knowledge of Spanish and Italian.
Perhaps if he had kept a diary, it would have been not
unlike that of Samuel Pepys, his approximate contemporary.

The Vitart couple, soon reinforced by the children who
are regularly ushered into the world by Madame Claude,
constitute the first normal domestic circle that Racine has
known. Until then, he had lived only with an old couple,
then with spinsters and bachelors. He watches with
admiration the lively young wife, tries teasing her and finds
she has a quicker wit than he, tries to flirt with her as he
sees other people doing and gets his ears boxed for his pains.
She was a Marguerite Le Mazier, and she came of a family
prominent in Parisian legal circles. Her marriage certificate
describes her as "a daughter of the honourable and discreet
person M. François Le Mazier, sometime attorney at law,
and of Marguerite Passart". When the still-distant time
came for Racine to settle down, a wife was provided for
him also from the Le Mazier stock. Marguerite Vitart
became the godmother of his first child.[1]

The Hôtel de Luynes of which Nicolas Vitart was the
deputy ruler was a court in miniature. Racine's place in
it is ill-defined, but he seems to have justified his presence
by assisting his cousin as a clerk. There was no rigorous
line drawn between the Vitart family and the lesser retainers
and hangers-on. Among the familiars were a M. l'Avocat,
who was a precisian in matters of literature and socially
something of a snob (Racine remarks that no prison is
worthy of him but the Bastille—"for a man of his consequence could only be a prisoner of State"), M. d'Houy, a

---

[1] According to the custom of the time, she is always referred to as
"Mademoiselle" Vitart. "Madame" was a courtesy title reserved for
noble birth or for women whose age earned them greater formal respect.
It did not necessarily imply marriage any more than "Mademoiselle"
necessarily implied celibacy.

humble copyist whom Racine tyrannizes ("M. d'Houy will copy my ode in the morning"—"M. d'Houy is drunk"—"Since I am out of reach you can slap my lieutenant M. d'Houy instead"), and a tantalizing list of female names of which little can be told except that their owners were all in love with the brilliant, the facile Le Vasseur.

This young priest—he was a society abbé of a type which became more prominent in the eighteenth century—was all that Jean Racine would have given his right hand to be. He makes a strange figure in a nominally Jansenist circle. Lightly erudite, a natural connoisseur of the new trends of poetry, pirouetting gracefully between the salon, the spa, and the stage-door, he is liked by men and adored by women, whom he seduces with the easy charm of the man-about-town-and-court. This at least is how he appears to the eyes of Racine which, it must be confessed, are slightly a-goggle. But it is undeniable that he had an easy way with him and—what was more important—an up-to-the-minute taste in literature. He provided the whetstone on which Racine could sharpen his verses, and the correspondent to whom he could write both more freely and more technically than to Vitart.

2

With Le Vasseur as a guide and Vitart as an ally, Jean Racine made his first attempts to obtain advancement by his pen. A year in Paris had been enough to show him that patronage was the surest road open to any man who hoped to distinguish himself in literature, and he saw but few established writers in any genre who were not supported by a royal or noble patron. Early in 1660, he tried to attract the notice of Cardinal Mazarin by a sonnet celebrating the triumphant conclusion of the Peace of the Pyrenees. The sonnet failed in its objective and brought down upon its author's head the displeasure of Port-Royal, which looked upon Mazarin as one of its bitterest enemies. Undeterred, Racine continued his search for a patron by aiming his next shaft at the highest of them all. In early

September of the same year he composed an ode on the marriage of Louis XIV, who had just ridden into Paris with his Spanish bride after long months spent on the frontier and in the slow journey back through the western provinces.

The sonnet to Mazarin has been lost, but the ode, *La Nymphe de la Seine*, survives to show how thoroughly the young poet had absorbed the lesson which such judges as Le Vasseur had taught him. As poetry, it is smooth and almost featureless, though here and there the grandiloquence which characterized the Port-Royal odes breaks out. Gone, however, is all their naïveté, and gone, too, their direct observation. If Racine saw the royal bride at all before writing in praise of her beauty, no hint of it appears in his verse. It was, in fact, better that he should not see the plump little Marie-Thérèse in order that his imagination might be more free to idealize her charms. The poetic prescription which he was following required him to be as abstract as possible and to handle classical allusions with grace and skill. In this convention, his ode was a notable success.

Nicolas Vitart acted as a kind of impresario. He knew, or obtained an introduction to, Chapelain, who, as an elder poet with an overblown reputation, acted as the official taster of literature. On his recommendations the royal bounty depended. He made periodical reports on the state of French literature to Colbert, who kept the purse. If the resultant pensions-list was headed:

"To Chapelain, greatest poet in the world, 3,000 *livres*", other talents were generously rewarded also.

Prompted by a sound sense of realities and more openly enthusiastic than the author himself, Vitart carried the poem to Chapelain. Chapelain delighted him by remarking:

"The ode is very fine, very poetic, and there are many stanzas which could not be better. If he revises the few passages which I have marked, it will make a very fine piece."

He ended the interview by pressing Vitart to bring the young poet to see him.

On leaving Chapelain, Vitart was unable to resist calling on another acquaintance, Charles Perrault. He also enjoyed a considerable reputation, but Racine prized his opinion less than Chapelain's and had been against consulting him. Perrault also praised *La Nymphe de la Seine* and in his turn suggested a number of improvements. He took particular exception to the comparison of the royal bride to Venus, since that goddess, he observed, was nothing better than a prostitute. This consideration, which seems curious to us, also startled Racine. The gods, he protested to Le Vasseur, are surely covered by a poetic convention, according to which they can do no wrong. If one started a factual examination of their records, they would all deserve to be burnt.[1] And then what would become of poetry?

He also chewed upon, but accepted, an objection raised by Chapelain against the introduction of Tritons into the River Seine. Tritons, it appeared, were found only in salt water. Racine was obliged to re-write an entire stanza. "Several times I have wished they had all been drowned for the trouble they have given me."

The young writer already realized that the literary game had rules. Unless he found them too outrageous, he grumbled but obeyed. If he shows a certain impatience under criticism at this early point in his career, it is by no means excessive. On the contrary, he bows in a reasonably docile manner to the opinions of more experienced, if not wiser, heads. Yet he does this without real subservience, seeing clearly enough what he is doing.

"These were the words of M. Chapelain," he writes privately to Le Vasseur, "I will repeat them to you as though they were the text of the Gospel, changing nothing.

[1] Sixteen years later he was to put a similar reflexion into the mouth of Oenone:

> Les dieux mêmes, les dieux de l'Olympe habitants
> Qui d'un bruit si terrible épouvantent les crimes
> Ont brûlé quelquefois de feux illégitimes.

PHÈDRE, Act IV, Sc. vi

[19]

And then again, *he is M. Chapelain*, as M. Vitart kept saying at the end of each sentence.''

In due course he was rewarded with a grant of one hundred *louis* from the funds which Colbert administered.

3

The only important ladder to literary success which did not depend on patronage was the theatre. The acceptance of a play was a matter of direct arrangement between the author and the comedians, who were concerned solely with its chances of drawing the public. They paid the author a proportion of the receipts, though for a first play the proportion was small and was sometimes omitted altogether. The number of new plays required each year was limited and there were more than enough established dramatists to supply them. Nevertheless, Racine was determined to try his hand.

In the summer of 1660 he completed a tragedy entitled *Amasie* which he submitted to the company of the Marais, one of the two established theatres in Paris. (The third, Molière's, was still struggling to consolidate its position.)

A few days, or at the most weeks, before Chapelain was shown *La Nymphe de la Seine*, Racine and his two supporters organized a small campaign to secure the play's production. While the Abbé Le Vasseur engaged the interest of Mlle. Roste, an actress of the company, Racine, accompanied by the faithful Vitart, called on the *orateur* of the troupe and read his composition to him. The *orateur*, who also acted as manager, was a certain Laroque. He appeared delighted with the *Amasie*, but asked if he might keep the manuscript by him for a few days to study it more carefully. Racine and his sponsors returned to the Hôtel de Luynes in high spirits, feeling confident that their combined manoeuvre had succeeded.

How great was Racine's disappointment when at the beginning of September he received a letter from Laroque criticizing the play unfavourably and regretting that he could not produce it. At the first shock he was inclined to suspect some covert motive for the rejection.

"I do not know with what intention Laroque has shown this change of front. M. Vitart gives several possible reasons, and does not despair. But for my part, I am afraid that the actors nowadays are only interested in balderdash, provided that it is signed by some great author."

The success of his ode, which followed immediately after, partly compensated him for this setback. In a calmer mood he must have recognized the soundness of Laroque's judgment, for he dropped the *Amasie*, which has disappeared without trace. But he never took the Marais another play.

In the following year he began to work on a project for the rival theatre, the Hôtel de Bourgogne, to which he planned to give a tragedy based on the *Amores* of Ovid. His contact this time was the actress Madeleine de Beauchâteau whom, as familiarity grew, he nicknamed *la déhanchée*, the * waddler. But in June 1661 he was still awed by her and reported to Le Vasseur that "in a letter which I sent her yesterday I called her the second Julia of Ovid".

The Beauchâteau was one of the more cultured actresses of the time and was in her forties when Racine made her * acquaintance. With her husband, François de Beauchâteau, she had had long professional experience at the Hôtel de Bourgogne. But she was a sound rather than a brilliant actress, and in all her career rarely played a leading part. She made up for her mediocrity on the stage by a reputation for taste and intelligence and had the further compensation of producing, among her six or eight children, one infant prodigy. This was her son Etienne who, at the age of twelve, published a collection of verses styled *The Lyre of Young Apollo or the Nursling Muse of the Little de Beauchâteau*, in which a long list of potential patrons were praised in youthful numbers. The book did for its author what Racine's sonnet had failed to do for him: it earned a grant of 1,000 *livres* from Cardinal Mazarin. In later life the little de Beauchâteau went altogether to the bad—according to Boileau—and finished by emigrating either to the colonies or to England and becoming a Protestant clergyman. We have not succeeded in tracing him further.

The mother of such a child could easily be persuaded to interest herself in a young and promising writer like Jean Racine. She seems to have taken considerable pains with him. She, or another member of the company, almost certainly proposed the subject—which acquits Racine of a monumental folly. She went carefully over his first plan and made a number of suggestions for its improvement. Accepting these, Racine returned to the Hôtel de Luynes and wrote out an entirely new draft in which he incorporated all the hints she had given him.

These details, which Racine himself gives in his correspondence with Le Vasseur, are interesting for two reasons. First, they show that he had grown wiser since the day he had walked into Laroque's room and declaimed his finished tragedy to a producer who had not asked for it. He knew now that, if he hoped to see his play acted, it was best to collaborate from the start with the people of the theatre. Secondly, he had hit, as early as this, on the method of working which he was to follow throughout his career as a dramatist. The action was planned first, in careful detail, and only when that was done did he begin writing the dialogue.

"I have made a fine plan", he writes to Le Vasseur, "of all that my child [the play on Ovid] is to do; his actions being properly ordered, it will be easy after that for him to say fine things."

That this remained Racine's constant practice is indicated by a sketch, found among his papers after his death, for the first act of an unwritten tragedy, *Iphigénie en Tauride*. In this, the exits and entrances are clearly disposed and the actual speeches of the characters are summarized in prose. Such instances illustrate the significance of the famous remark attributed to Racine: "My tragedy is done. Now I have only to write it."

His second experiment in play-writing was not brought to a conclusion. More urgent affairs may have interrupted him. He was ill for a time in the late summer or autumn. By November he had left Paris and was beyond the reach of Mademoiselle de Beauchâteau's encouragement. Nothing more was ever heard of the "fine plan" which he had drawn up with her help.

But someone at the theatre was more persistent than he. They had decided that the Loves of Ovid would appeal to the public and they clung to their inspiration. Two years later the red play-bills of the Hôtel de Bourgogne announced a *pastorale* in five acts by the minor playwright Gilbert. Its title was *Les Amours d'Ovide* but there is no record of its success.

4

These excursions into literature could hardly be kept secret from Port-Royal, though Racine felt it important that they should be. While revising *La Nymphe de la Seine* in the light of Chapelain's recommendations, he had felt badly in need of a second opinion on the changes he had made. Le Vasseur was away temporarily in the country, Vitart was occupied. The haughty M. l'Avocat had been consulted already on the original version, and "he hates to read a piece more than once, however good it is". At his wit's end, Racine was about to ask the opinion of an old serving-woman, when he remembered in the nick of time that she was a Jansenist like her master, the Duke. She might betray him, "and that would mean my complete ruin, for I still receive every day letter upon letter, or rather excommunication upon excommunication, because of my unfortunate sonnet".

From whom in particular did these "excommunications" come? Not from Antoine Le Maître, for he was now dead. Hardly from the mild Hamon or from Racine's homely grandmother. More probably they were written by his aunt Agnès, or by Lancelot or the disputatious Nicole, or even by all three in turn. All of them would have felt as a betrayal his attempts to win patronage from their adversary. But when he followed this with an approach to the playhouses, which they regarded with genuine horror, their sorrow and their anger can have known no bounds. Just as they were entering on a new period of tribulation—the worst that they had so far experienced—one of their most brilliant pupils was defying their teaching and courting the enemy.

No less understandable was Racine's resentment against the people who seemed to be doing their best to hold him back from success. They could ruin his prospects by denouncing him to the Duc de Luynes—at this stage Racine regarded de Luynes merely as a crushing weapon in the hands of Port-Royal; he had not yet perceived the advantages which might come from the patronage of such a powerfully-connected nobleman—or perhaps he was too bewildered to look for them. On the other hand, what could Port-Royal do for him if he submitted? They had, presumably, made it easier for Vitart to introduce him into the de Luynes household. But what more could he hope for? Of what use were his education and his talent if he was to remain a petty official in a great house?

Highly ambitious and conscious of his own great gifts, young Racine could not accept so humble a future. What followed was inevitable.

Behind the great de Luynes's back he stuck out his tongue at him, blasphemously nicknaming him 'the Holy Spirit'. (It was a joke which he shared with Le Vasseur and with Mademoiselle Vitart, but apparently not with Nicolas Vitart.) Much worse, because it touched people closer to him when they were in distress, he mocked his great-aunt Vitart for her concern at the new persecution of Port-Royal. The nuns of the Paris house had refused to sign the formula of submission devised by Pope Alexander VII and had been driven from their convent. In the midst of this persecution the Abbess Angélique, founder and pillar of the community, died. At Port-Royal des Champs, the *petites écoles* were closed for good; the *solitaires* were dispersed; and the nuns' beloved director, Singlin, hunted by his enemies, lay in hiding in the house of one of the ever-generous Vitarts.

At this apparently desperate moment in the community's history, Racine writes to Le Vasseur:

"I am going this afternoon to call on Madame our holy aunt [Madame Claude Vitart], who was looking for no further joy since the loss of her holy father—or, as M. de Gomberville called him, her future spouse [Singlin]. Indeed he is no longer on the throne of St. Augustine and he has avoided, by a prudent retreat, the displeasure of receiving a *lettre de cachet* sending him to Quimper. The seat was not vacant for very long. The Court—without, it seems, consulting the Holy Spirit—has elevated to it a certain M. Bail . . . No doubt you know him and perhaps he is one of your friends. On the creation of this new pope, the whole consistory seceded. They have withdrawn to various points and continue to rule themselves by the edicts of M. Singlin, who is now considered as the anti-pope. *I will smite the shepherd and the sheep shall be scattered abroad.* This prophecy has never been more perfectly fulfilled, and of the whole multitude of *solitaires*, only M. Guays and Maître Maurice are left."

The passage is part of a letter written by one bright and cynical young man to another bright and cynical young man whom he desires to impress. His delight in his own wit has no doubt carried him beyond his real feeling. Yet this does not completely explain the cutting irony of his language. There seems no doubt that now, less than three years after he had left it, Port-Royal rankled painfully in Racine's mind. His exasperation would grow until there appeared to be no common ground left.

5

Racine's attack on Singlin was made in June 1661, in the same letter in which he spoke of his work on *The Loves of Ovid*. During the remainder of the summer it became clear to his relatives that he was wasting his time in Paris. He was making undesirable acquaintances and incurring debts which he had no good prospect of paying off. He must at all costs be established in some respectable employment.

It was decided that it would be an excellent thing if he could obtain a benefice. With all the bishops of the kingdom against them, Port-Royal could not help him here, and, for the time being, the Vitarts had done their share. But his mother's family, the Sconins, who were not Jansenists, had good ecclesiastical connexions. They offered, or were persuaded, to come to the rescue. One of his uncles in the north vaguely and somewhat grudgingly arranged the preliminaries. A second uncle, Antoine Sconin, agreed to substantiate the project. As a canon and Vicar-General of the diocese of Uzès in Languedoc, he enjoyed considerable influence which he was willing to use on his nephew's behalf.

CHAPTER III

UZÈS

HIS hopes and spirits high, Racine set out at the
end of a bright October to join his uncle in the
south. He rode on horseback as one of a cheerful
troop of travellers who had joined forces in
Paris for greater safety on the roads. Among them were
two of the King's Musketeers, two of his Secretaries, some
Italians, and an Englishman.

Italians were common enough as both visitors and
residents in the France which had been virtually ruled by
Mazarin for the best part of twenty years. Although the
Cardinal had died that spring, their cultural influence
remained, too firmly rooted to depend on political considerations. The ambitious inhabitants of the Peninsula
still found a ready market for their talents among the
prosperous and slower-witted French. Benefiting indirectly
by the vast cultural prestige of Ancient Rome, they set the
modern tone in artistic matters: in painting, architecture,
music, and partly in literature. On the other hand they
preserved, through the freebooting Italian families which
had intermarried with the French aristocracy, a certain
tortuous influence which went well with their reputation
for decadence.

As for the Englishman, he may have been a merchant on
his way to Lombardy to deal in cloth, or a gentleman
touring the Continent as Evelyn had done a few years
earlier, or even a Papist bound on a secret mission to Rome.
For now that the Antichrist Cromwell was dead and the
Stuarts had recovered their throne, Rome was beginning to

look towards the northern island with a renewal of hope. But whatever the English traveller's business, he certainly disapproved of the conduct of the exuberant young Frenchman. Every evening, when they were about a league from their destination, the young man would clap spurs to his horse and disappear in a cloud of dust. When the rest of them arrived half an hour later, there the fellow would be sitting at the inn table before a mug of wine, having bespoken the best bed for himself, and showing by his triumphant grin that he was in no way ashamed of his behaviour.

At Lyons the company broke up. Racine joined forces with the Musketeers and between them they hired a boat to take them down the Rhône. Since the autumn had been dry the river was low and the current which travellers so much dreaded was less dangerous than usual. Nevertheless they took the precaution of chartering the best craft and skipper that they could procure. Two days on the Rhône brought them to Pont Saint-Esprit, where Racine disembarked to make his way overland to Uzès.

Beyond noting their professions or nationalities, he seems to have paid little attention to his fellow-travellers. He was more interested in the changing scenery and in the struggles with the Provençal language which soon confronted him. These inspired a cheerful letter which he wrote on arrival to his friend La Fontaine:

"After Lyons I almost ceased to understand the language of the country or to make myself understood. At Valence things grew worse, and God so willed it that, having asked the servant for a chamber-pot, she put a chafing-pan under my bed. You can well imagine the sequel of this unfortunate episode and what can happen to a sleepy man who uses a chafing-pan for his night necessities. But at Uzès it is even worse. I swear that I have as much need of an interpreter here as a Muscovite would have in Paris. Nevertheless I am beginning to see that the jargon is a mixture of Spanish and Italian and, as I have a tolerable acquaintance with both those languages, I sometimes use them to understand what is being said to me, and to make myself understood.''

Still in exuberant vein, Racine cannot resist giving his impressions of the women of the province:

''I had heard them highly commended in Paris,'' he observes, ''but all I had been told was nothing compared to what they are really like—both in number and excellence. There is not a village girl, not a cobbler's daughter, who could not dispute the palm with the most famous beauties of the Court. If the landscape were a little more delicate and the rocks a little less numerous, it would be a true country of Cythera. *All* the women are dazzling and they dress in a fashion which suits them like a charm. As for their persons:

'' *Color verus, corpus solidum et succi plenum.*[1]

'' But as this is the first thing I have been warned to beware of, I will say no more about them. Also, I should be profaning the incumbent's house in which I am if I made a longer discourse on this matter. *Domus mea, domus orationis* —my house is a house of prayer. So you must not expect to hear any more from me on the subject. I have been told: Be blind. If I cannot be quite blind, at least I can be dumb, for—you understand—I must be ecclesiastical with the ecclesiastics just as I have been a wolf with you and the other wolves, your brothers. *Adiousias.*''

The letter he writes to Vitart is concerned with more serious matters, but here also a note of youthful optimism predominates. He is delighted with the welcome given him by his uncle, Canon Antoine Sconin, who would in fact have sent his horse and valet to meet him at Pont Saint-Esprit had not his other uncle, Dom Cosme, bungled matters by writing to say that he would not arrive until two days later. Now that he is at Uzès, his hopes of a benefice run high. Canon Sconin has already taken him to see the pleasant new presbytery which he has built outside the town to house the incumbent of a living which belongs to him. Perhaps the nephew cannot aspire to this just yet,

---

[1] The complexion good, the figure firm and full of freshness.

nor to such a plum as the benefice held by the Dean of the Chapter, which is worth 5,000 *livres* a year. Yet the old man is seventy-five and a particular friend of Canon Sconin. Meanwhile, the Canon wants him to begin his theological studies and is ready to take him to Avignon to be tonsured just as soon as Dom Cosme in the north forwards the necessary authorization from the Bishop of Soissons, in whose diocese Racine's native parish of La Ferté-Milon lay.

There seems no reason why his hopes should not quickly mature. His uncle Antoine is Vicar-General of the diocese of Uzès. He is an influential member of the Chapter, whose affairs he administers. Eight years' residence at Uzès have given him an excellent understanding of the intricate world of the cathedral, with its cliques and rivalries. He knows the importance of enlisting the highest authority of all on his nephew's behalf. Monseigneur Jacques Adhémar de Monteil de Grignan is a power in the district not only because he is Bishop of Uzès but by virtue of his family connexions. His brother is Archbishop of Arles. His nephew—the secular head of the family—is Lord-Lieutenant of Languedoc and will be welcomed with delight when, seven years later, he approaches Madame de Sévigné with a request for her daughter's hand. The de Grignan family, by reading the signs of the times and substituting suppleness for defiance in their dealings with the throne, have to a certain extent assumed the local authority lost by the stiffer-necked Dukes of Uzès. They nurse their position by frequent visits to the Louvre and Versailles, for even prelates feel safer after paying their court to the energetic young king and his advisers, while to the secular aristocrat it is essential.

The parallel between a powerful ecclesiastic waiting upon His Majesty and an unknown young man, tainted with Jansenism, endeavouring to catch the eye of the same ecclesiastic, is so wide that it can never have occurred to Canon Sconin to draw it. Inevitably, however, he follows the same system on his more humble level. He had prepared the ground by sending to the Bishop a copy of his nephew's ode on the King's marriage, explaining as he did so that the poem had won very favourable opinions at Court, including the approval of no less a critic than M. Chapelain.

We do not know what Monseigneur de Grignan thought of *La Nymphe de la Seine*, or whether he even read it, but the fact that he had accepted a copy was almost as important as his opinion upon it. On arrival at Uzès, Jean Racine finds that his reputation as a poet has preceded him. The whole Chapter are anxious to read the verses which have been so graciously filed in the Bishop's secretariat. Racine asks Vitart to send him any copy of the ode that he can lay hands on, but before dispatching it to be careful to cut off the margins. Perhaps he is afraid that some comment by Perrault or Le Vasseur, or some counter-comment of his own, might by inadvertence shock the pious canons. But he needs the ode. His uncle wishes to show it to his friend the Dean of the Chapter. He wants it himself to maintain his prestige in this small but polished society. With what extravagant grace they bow to him, with what more-than-Italian courtesy they compliment him in long speeches of which he does not understand a word. Surrounded by so much smooth and garrulous civility, he is very conscious of his gawky northern manners. All he can do is to bow in return and utter the only word of Provençal he ever seems to have learnt: *Adiousias*. His ode, if he had it, would furnish tangible proof that he is not "uncivil or unlettered". With it to stay him over, he might acquire in time some of the graces necessary for a man not to pass for a boor in Uzès, " where I assure you", he writes to Vitart, "people have more refinement than anywhere else in the world".

Racine's respect for this provincial urbanity presents a curious contrast with the impressions formed by other travellers from Paris at much the same date. Thus, Molière's friend Chapelle who, in collaboration with Bachaumont, published a *Voyage en Languedoc et Provence* in 1656, saw in the cultured circles of Montpellier only a ridiculous aping of Parisian manners. The Abbé Fléchier, in his account of a journey through the Auvergne in 1665, was chiefly struck by the simpering silliness of the local literary ladies.[1] These travellers judge the southern refinement with a contemptuous smile. But Racine has not yet climbed to a height from which he can look down with amusement at the antics of the provincials. He has seen culture and fashion in the capital, but has not yet made them his. He is so far from feeling himself a Parisian man-of-the-world that he is dazzled by the Uzétiens and almost despairs of ever rising to their level. Such, at least, are his first reactions.

2

During the first few weeks, the business of the benefice appears to be making good progress. Canon Sconin is friendly and active on behalf of his nephew, who plays his part of an aspirant to holy orders with a nice discretion. He goes to Nîmes with a reverend father of the Chapter to see a firework display in honour of the Dauphin's birth. Many are the lovely faces momentarily revealed by the flashes of the fireworks, but Racine, crushed in the crowd beside his severe companion, keeps his eyes downcast like any well-drilled seminarist. Had he been alone, and dressed like a gallant instead of in the suit of black Spanish cloth which his uncle buys him at the cost of twenty-three *livres*, it is still doubtful whether he would have dared to approach the full-blooded southern beauties. The Latin compliment, "by a gallant of the time of Nero", which he imagines as a suitable entry into conversation, is pure literature. In describing the temptations to which he has been exposed at the firework display, he is writing to Le Vasseur the things which he thinks Le Vasseur will appreciate. His proclivity to amorous adventure seems as imaginary—or at least as exaggerated—as the memory of his escapades with La Fontaine. All his correspondence of this period bears the mark of inexperience in affairs of the heart, but a much surer grasp of business matters.

[1] *Mémoires sur les Grands-Jours d'Auvergne.*

The first flush of optimism passes. Racine never doubts that his uncle is doing his utmost for him, but to secure a benefice with a good stipend proves a more complicated matter than he had supposed. Before he has been three months in Uzès, a note of uncertainty appears in his correspondence. And with his first doubt of success in business comes a feeling of revulsion against the climate and people of Languedoc.

The delicious southern winter which inspired him to write the limpid line: *Et nous avons des nuits plus belles que vos jours*, changes within a week to rain and mud. The polished jewel of Uzès is transformed into a wet, windy, provincial town on a hill. And with it, the inhabitants undergo a change.

"This is the most accursed town in the world," he writes to Vitart (24th January 1662). "They spend their whole time killing each other or getting themselves hanged. The place is full of police officers. That is why I avoid making any acquaintance, since by making one friend I should make a hundred enemies. But do not think that I have not been invited time and again, or that they have not been to beg me—unworthy me—to join their companies. For my ode has turned up in the salon of a lady of the town, and people have been calling here to see the author. But all to no purpose. I refuse to go out."

Ten days later his opinion has hardened still further. He writes to Le Vasseur:

"I am shut up in a country somewhat less sociable than the Pontus Euxinus. Common sense is rare here, constancy is entirely lacking; you do not know whom to trust. A quarter of an hour's conversation is enough to make you detest a man, so hard and selfish are hearts in this town. They are all bailiffs. And so, although they have been a hundred times to invite me to go into company, I have so far been out nowhere. In short, there is no one for me here."

The honeymoon phase is over. Henceforth Racine will approve of only two things at Uzès: his uncle's generous nature and the climate—which soon afterwards picks up and produces green peas and roses as early as March.

What has happened? It is unlikely that he has been disillusioned in any newly-formed personal friendship. His own words show that he has received no social rebuff. Unfavourable though the conclusion is to Racine, one is driven to suppose that his general disgust with people and things springs from the frustration of his hopes of a benefice. Evidently he has over-estimated his uncle's influence. Other interests, other candidates are working obscurely against him. The Bishop seems to be deaf to his Vicar-General's hints and has said nothing that could be construed as a word in the young man's favour. To crown all, Dom Cosme still delays sending the letters dimissory from the Bishop of Soissons. Should a living be offered which could only be held by a priest in orders, Racine would not be in a position to take it.

By the end of April he is still more depressed. The Bishop, deciding to handle his prickly Chapter of 'reformed' canons with velvet gloves, has surrendered to them his right of appointing new incumbents and with it has virtually gone the influence of his Vicar-General. These developments in diocesan policy make it impossible for Racine to expect anything better than some chapel worth twenty or twenty-five crowns a year. "As though that was worth all the trouble I am taking!"

"Nevertheless," he continues to Le Vasseur, "I am resolved to go on leading the same life, and to stay here until my cousin recalls me for some better prospect. One gain at least will be that I shall study more and that I shall learn self-restraint, of which I used to be quite incapable."

Since the prospects look so black at Uzès, his thoughts turn to the chances of finding a benefice elsewhere. There is, it seems, a possible vacancy at Oulchy-le-Château, a parish near to La Ferté-Milon over whose disposal the Vitart family have some influence. To obtain at least a share in it, Racine tells Vitart that he is ready to abandon his

former scruples "concerning black robes and white robes"—
he is ready to enter a religious order if necessary. He wishes
that he could conclude his novitiate, which he has now
begun, at Oulchy instead of at Uzès. Le Vasseur, however,
is also a candidate for Oulchy and, in writing to him,
Racine suggests the following arrangement:

"Whatever transpires, be assured that, if the negotiation
succeeds, 'the edifice I am building is yours'. I might be the
only titular incumbent, but at least four of us would be
beneficiaries. You will be Monsieur l'Abbé or Monsieur le
Prieur—for I believe that M. Vitart and M. Poignant will
readily cede their authority to you."

At the same time, the Sconin family are engaged in complicated negotiations over a living in Anjou, to which they
have a claim. This claim is obscured by prolonged legal
proceedings, but Racine is ready to clutch at any straw. He
finds that Canon Sconin is willing to surrender his share in
the title, in which case it might be transferred to Vitart
and ultimately to Racine. The chief obstacle consists in the
hesitations, and indeed the ill-will, of Dom Cosme, who
also holds in the disputed title a share which he appears
quite unready to give up.

The identity of Dom Cosme, to whom we have already
referred several times, has not been satisfactorily established.
From the evidence of Racine's letters, he is clearly a
brother of Canon Antoine Sconin. The difficulty of
biographers begins when it is found that none of the eight
Sconin brothers bore the name of Cosme. The best solution
that has been proposed is to regard 'Dom Cosme' as a nickname given by Racine and Vitart to one of two persons.
The first is Adrien Sconin, who was in orders and later
became Principal of the Jesuit College at Soissons—but he
was only a year older than Jean Racine and seems much too
young to have exerted the baleful influence attributed to
Dom Cosme at Uzès. The second is Pierre Sconin, a man
in middle life who was an official in the salt-tax office at
La Ferté-Milon, and might easily have had a finger in
several legal and ecclesiastical pies. If, as seems most

probable, this was the man, he was not in orders and the significance of his monkish nickname is obscure.

Whatever his true identity, there is no doubt that Dom Cosme was real enough to Racine. He becomes a stumbling-block to all his designs; he is dilatory, unhelpful, and finally displays, in Racine's view, active malevolence. His shadow lies across all the letters from Uzès and contrasts with the shining charity of Canon Antoine Sconin.

By the summer of 1662 Racine was clearly smarting under the lash of disappointment, and was ready to turn to any quarter that would relieve him. He was at an age when time seemed to be winging ahead of him at ever-increasing speed. He could settle to nothing because he was too worried by business matters. He was conscious of his unpaid debts and brooded on his obligations to Vitart which he could not discharge. Was he always to be dependent on others, a man without parents or inheritance, with no fixed position in the world, obliged to beg when his talent fitted him to command? Sensitive and baffled, he turned inward upon himself. What was wrong with him, that everything he touched led to failure?

"I seem to bring disaster to every affair in which I am concerned," he cries. "I do not know whether *my ill-luck* will not once again ruin the negotiations which my cousin is undertaking for Oulchy."

This touch of self-accusation serves to exasperate him still more against the outer world. Not only does he sulk when the good people of Uzès press him to visit their houses, but he rages against the ignorant and intriguing monks of the cathedral and his bitterness against everything religious bursts forth in a letter to Vitart who has been urging him to write to his pious relatives.

"I will try to write this afternoon to my aunt Vitart and my aunt the nun, since you complain about this. But you must excuse me if I have not yet done so, and so must they; for what can I say to them? It is quite enough to play the hypocrite here, without doing the same thing in Paris by letter; for I call it hypocrisy to write letters in which you must speak of nothing but devotion and continually ask to be remembered in their prayers. Not that I do not badly need praying for, but I wish that they would do it without my having to ask so often. If God wills it that I should be a prior, then I will say as many prayers for other people as they have said for me."

It is always the same thing that makes him wince: the burden of an obligation which he cannot discharge. He must beg for money, for patronage and advancement. And now even prayers—of which he does not feel so urgent a need—are only to be doled out at his humble request.

3

A temporary revival of hope comes soon after. The Bishop is coming to visit the new presbytery which Canon Sconin has built at Saint-Maximin-lès-Uzès. Perhaps his visit will mark a change of fortune? Racine is entrusted with the delicate business of arranging the dinner of four courses, "without counting the *entremets* and the dessert", which is to be offered to the Diocesan. Meanwhile his uncle hurries to Avignon to buy whatever delicacies cannot be found in Uzès. But nothing comes of the dinner except the Bishop's general good will. "He has hungry people round him to whom he gives everything", and among these ravening suitors the Canon's nephew would be torn limb from limb if he were singled out for preferment.

The Canon falls ill and, ashamed at proving such a broken reed, makes a proposal which fills Racine with dismay. He offers to resign his own benefice in favour of his nephew.

"It made me tremble, seeing the present state of affairs. But I managed to prove to him so clearly that it would mean involving myself in lawsuits, and in the end remaining a monk with no title and no freedom, that now he is the first to dissuade me from it. Besides," adds Racine, piling argument on argument in face of the threatened danger, "I am not old enough, since I should have to be ordained

first. And, although it would be easy to obtain a dispensa-
tion, it would form a new subject for lawsuits and I could
expect no mercy at the hands of the reformed clergy.''

Canon Sconin then suggests another arrangement. He
thinks that the Bishop's chaplain could easily be persuaded
to exchange a prior's living which he has in Languedoc for
the disputed living in Anjou. This would suit everyone,
except no doubt Dom Cosme, who would have to abandon
his part-claim before the negotiation could be put through.

Reporting this, Racine begs his cousin Vitart to keep his
eyes open for any living that falls vacant ''in your direction''
—he is still thinking of Oulchy—without prejudice, of
course, to the interests of Le Vasseur.

''I don't think they would grumble at P.R.,'' he observes naïvely, ''since they must see that I am very devoted
to the Church down here.''

It is a niggling business, though Racine clearly feels that
it is his duty to pursue it. But he is disgusted with the
delays, with the petty intrigues which he sees all around
him, with his own ineffectiveness. To top all, it is mid-
June, and the hot weather has come with a vengeance. It is
impossible to go out into the ovenlike heat and ''I am
deafened the whole day long by an infinite number of
cicadas which never cease chirping on every side—but with
the most piercing and importunate note in the whole
world.''

Into this world of baked fields and dazzling skies falls the
final blow. Its exact nature cannot be determined from
Racine's indignant letters, but it is plain that he holds Dom
Cosme responsible for some spectacular failure in his plans.
Probably Dom Cosme's ''treason''—as he calls it—concerned the Anjou living, on which he had been building a
new castle in Spain. The disaster provokes Racine's
often-quoted condemnation of his mother's family, which
must be read in its true context if it is to be properly
understood.

''I cannot write to anyone else except you to-day,'' he
writes to Nicolas Vitart. ''My mind is too troubled, and I

[38]

am not in a state to speak of anything but lawsuits. Perhaps that would shock the people to whom I usually write. Everyone has not the patience which you have to suffer my follies, besides which my uncle is ill in bed and I am attending him. He sends you his sincerest regards and would entrust his interests to you more· confidently and more gladly than to his brother. He is the soul of kindness, I assure you, and I think he is the only one in his family who has a tender and generous heart, for all the others are just plain boors. Except the father [Racine's grandfather Sconin], and he is not quite without taint. I would not say so much, but for the anger I feel at the ugly trick they have played on you."

And Racine concludes, in a tone as sincere as the rest of the letter:

"I can assure you that I am not greedy for benefices. I only hope for one in order to pay you back at least some poor part of what I owe you."

So matters stood in June 1662. After eight months at Uzès the main object of his journey seemed more remote than ever. Every door had been slammed in his face. He looked at his good uncle and wondered how to tell him that he was not willing to stay at his side indefinitely, helping him with the business side of his duties and quietly studying to be a priest. He was loath to forfeit the Canon's good opinion of him, yet there was neither material nor spiritual profit to be had in remaining at Uzès much longer.

4

Racine's life at Uzès added little to his direct experience of humanity. Mindful of the recommendations of his uncle and of Nicolas Vitart, and obeying also his own basic inclinations, he led a retired and studious existence. He did much reading, partly of the theological books which he found in Canon Sconin's library, and partly of the profane poets—Homer and Pindar, Virgil and Horace—which he annotated as he read. But looking up sometimes from his

Odyssey or his Lives of the Saints, he examined briefly the living people around him and his own tentative response to them.

In the middle of a heavy teasing of Le Vasseur, who has fallen in love with a new flame, Racine suddenly lets fall a sentence which might serve as the text for his future plays, and which throws a light on his reluctance, as a young man, to commit himself to any emotional adventure.

"I admire you", he says, "for making so excellent a choice, and for falling in love with so much discernment, *if there can be discernment in love.*"

There, as much as in his eminently reasonable desire to observe the discretion expected of an aspirant to the priesthood, lies the explanation of his coldness—as some would say, of his inhumanity. He is afraid of the dangerous whirlpool of the passions which lies before him, afraid of losing control of himself and his destiny if he lets himself be drawn in. Le Vasseur can lose his heart half a dozen times in a year and still remain Le Vasseur. He is at once more 'tender' and thicker-skinned. But Racine, the intellectual, the lucid analyst, feels instinctively that his own integrity will be irreparably damaged if he once allows his foot to slip. Since so much is at stake, he is careful, even calculating.

"Thank heaven I am still free", he writes to Le Vasseur, after six months at Uzès. "If I left this place, I should bring back my heart as sound and as whole as I brought it here. Yet I must tell you quite an amusing story in this connexion."

He then recounts his own curious and stilted approach to a young woman. The words he chooses to tell the story show that the warm-hearted, impulsive Racine has not yet come into being—if, indeed, he is ever to exist.

"There is here", he relates, "a very well-built young lady with a most handsome figure. I had never seen her at a closer distance than five or six paces and I had always thought her very good-looking. Her complexion struck me as bright and glowing, she had fine big dark eyes; her throat and the rest—which is uncovered very freely in this part of the country—was very white. I had always been rather struck by her and felt something approaching an inclination; but I only saw her in church.''

The young man decides to discover if this apparent beauty is really worthy of his admiration. He seeks out a "perfectly respectable opportunity" of speaking to her. "My only intention", he assures Le Vasseur, "was to see how she would answer me. So I spoke to her on some trifling matter; but no sooner had I opened my mouth and looked at her closely than I was struck almost speechless. I saw on her face certain blotches, as though she had just recovered from sickness, and this caused a rapid change in my ideas. However, I did not dry up, and she answered me in a very gentle and obliging manner. To tell the truth, I suppose I must have seen her on one of her bad days, for in the town she is considered very beautiful and I know many young men who sigh for her from the bottom of their hearts."

"In any case," he concludes, "I was very glad of this encounter, for at least it served to free me from the beginning of an anxiety. I am endeavouring to live a little more reasonably now, and not to let myself be carried away by all sorts of objects.''

It is difficult to believe that Racine had ever been carried away very far. At twenty-two his imagination well outran his experience.

It is possible that the puritanism of some of his relatives and teachers was still working in him, in spite of his efforts to be more "emancipated". But, although Port-Royal may have marked him against his will, it is much more probable that the factor which held him back was his innate mistrustfulness. He is in turn timid and arrogant, but always withdrawn. Typically, he speaks of a young man whose acquaintance he has made as being "very handsome, *but* passionately in love". This unusual young man brings letters and verses to show him before sending them to his lady-love. The two of them then go out together to catch a glimpse of her sitting at a window, and afterwards walk to a farm belonging to his acquaintance, where they eat the first cherries of the year.

For Racine, the case seems worthy of description and comment. "In this country one sees but few temperate loves; all the passions are excessive; and the people of this town, who are frivolous enough in other matters, commit themselves further to their desires than in any other part of the world."

Thus the cool northerner, the continent adolescent and, in part, the professional writer, observing his human specimens and noting down, without much insight yet, their emotional reactions.

With the same objectivity, obeying again an instinct which tells him that the case may be significant although he does not yet understand how, he records one more occurrence.

"I must tell you another little story which is less important [he has just been describing the intrigues of the Jesuits] though it is sufficiently curious. A girl in Uzès, who lived quite near us, poisoned herself yesterday with arsenic, to be revenged on her father who had scolded her too violently. She had time to be confessed and only died two hours after. It was thought that she was pregnant and that shame had driven her to this desperate course. But she was opened up and never was a maid more a maid. Such is the temper of people in these parts: they carry their passions to excess."

The novel environment of Languedoc could not startle Racine out of his detachment. Neither man nor nature moved him profoundly: they were just worth recording. His interest in affairs was at least as strong as his interest in emotions. As for his own emotions, they hardly seem to have been awakened.

The half-retirement in which he lived contributed, however, to the crystallization of his character. It gave him leisure to meditate on himself and, if no clear-cut determination emerges from his correspondence, it would be rash to assume that he was not seeking one. He was obsessed with the feeling that he was not as other men: either he was higher or he was lower, but in any case he was different. This feeling produced two principal effects—in appearance contradictory, but in fact complementary. On the one hand he was continually reaching out for reassurances of affection. Has Le Vasseur forgotten him? Will Vitart grow weary of his greenness and importunity and abandon him? Could not Marguerite Vitart spare the time to write him a few lines instead of merely addressing the envelopes of her husband's letters? He humbles himself whenever he thinks that he has given offence, as though afraid of losing the tenuous thread which links him to humanity.

On the other hand, he is self-assertive and susceptible. He reacts spontaneously to any fancied insult or neglect. In his desire to amuse his friends, he can be malicious and sometimes wounding in his criticisms of people who have done him no wrong. There is a certain gratuitous cruelty in the comments which he makes to Mademoiselle Vitart on the forthcoming marriage of the inoffensive but bibulous M. d'Houy. The bride is a woman afflicted with dropsy. With ready wit, Racine sees the match as a marriage of wine and water, but he develops the point a little beyond the bounds of charity. And when Marguerite Vitart herself fails to reply to his letters (she was pregnant with her third child at that time), he remarks very drily to her husband: "I have great difficulty in believing that she has the least curiosity to see anything written by me, since she has sent me no word for over six months."

Racine's strength and weakness, his bold powers of lucid judgment and his more cautious regard for the opinions of friends and critics—features which, alternating through his career, will be the outward signs of a personality compounded in proportions peculiar to itself of assertiveness, susceptibility, and subservience—are perfectly illustrated in his criticism of an ode by Charles Perrault which Le Vasseur has sent him. No doubt he still remembers Perrault's reservations on *La Nymphe de la Seine*.

"I have had full leisure to read M. Perrault's ode," he writes. "In fact I have re-read it several times. I had

[43]

great difficulty in recognizing his style, and I still would not believe that it was his if you and M. Vitart did not assure me of the fact. I could not seem to find in it that natural facility which he always had; I could see in it no trace of a mind as clear as his has always appeared to be, and I would have wagered that this ode had been hewn with a hammer by some man who had never written good verse. But'', he adds, ''I expect that M. Perrault's talent is still the same and that it was simply the subject which betrayed him.''

Suddenly he remembers that he himself is a novice in literature and that he is writing to Le Vasseur.

''But I forget myself, and I did not reflect that I was saying this to a man more qualified to judge than I am. You must excuse me for having taken this liberty. I was speaking with the same frankness that we used together in your study or along the galleries of your staircase. If my judgment is faulty and my opinion at variance with yours, you must put it down to the barbarity of this country and to my long absence from Paris which, separating me from you, has perhaps entirely deprived me of a right perception of things.''

This is not mock humility, though Racine at this age is sufficiently unstable for it to be just possible that there is a grain of irony in it. Uncertainty about the world and himself drives him infallibly to paradox, and a tenacious sense of his own talent is embittered by the realization that it is finding no worthy outlet.

But if that were all, Racine would not differ from many an ambitious young man whose dreams overleap reality. What distinguishes him is that at moments he can stand outside himself and see the situation with perfect clarity, yet without ceasing to suffer from it. Again, his ambition is tougher and more ruthless than the average. Where it will lead him he does not yet know, but he has felt its pull and is obliged to follow it, even—this he has still to accept—at the cost of his human relationships. ''I shall learn self-restraint, of which I used to be quite incapable,'' he had written. Policy, not humility, prompted that resolution. Racine, with his calculated self-restraint, will presently be a dangerous man to those who stand in his way.

5

Racine's finished literary output at Uzès was negligible. If we except a 'petit mémoire' on a firework display which he wrote soon after arrival and sent to Paris for publication in the *Gazette*, everything else was intended only for the private eye of his friends.

He sprinkles his letters with occasional verses: compliments addressed to Marguerite Vitart, good wishes for her two small girls, Manon and Nanon, and for the third child who is soon due to arrive; more stilted lines to Le Vasseur in which he attempts to combine a forced sprightliness with an observance of the rules of polite poetry; to La Fontaine he sends a long set of burlesque verses on a classical theme. Finding little new matter to inspire him, he takes out a piece which he had composed in Paris, entitled *Les Bains de Vénus*, shows it to some acquaintances at Uzès who praise it, then sends it to Le Vasseur for a true Parisian opinion. "But," he begs him, "if you show it round, do not give the name of the author. My name damages all that I do."

He awaits with impatience Le Vasseur's criticism and is disappointed to receive only a few words of general praise. He fears that there must be something wrong with his poem. Probably it is so bad that Le Vasseur has found it easier to commend it *in toto* than to mark all the passages which require correction. Racine evidently set some store on this composition, for he sent it next to La Fontaine, asking him to "tell me what your academy at Château-Thierry think of it, and particularly Mademoiselle de La Fontaine".

The opinion of Château-Thierry—if it was ever given— has been lost, as has the poem itself.

As for the *Stances à Parthénice*, a smoothly-flowing composition which it would be pleasant to claim for the young poet, there is no sufficient reason for attributing it to him.

To judge by the self-conscious verses encrusted in his prose, Racine was then at the least attractive stage of his development as a poet. He had lost the fresh outlook of a boy and had not yet acquired the skill or the experience of an adult. For a classical writer, the early twenties are of necessity the *âge ingrat*. Only the prose of his letters, when he is not attempting to be 'literary', is supple, sinewy, compact, pointed here and there with the stinging phrase which he can never resist writing.

The tradition that at Uzès Racine wrote his earliest extant tragedy, *La Thébaïde*, can be no more substantiated than the rest of the charming legend which pictures him at work in the little stone pavilion overlooking an orderly landscape of olive-trees, cypresses, and grey rocks which Poussin would have loved to paint. *La Thébaïde*, as Racine's later correspondence shows, was being composed act by act in November-December 1663, after his return to Paris.

The slender foundation on which the tradition is based can be discerned in his correspondence. In July 1662, for the first time for a year, and stimulated by a letter from La Fontaine, his thoughts turned again to the theatre, and he wrote to Le Vasseur:

"I am looking for a subject for a play and I might be quite disposed to work on one; but I have too much cause to be melancholy in this place and my mind would have to be freer than it is. And then I need someone like you at hand who could give an opinion on what I am writing while I am actually doing it."

On the same day he complained to Vitart: "I cannot settle down to writing."

Three weeks later he had given up all hope of a benefice at Uzès and was mentally prepared to leave the place. It is highly unlikely that after this he would have started work on an important literary project. There is no evidence that the play he had vaguely contemplated was ever begun at Uzès; still less that it was *La Thébaïde*.

Racine returned to Paris at some date between 25th July 1662, when he addressed to Vitart the last letter from Uzès that has been preserved, and 22nd June 1663, when Chapelain reported to Colbert that: "I shall have in a few days a French ode by a young man called Racine, which he has brought me and which he is repolishing on my advice. The subject is the convalescence of His Majesty." (Louis had just recovered from measles.)

If Racine was free to follow his own inclinations, his return no doubt took place much nearer to the first date than to the second; in that case, the Uzès interlude lasted approximately a year. According to a local tradition, he revisited the town twelve years later, in 1674, but the tradition rests rather on the desire of the people of Uzès to honour the poet by stressing his association with them than on any basis of known fact. It is unlikely that his kindly uncle ever saw him again in the long span of life which remained to him. Canon Sconin died in 1689 at the age of eighty-one, and is buried in the choir of Uzès cathedral. As for Dom Cosme, he—or at least his name—disappeared for ever from Racine's horizon.

The young poet came back empty-handed from his benefice-hunting and—it seems fairly certain—without being ordained. His hopes of obtaining Oulchy also came to nothing. The living went some years later to Le Vasseur, who was appointed Prior of Oulchy in 1671 and remained there for the rest of his life. His fine literary taste never deserted him and he became a valued member of the Academy of Soissons.

Is it an exaggeration to say that Racine barely escaped a similar destiny? There seems no doubt that he would have accepted Oulchy eagerly had it been offered to him in 1662. With equal readiness he would have accepted a living in Languedoc, with residence, even with entry into a religious order if it had been required of him. His literary vocation was not so irresistible at that time that he would have refused a remunerative provincial incumbency. In it, he might have continued to write elegant *vers de circonstance*, turning perhaps, with advancing years, to works of meditation, but the theatre would never have known him.

With worldly success, the elusive benefices rapidly came his way. Within ten years of leaving Uzès he secured at least three. One, Saint-Jacques de la Ferté, was near his birthplace. Another, Sainte-Madeleine de l'Epinay, was in Anjou and was almost certainly the benefice of the letters. It had been held previously by Antoine Sconin and was in the gift of Mgr. Jacques Adhémar de Grignan, so that its acquisition by Racine was not unconnected with his stay in the south. But he would never have obtained it by remaining humbly in Languedoc to complete his novitiate. Traditionally, this was the benefice which he lost again in the lawsuit which inspired *Les Plaideurs*.

He enjoyed all these benefices as a layman and without residence, as was the common practice among his contemporaries. They were the recognized perquisites of success. If, when they fell to him, he no longer needed them desperately as he had done in his twenty-third year, at least they formed a useful addition to his income.[1]

[1] In a recent study (*La Vie privée de Racine*. Paris, 1949), M. Pierre de Lacretelle has sought to prove that Racine could have held none of the benefices attributed to him in the five legal *actes* signed between 1668 and 1674, as well as in the *privilège* of *Andromaque*, and he concludes: "Il faut donc ranger ces petites supercheries parmi les 'scandales' dont Racine, avant de mourir, s'est accusé dans son testament sans toutefois les énumérer." But M. de Lacretelle's arguments are negative and hardly conclusive; on at least one point he is certainly in error. The documentary evidence, though it may be incomplete, added to the transparence of such "petites supercheries" in the eyes of Racine's contemporaries, and above all their pointlessness, surely absolve Racine of this charge.

PART II

Through the Jungle

CHAPTER IV

THE THEATRE IN 1663

AT the date when Racine returned from Uzès there were three regular companies of French players in Paris. Two of them had been established since the early years of the century and at one period had been keen rivals, though for some time now the tide had turned against the Company of the Marais in favour of the Hôtel de Bourgogne. The Marais had enjoyed its heyday in the sixteen-thirties and 'forties, had created the first plays of Pierre Corneille—the Great Corneille, as he was now beginning to be called—and of his younger brother Thomas Corneille. But after *Le Cid*, *Horace*, *Cinna*, and *Polyeucte*, it had ceased to be the chief home of tragedy. The roaring days of Richelieu died with him, the Fronde came to purge French society, or at least to divide it clearly into two unequal parts: the goats, headstrong and individualistic, inescapably redolent of the old régime; the sheep, more docile, in their scented own or borrowed skins, flocking to enter the pen of Versailles. A politer public noticed for the first time that the Marais was almost opposite an open drain and began to complain of the remoteness of the theatre's situation in the Rue Vieille-du-Temple—a sign that the fashionable centre of Paris, as of London, was slowly moving west. West also went the best actors and authors, both following the tide and helping to swell it. Perhaps the greatest single influence in the decline of the Marais, after the retirement of Mondory, had been the defection of the actor-manager * Floridor. He had gone over to the rival theatre in 1643 and had been succeeded by Laroque who, ironically, would hardly be known to history if he had not turned down Racine's first and probably unactable effort. Had he produced it, however, the ultimate result would hardly have been different. Racine at his height would still have been acted by the Hôtel de Bourgogne. The position of the Marais in the sixteen-sixties was in one sense similar to that of a modern outlying theatre compared to the greater talents and profits of the West End. It was a testing-ground of rising writers and players who afterwards transferred to the Hôtel. Long after the Corneilles and Floridor, the Champmeslé couple followed the same well-marked path.

Yet, although it was generally agreed to be languishing, the Marais survived as an independent theatre until 1673. The stream of talent occasionally flowed back towards it. Actors and actresses, such as the Du Parc and her husband, joined it temporarily if they fell out with their own company. Authors, who could transfer their allegiance more easily than players, had recourse to it when disappointed in the production of their plays elsewhere. The chief factor in the prolonged vitality of the Marais, however, was the popularity of a new genre, the *pièce à machines*, which for a time it made its own. These spectacular shows, mixing music and sometimes rudimentary ballet with spoken lines of verse, made their chief appeal to the public by their ingenious scenic effects: lavish décors and surprising scene-changes, cars of nymphs and goddesses rolling in from the wings or descending from the flies, Egyptian mummies so macabre that they frightened the chorines, a real horse. All these visual adjuncts to the drama were dubbed *machines*, but, although they drew Parisians back to the theatre in the Rue Vieille-du-Temple, their use was not fully exploited until the 'seventies when the Florentine Lully blended them in proper proportion with singers and orchestra and established the opera in France.

The Hôtel de Bourgogne used no *machines*. It did not need them. On its austerer stage walked the greatest tragic

[51]

LES COMEDIENS DV ROY
ENTRETENVS PAR SA MAIESTÉ

COMME les diuertissemens enjoüez sont de saison, nous croyons vous bien regaller en vous promettant pour demain Mardy iij. iour de Feurier, la plaisante COMEDIE du IODELET MAISTRE, de Monsieur SCARON: Auec vne DANSE de SCARAMOVCHE, qui ne peut manquer de vous plaire beaucoup.

A Vendredy sans faute les AMOVRS du CAPITAN MATAMORE, ou l'ILLVSION COMIQVE, de Monsieur de CORNEILLE l'aisné. En attendant les superbes Machines de la CONQVESTE de la TOISON d'OR

C'est à l'Hostel du Marais, vieille rue du Temple, à deux heures

Playbill of the Marais, *circa* 1660, from the Musée de l'Opéra.

actors of the time, Montfleury and Floridor, and with them
Hauteroche and La Fleur. The leading female parts were
usually played by the Des Oeillets, an experienced and
gifted player (though "she was not so lovely by day as she
was by candlelight"), while the second parts went to the
Beauchâteau. These were soon to be joined by Brécourt, a
young actor from Molière's company, and by the rising
young actress Mademoiselle Dennebaut.

This company owed its prestige to the personal talents
of its actors. Their resources were voice, intonation, pose,
gesture, the expression of emotion by the human instrument
performing with practically no external aids in a confined
space. On both sides they were hedged in by the chairs of
the spectators who sat on the stage. In front of them
stretched the auditorium, a narrow rectangle whose floor
was packed with a restless, critical audience made doubly
so by the fact that most of them were standing and that
those at the back had only the scantiest view of the stage.
Other spectators sitting in the boxes which ran round the
three sides of the auditorium could see and hear in more
comfort, but even for them the actors had to keep well to
the front-centre of the stage and declaim boldly the most
telling lines that their authors could give them. In these
conditions, the 'grand style' was almost inevitable. A
player who was not capable of tearing a passion to tatters
would not only fail to hold, but even to reach, a large part
of the audience. There was no scope for underplaying,
for fugitive expressions and gestures, and certainly none for
complicated 'business'. The personality of the actor was
everything, since on his interpretation alone the appeal of
the spectacle depended. In fact, it was the spectacle,
unsupplemented by changes of scenery, or by effects of
lighting. The costumes generally were contemporary
French court dress, to which was added a few 'Greek'
or 'Roman' accessories. Only occasionally, as in the
Turkish costuming of *Bajazet*, was any consistent attempt
made to dress a play in the style of a specific period or
country.

The company of the Hôtel de Bourgogne were, with some justice, proud of their professional skill. Their standing as interpreters of tragedy was hardly in dispute. Moreover, as the *Comédiens Royaux*, or the *Grands Comédiens*, they enjoyed the advantage of being the only troupe in France which had the King's official patronage. This carried with it, besides protection against the not inconsiderable enemies of the theatre, allowances paid to actors from the royal purse and a pension on retirement. Comparable advantages were enjoyed by their authors and attracted, besides the brothers Corneille and the Abbé Boyer, the most promising younger writers, such as Philippe Quinault.

In this period of ascendancy, the *Grands Comédiens* found themselves challenged from a new quarter. Molière, who had returned triumphantly to Paris after thirteen years of wandering in the provinces, was raising comedy to such a level that it drew audiences as numerous and as select as tragedy. He had made his bow in the winter of 1658–9, using for his performances the hall of the Petit-Bourbon which the protection of Monsieur, the King's brother, had procured for him, and which he shared with the Italian Players. Both Court and Town caught the fashion of flocking to the new comedy, until one Monday morning in October 1660, near the beginning of the theatrical season, when a gang of workmen arrived and set about demolishing the hall. The comedians sought desperately for someone in authority. They found a Monsieur de Ratabon, Overseer of the King's Buildings, who informed them that the demolition of their theatre was part of a long-term plan for extending the Louvre. He added that the scheme had such obvious priority over the interests of a band of players that the necessity of warning them in advance had never occurred to him.

It is possible that Molière's expulsion from the Petit-Bourbon was a result of the normal workings of bureaucracy, but it is also possible that the instigators were to be found at the Hôtel de Bourgogne. Montfleury and his faction

would have gone to greater lengths to scotch their competitor. Even if M. de Ratabon was incorruptible, he was ahead
of schedule. The new colonnade of the Louvre for which
he had cleared the ground was not begun until five years
later. In the upshot, Molière was the gainer. The King
himself, whose unofficial protection he now enjoyed,
allotted him a hall in the Palais-Royal which had been
specially constructed for theatrical performances in the
time of Richelieu. This hall, opening on the Rue de
Valois, was at least as central as the Hôtel de Bourgogne
which was situated half a mile further east in what is now
the Rue Etienne-Marcel. M. de Ratabon was ordered to
carry out the necessary structural repairs. This done,
Molière moved into the Palais-Royal where, still alternating
with the Italian Players, he was to remain for the rest of his
life.

The Italians, who constituted a fourth regular troupe in
the capital, occupied a special position in the affections of
Parisians. Using the stock characters of the *commedia dell'
arte*, they played farces in which the spoken lines, freely
improvised by the actors, were incomprehensible to the
majority of the spectators. But the situations which they
mimed were clear enough and their broad humour and
satirical intention often delighted their audiences. Occasionally they overstepped the mark and were temporarily
banned by the authorities. But official displeasure was
the only danger they ran. They lived in amity with the
French companies and were not involved in the bitter
quarrels which arose between these.

2

The year 1663 was memorable for the theatrical quarrel
which contemporaries dubbed the Comic War and which,
in the space of a few months, brought to the surface a whole
world of personal and professional animosities. The immediate cause of war was Molière's comedy *L'Ecole des
femmes*, which opened on 26th December 1662, ran

without a break until the Easter vacation and was performed
frequently during the summer—an exceptional run for the
time. From the first, *L'Ecole des femmes* was subjected to
violent attacks by several groups of persons. The religious
moralists, always ready to condemn the theatre, claimed
that this satire on an old man who brings up his young ward
in cloistered ignorance with the object of making her his
submissive wife was an offence against the sanctity of
marriage. The feminine leaders of Parisian culture and
their male satellites, already ruffled by the *Précieuses
ridicules*, exclaimed in disgust at the naïvely coarse expressions which they found in Molière's latest play. The whole
hive of authors, critics, literary dilettanti, and camp-
followers who clustered round the Hôtel de Bourgogne or
round the salons which Molière had offended, stirred,
buzzed, and prepared to sting. Even the Great Corneille
attempted to organize a *cabale* against him. Like everything
he did in these days, it was mistimed and ineffective. He
might well have left Molière and his own established reputation to flourish in peace, each in their separate spheres,
for, although Molière had shown signs of an ambition to
write tragedy there could be no question of a serious rivalry.
The quarrel seems to have had a very trivial origin. Molière
had borrowed for his comedy a line from Corneille's latest
tragedy, *Sertorius*:

> *C'est assez.*
> *Je suis maître, je parle; allez, obéissez!*

had cried Corneille's character with all the dignity of
a Roman commander. At the Palais-Royal, the same words
were declaimed by a self-infatuated bourgeois seeking to
impress his mutinous servant-girl. A different author might
well have accepted the good-natured parody as a homage
(Molière was one of his sincerest admirers), but Corneille
had all the susceptibility of failing genius and all the
fatuity too. The fact that his fustian had been put to baser
uses than he intended no doubt struck him as an outrage.
He launched his *cabale*, missed, and retired to brood over

the half-failure of his next tragedy, *Sophonisbe*, which was winning but grudging applause at the Hôtel de Bourgogne.

The first printed attack on Molière's play was made by a young man so far unknown to fame, but determined to rise at all costs. This young writer, Donneau de Visé, provides a classic example of the literary careerist. He had considerable talent, not too many principles and a strong sense of opportunism. The son of an official in Monsieur's household, he abandoned a study for holy orders in favour of the world of letters. He was of the same age as Racine whose career he paralleled on a lower, flashier level. At twenty-three he began his campaign of conquest by publishing a literary miscellany called *Les Nouvelles Nouvelles*. As the third number was going to press, the storm broke over *L'Ecole des femmes*. De Visé halted the printers, hastily wrote a long notice, and came out with the first published comments on the much-discussed play. If as criticism it had small value, it was excellent journalism.

But Molière also had a sense of the topical. Derisively gathering up the spoken and printed criticisms of his work, he moulded them into a one-act sketch and presented them in the light he himself chose in *La Critique de l'Ecole des femmes*. It was a nimble manoeuvre, this second thrust delivered before the adversary had parried the first. Its timing pointed the contrast between Molière's rapid mind and the stolid thinking of his rivals at the Hôtel de Bourgogne. On the day when Molière first presented *La Critique de l'Ecole des femmes*, Montfleury's company opened with Gilbert's completely untopical pastoral, *Les Amours d'Ovide*, which, as we have seen, they had been contemplating for at least two years.

Molière's most mobile opponent was undoubtedly de Visé. In August, two months after the production of Molière's *Critique*, he published a comedy which he entitled *Zélinde, ou la Véritable critique de l'Ecole des femmes*, which does not seem to have been acted. Clearly, however, he was aiming at a production by the Hôtel de Bourgogne. He was inspired by a desire for rapid notoriety rather than by any convinced hostility against Molière—to whom, later, he pandered. He was not, however, to reach his goal just yet. Another young writer was active in the same field, and it was his comedy which Montfleury preferred when at last he was ready to counter-attack.

The Hôtel de Bourgogne's new author was Edme Boursault, another almost exact contemporary of Racine. Like de Visé, he was a literary journalist, an opportunist also but with a greater sense of humour and less ruthlessness. His talent was for criticism and pamphleteering; the plays he wrote were adaptations and topical skits rather than original creations. Years later, after his retirement, Racine felt tempted to couple Boursault with Pradon in suggesting that the sewage-dump at Clignancourt would make a suitable theatre for the works of both of them. But the time when these two were to clash was not yet and Boursault could unleash the whole of his satirical verve against Molière, not omitting a distasteful allusion to the private life of the great comic dramatist. Molière had recently married Armande Béjart, a young actress of his company who had been with him since her childhood and whom the extreme of slander alleged to be his daughter. Boursault stopped short of this, but he remarked that the part of Arnolphe, the old man in L'Ecole des femmes who attempts to form his young ward in the image of his desires, would be an easy rôle for Molière to play since it would come so naturally to him.[1]

These unpleasant insinuations by the faction of the Hôtel de Bourgogne drew from Molière the almost instant rejoinder of the Impromptu de Versailles. The main interest of the Impromptu—and the most memorable statement that emerged from the whole Comic War—lies in Molière's description of how tragedy should be acted. Like Hamlet in his advice to the players at Elsinore, Molière would have his actors avoid ranting and hold the mirror up to nature. As an example of how not to do it, he mimics the actors of

[1] Boursault later withdrew these personal allusions. They do not appear in the printed version of Le Portrait du peintre.

[58]

the Hôtel de Bourgogne: Montfleury striking heroic
attitudes and ringing out his final lines as a signal for the
audience to applaud; the Beauchâteau, charming the public
with her fixed smile while declaiming a heartrending
passage.

This was parody, but behind it Molière went to the root
of the matter. He disliked actors in the heroic manner on
the same grounds as Shakespeare: that they imitated nature
so abominably. His remedy was naturalness, and again
naturalness. But however attractive his views, particularly
to the modern English mind, they brought no response
from the seventeenth-century French public. Molière, both
as author and actor, failed in tragedy before the same audiences which adored him in comedy. 'Naturalness' in the
first was neither understood nor desired and it certainly
appeared out of key in the pieces of Corneille and his disciples. This was not the way to attain 'the sublime'.
A certain artifice was necessary in order to achieve the
larger-than-life effects of the tragic stage. The point is
important because, had Molière's conception of tragic
acting become the rule, it is doubtful whether Racine
could have met its requirements successfully. Certainly
he never fell into the fustian of Corneille at his worst; he
was too self-conscious an artist for that. But he worked
best in a stylized framework and, however 'natural' the
passions of his characters (however close to psychological
truth), they demand, at the great moments of tension, to
be interpreted in the grand manner. This only the players
of Montfleury's troupe could do, for—apart from certain
exaggerations and absurdities which Molière's quick eye
had seized—they represented a school of acting which will
always flourish where audiences demand to be moved rather
than amused. Their excesses were laughable, and in the
eyes of any intelligent spectator defeated their own ends,
but the main tradition which they followed was sound
enough. It has too many triumphs to its credit to be lightly
disregarded.

Such fundamental differences of dramatic theory did not,

however, become a central issue in the Comic War. All that Montfleury, the exponent of artifice, saw was that his noblest manner had been caricatured by a pack of comic actors and, in addition, that this man Molière had publicly called attention to his fatness. If Montfleury had had any reservations before, he now cast them aside. After the *Impromptu de Versailles*, he was prepared to use any weapon that came to hand against his enemy.

His fury served Donneau de Visé, whose third contribution to the controversy—a sketch entitled *Réponse à l'Impromptu de Versailles*—was written, rehearsed and produced at the Hôtel within six weeks of the first performance of Molière's skit. The young writer thus achieved his ambition of being acted by the *Grands Comédiens*, even though his play was a one-act comedy with no other merit than its topicality. De Visé published it while it was still fresh, together with a preface in which he repeated all the criticisms already formulated by others against the *Ecole des femmes*. When his play finished its short run to make way for yet another attack on Molière written by Montfleury's son, de Visé may well have looked back with satisfaction over a busy and not unprofitable year.

At the close of that year, the Comic War disappeared from the boards of the Paris theatres. With 1664, the chief antagonists were preparing to engage on different ground. Molière was now meditating *Tartuffe*, which would raise up more powerful enemies against him than players and pamphleteers. He was working assiduously to ensure the support of the King, without which all his genius could have availed him nothing.

In the circumstances, the first steps of a young, untried dramatist must have seemed of minor importance to nearly everyone except Racine himself.

CHAPTER V

RACINE'S DEBUT

LA THÉBAÏDE and *ALEXANDRE*

IF, as is probable, Racine returned from Uzès in the autumn of 1662, he could have witnessed the first performance of the *Ecole des femmes*. He was quite certainly in Paris by June 1663, the month of the *Critique de l'Ecole des femmes*, and he must have followed with a close and perhaps personal interest the most envenomed phase of the Comic War. By the autumn at the latest he had made the acquaintance of Molière. His first reference to his great contemporary occurs in a letter to Le Vasseur dated November 1663.

"At the King's *levée* to-day I found Molière, whom the King praised very highly. I was very glad for his sake. He was very glad, too, that I was there."

In December, he writes, somewhat obscurely, that it is a week since he has seen either Molière or the *Impromptu*—of which the Paris première was on the 4th November. But he intends to see them soon.[1]

These references suggest a certain familiarity with the fashionable playwright which Racine is proud to display, but there is no sign that an intimate friendship has been formed. At the end of the December letter Racine remarks as though casually giving a small item of news:

"Montfleury has made out a petition against Molière and has given it to the King. He accuses him of having

[1] "Je n'ai point vu *l'Impromptu* ni son auteur depuis huit jours; j'irai tantôt."

married the daughter and of having formerly slept with the mother. But no one at Court listens to Montfleury. Good-bye. Please do not send your lackey back without charging him with a letter for me. You have more time than I have.''

This incidental sentence of Racine's is the only surviving evidence that Montfleury had carried the vendetta to the ultimate attack on his enemy's personal character. The insinuation of incest, (for, even as it stands, the sentence can bear that reading[1]) was taken up independently by later slander-mongers and made into a precise accusation. It seems to have been finally disproved by the discovery of documents describing Armande Béjart, Molière's young wife, as the sister and not the daughter of the older actress, Madeleine Béjart. The question belongs to the biography of Molière rather than of Racine; but since Racine is frequently blamed for having repeated a monstrous accusation against a close friend, it is necessary to point out that Molière hardly was a close friend. Le Vasseur, on the other hand, was, and Racine was sending him a rapid review of current gossip in a letter which he never expected would be published. Had he added: "But of course it is absurd," he would be held blameless. He wrote instead: "But no one at Court listens to Montfleury." Who can say that in his mind the two sentences were not equivalent?

The letters which contain these brief allusions to Molière are full of another subject which Racine naturally found more absorbing. He was working over the fourth and fifth acts of a new play in close touch with the Hôtel de Bourgogne. *La Thébaïde*—for in a third letter he names it—is an experimental business for its author. Shall he let his characters threaten each other with drawn swords on the stage? But by then such ostentatious physical gestures were out-of-date on the French stage and Racine, in consultation with the company (among them the Beauchâteau, for whom he intends the part of the young

[1] Louis Racine, publishing an expurgated edition of his father's letters in the eighteenth century, bowdlerized the sentence as: "He accuses him of marrying his own daughter," and so made things worse.

princess Antigone), decides against it and has to cut more than two hundred lines which he has already composed.

His last act contains another out-dated feature: a soliloquy cast in the form of lyric stanzas which his heroine is to recite. Racine is sufficiently pleased with this soliloquy to quote part of it to Le Vasseur, adding: "But please do not show it to anyone; because if people see it they might remember it, and so they would be less surprised when it is recited."

A few days later he has decided to sacrifice these very lines, recognizing that they are not dramatic: but "perhaps I shall be able to use them elsewhere". Finally, the whole soliloquy is reduced to three ten-line stanzas. This was the last time until *Esther* (with the unimportant exceptions of the letters in *Bajazet* and the words of the oracle in *Iphigénie*) that Racine departed from the exclusive use of the Alexandrine couplet in his plays.

Some time in December, *La Thébaïde* was finished. The Hôtel de Bourgogne would produce it, but "they only promise it after three other plays". They were then engaged in firing their last shot in the Comic War. They had a five-act comedy by Boursault in prospect and the promise of tragedies by Pierre Corneille and by Quinault. The new dramatist was expected to wait his turn. To Racine the probable delay of some twelve months must have appeared very long. He began to consider Molière as an alternative producer.   *

Meanwhile, he had been active in other directions. He had written two odes, which had increased his consideration as an official poet and brought him a new pension and a patron. The *Ode on the King's Convalescence*, which Chapelain had mentioned in his report to Colbert of June 1663, was rewarded shortly afterwards by a pension of 600 *livres*. *La Renommée aux muses*, a panegyric of Louis not linked to any particular event, won the approval and interest of the Duc de Saint-Aignan when it was shown to him (perhaps by Vitart) in November of the same year.

Saint-Aignan was an enlightened patron of letters and a man whose credit stood high at Court, unlike that of the morose Duc de Luynes. Nevertheless, he belonged to the same circle. His son Paul, Duc de Beauvilliers, was the intimate friend of de Luynes's son, the Duc de Chevreuse—the 'Marquis' of Racine's letters. Both the young noblemen married daughters of Colbert, who through his sons-in-law found a genuine alliance with that aristocratic blood to which he himself pretended more doubtfully by claiming descent from the ancient Kings of Scotland.

Thus, by going just a little way out of the household overshadowed by the stern 'Holy Spirit', but without leaving the orbit of a lettered and high-minded section of the nobility, Racine found his first protector. Saint-Aignan may have helped to secure for his poet the benefices which had seemed so elusive at Uzès. When *La Thébaïde* came to be published, it was dedicated to him.

For Racine, as for de Visé, 1663 had been an active year. He had resumed his relations with the theatre people, had secured the support of Chapelain and of Saint-Aignan, and was, moreover, becoming familiar with the ante-rooms of Versailles. He was modest about this last achievement. "You see", he remarked to Le Vasseur, "that I am half a courtier. In my opinion it is a pretty boring business." But still it was a beginning.

At the Hôtel de Luynes, where he is still lodging, Racine seems to enjoy a higher standing than before. He speaks with some authority of the business matters with which Vitart entrusts him. He uses less 'elegant supplication' in writing to Le Vasseur, whom he now treats as an equal. Perceptibly, he has shed most of the self-mistrust which afflicted him at Uzès. This may be a result of the success which is beginning to come to him, and at the same time a sign that his adolescence is over. While it would be premature to say that he is now determined to be a dramatic poet, it is at least clear that he intends to devote his future to letters in general. Without the picaresque temperament of a de Visé, yet equipped with a determination no less strong, he is learning to pick his way through the complexities of the material world.

The three letters written in November and December 1663 are his last for over twenty years that have been preserved, except for a few scattered letters to his sister. Beyond these, no personal correspondence remains from his period of greatest production and fame. His story is now taken up by his plays and other published writings, by his contemporaries and by the testimony of events. But he has already portrayed himself well enough to be recognizable in his actions.

2

Tired of waiting on the Hôtel de Bourgogne, Racine gave *La Thébaïde* to Molière, who produced it at the end of a crowded theatrical season. For the company of the Palais-Royal, the main event of the summer had been their appearance at Versailles in *Les Plaisirs de l'île enchantée*, a series of fêtes lasting a week of which the general plan was drawn up by the Duc de Saint-Aignan. Throughout the week Molière's company paraded, danced, acted, and recited. They presented four plays, beginning with *La Princesse d'Elide*, a spectacular 'comedy-ballet' written and directed by Molière, with music by Lully. On the sixth night they gave the first performance of *Tartuffe, ou l'Imposteur*, which immediately provoked such a storm among the devout that the King felt obliged to forbid its repetition. That was in May. On 20th June, Molière produced *La Thébaïde* in Paris, performed it twelve times between then and 18th July, then packed up his properties and costumes in readiness to go to Fontainebleau, where he had been summoned to repeat *La Princesse d'Elide*. He boldly profited by this occasion to read *Tartuffe* to the Papal Nuncio. The Italian prelate heard the attack on false devotion without displeasure, until its dangerous undertones were pointed out to him by his advisers.

While at Fontainebleau, Molière gave one performance of *La Thébaïde*. He produced it three times in Paris on his return there in August, once again before the King and Monsieur in September, and then put it in his repertoire for occasional production during the winter. No doubt he did his duty by the new author, and a score of performances in all represented reasonable success for a first play.[1] But from Racine's point of view, the handling of his tragedy may well have been a disappointment. The actors were probably tired when they first came to it; their minds were certainly full of more important and exciting matters. Molière himself was preoccupied with the ban on *Tartuffe* and with his attempts to have it lifted. And even at their freshest, could the troupe of the Palais-Royal have done justice to a piece originally conceived for the majestic tragedians of the Hôtel?[2] If Racine felt that the production of his play had been scamped and that it had been used mainly to fill a hole in the repertoire, his reaction would be understandable. The plays of established authors were launched only in the winter, when the Court was in residence at the Louvre or Saint-Germain. The summer and early autumn were regarded as out-of-season times and reserved for revivals, or new ventures for which no great success was expected.

3

La Thébaïde, ou Les Frères ennemis was of this order, but it was not until later that Racine saw its weaknesses. "I was very young when I wrote it," he says in his Preface of 1676. And he goes on to explain why "love, which normally fills so large a place in tragedies, has hardly any in this one."

[1] Twenty *consecutive* performances would have spelt an unqualified success. Thirty to forty meant that a play was outstanding and that, with a limited theatre-going public, many of the audience were seeing it for the second or third time. The theatres normally opened on only three days of the week—Friday, Sunday, and Tuesday. Hence, thirty performances would represent a run of ten weeks, or half the main theatrical season.

[2] The statement that Racine originally wrote *La Thébaïde* for Molière, given by Brossette and Grimarest, with other (inaccurate) circumstantial details, is shown to be false by Racine's own correspondence.

The significance of such an apology, made by the experienced playwright of thirty-six for the first work of his impulsive youth, has been disregarded by most critics. It throws yet another blot on the portrait of the 'tender', or naturally amorous, Racine. Although we must avoid the other extreme of believing that he became an exponent of erotic themes through calculation (his sentimental education was in the same direction as his literary development, but its pace was much slower), we are faced with the evident truth that his first tragedy was 'political' in design and treatment.

His subject is the final extinction of the ill-starred house of Oedipus. In the last act, nearly all the principal characters die: Oedipus' twin sons, Etéocle and Polynice, kill each other in battle; their mother Jocaste and sister Antigone commit suicide; Antigone's lover, Hémon, is killed in an attempt to prevent the brothers from clashing. This general slaughter was not, of course, invented by Racine. He was following the Greek dramatists, to whom he acknowledges his debt in his Preface. In spite of so much blood, however, the sense of horror is not aroused. To the audience, it does not greatly matter who perishes or who survives.

Yet La Thébaïde has several interesting features. Racine saw that it was essential that the climax should not come too early. He reserved the key scene—the meeting of the rival brothers—for the fourth act, after which the play falls surely into the dénouement, the final resolution of the knot in blood and violence. This is already the Racinian formula, the pattern on which all his great plays will be built, in fact soon the accepted pattern of French tragedy. The weakness of La Thébaïde is that it remains a formula and that the climax is only delayed until the fourth act by complicated plot-juggling and transparent devices which cause the first three acts to appear forced and mechanical. Racine the intellectual clearly understood his medium; Racine the artist had not yet acquired the skill to handle it in practice.

Nor had he yet established his system of characters which ran like a *motif* through the later plays, each one counter-balancing or completing another. The characters in *La Thébaïde* are untidy, uncorrelated; they wander about the plot without a clear dramatic purpose. Because of this aimlessness they have a certain individual interest. Unable to utilize them fully, Racine has begun to paint them. One at least is a sketch for a tremendous portrait.

Jocaste, the mother of Oedipus and his incestuous wife (Racine follows Euripides in making her live on into old age), is one of those dark, elemental personages which the Greeks, blending myths and humanity, could conceive more easily than we. On the one hand she is human, essentially and symbolically so, following out her desires to their furthest conclusion, concentrating on one object the two intensest forms of love. On the other hand, because of the intervention of the gods in her story, because of the doom which she cannot escape and because of the retribution (so terrible that it is almost ritualistic), which overtakes her, she shades into the supernatural until it is difficult to say where the woman ends and the myth begins. Writers of the modern world, accustomed to a cleaner division between the natural and the supernatural, have lost the secret of this type of character. Their culture does not provide the atmosphere of lyric ignorance in which alone such monsters can thrive. But they can be fascinated by them and can try to imitate them from the Ancients. No doubt in Racine's mind the conception of the mature woman, a prey to the strongest passions of her sex, had been implanted by his schoolboy reading. And because he first encountered her at Port-Royal, clothed in the poetry of the Greeks and of his own adolescent mind, he would never entirely separate her from those shimmering associations. However well he came to know his contemporary world, he would never attempt the realistic portrayal of an elderly harpy or a middle-aged nymphomaniac drawn from observation like a character from Balzac or Flaubert. His conception was more poetic and, in the end, more terrible.

Jocaste in *La Thébaïde* is little more than an indication. The drama is not built around her, but she is constantly there, an unhappy presence. She opens the play, pronouncing the first of Racine's words to be uttered on a stage. She invokes the sun and speaks of the horror of her own incestuous race, doomed, it seems, to work evil. She struggles to avert the catastrophe and, when she fails, kills herself. That is all. But one day this atavistic character who was intended only as a piece of dramatic machinery will swell to gigantic proportions in the poet's mind until she crowns his work and all but exhausts her creator.

In dedicating his first tragedy to Saint-Aignan, the young author showed his mettle in typical fighting words:

"Whatever enemies it may have, I fear nothing for it, since it will be assured of a protector who is not accustomed to be daunted by the number of his enemies."

Examined coolly, the boast might appear a little fatuous. But it showed a braver spirit than that of the curiously humble Boursault, who at much the same date was deploring his first full-length comedy, *Les Nicandres*, as "the worst play that has ever been inflicted on the public". It showed, too, a less tortuous approach than de Visé's, who later wrote anonymous puffs for his own plays in *Le Mercure Galant*.

4

Eighteen months later, Molière produced Racine's second tragedy, *Alexandre*. This time the première was in December (1665), in the most favourable part of the season, with time ahead, if necessary, for a four-months run before the Easter break.

Dramatically, *Alexandre* was an advance on *La Thébaïde*, an altogether neater, more coherent piece of work. The plot follows a well-defined curve and the characters include no suggestive eccentrics like Jocaste. In spite of their names borrowed from Ancient History, they are types of the seventeenth-century Court, or at least idealizations of that society, expressing in the language of the salons sentiments drawn from the pastoral romances. Petrarchan love, which Racine had found so difficult to introduce into the legend of the house of Oedipus, is here supreme. Alexander the Great, while engaged on the conquest of India, languishes for the love of Cléofile, the sister of the Indian king Taxile. A second king, Porus, aspires to marry Axiane, "Queen of another part of the Indies", and, thanks to the magnanimity of Alexander, is able finally to do so. The tragedy thus has a partially happy ending. Only the vacillating Taxile is killed in battle and Alexander remains temporarily unsatisfied in his love though admired for his noble heart.

The play was excellently suited to the taste of the time and had the further merit that the character of Alexander was a projection of Louis XIV, though the latter was not, at this date, notably frustrated in his loves. It was, on Racine's part, an intelligent piece of play-making, an almost certain bid for contemporary success, though too fashionable to be in other ways memorable. A Frenchman considering it from London put his finger shrewdly on its weak points.

"Two kings", wrote Saint-Evremond, "are robbed of their proper characters to be thrown at the feet of purely imaginary princesses. Porus is not forced into battle by the highest and dearest interests which motivate men— the defence of their country, the preservation of a kingdom —but solely by the beauty of Axiane. Thus are knight-errants depicted . . ."

And he goes on to condemn Racine's omission of all trace of local colour:

"The Indian hero ought to have a different character from ours. Porus, however, is purely French in this play."

But Saint-Evremond was in London, exiled from the mental climate of the work he was reviewing. He was out of sympathy with the subtle change of taste which the new playwright was exploiting. For his immediate public, Racine had struck the right note.

He was no doubt aware of this. He had been reading parts of *Alexandre* to friends and critics for at least ten months

before its production[1] and noting their reactions—
following in this the usual custom of dramatic authors and
arousing, as far as lay in his power, an advance interest in
his play. He looked forward confidently to a triumph
which he had been at great pains to prepare. That much
must be said to attenuate an action which stands to his
professional discredit.

On the 4th December, the play opened at the Palais-
Royal before a brilliant audience which included the
King's brother, Monsieur, Monsieur's wife, Henrietta of
England, Condé and his son the Duc d'Enghien. Molière
did not act himself, but cast La Grange as Alexandre and
La Torillière as Porus. The female parts went to his two
most lovely actresses: Axiane to the Du Parc and Cléofile
to his wife Armande. How they interpreted the play is not
known, but it is fair to assume that a tragedy produced by
Molière would obey his theory of 'naturalness' and shun
excessive emphasis.

Meanwhile, the rivalry between the Palais-Royal and the
Hôtel de Bourgogne had not diminished. After the Comic
War, the two theatres had continued in bitter competition.
Just before *Alexandre* they both produced comedies with
the same title of *La Mère coquette*. Quinault at the Hôtel
and de Visé at the Palais-Royal claimed paternity of both
title and idea with equal vehemence. The resultant public-
ity harmed neither. De Visé's comedy ran for six weeks
until it was taken off to make way for Racine. At the same
time, the Hôtel replaced Quinault's play by an eighteen-
year-old tragedy by Boyer entitled *Le Grand Alexandre ou
Porus*. This revival was apparently the best riposte they
could make to the Palais-Royal production, and cannot in
itself have constituted a very serious threat. Molière
seemed to have moved ahead of his rivals and to be well
placed for a profitable run.

Ten days after the opening night, however, a private
performance of Racine's tragedy was given at the Countess
of Armagnac's house. Monsieur and Madame were again

[1] Assuming that Pomponne's letter was genuine. *See* p. 160.

present, but this time a still more distinguished spectator was with them in the person of Louis himself. The actors were not Molière's company but Montfleury's troupe. Four days later public performances of the play began at the Hôtel.

The event is noted with dignified restraint in the register of Molière's theatre kept by La Grange:

"On 18th December, the troupe were surprised to discover that the same tragedy was being played at the Theatre of the Hôtel de Bourgogne. As the new arrangement had been made in connivance with Monsieur Racine, the company did not feel bound to pay him his share as author, since he had used them so ill as to give his play to another theatre."

Even the skilled actors of Montfleury's troupe would hardly have been capable of learning their parts and working up a five-act tragedy to production pitch at a day or two's notice. The conclusion that they began to rehearse *Alexandre* very shortly after Molière's première on the 4th December is inescapable. Who approached whom? Was Montfleury the tempter, luring the young author with promises of a more brilliant interpretation? Or did Racine, disappointed with the first performances at the Palais-Royal—which yet were a box-office success—approach Montfleury? Furetière, who was acquainted with both Molière and Racine, says that it was Racine who took his play to the Hôtel, acting on the advice of his friends. Whatever the exact nature of the negotiations, they were to Racine's ultimate benefit. By a manoeuvre by no means unique in the theatre of his time, he had attained the *Grands Comédiens*, who henceforth produced all his plays. There is small doubt that sooner or later he would have been bound to go over, or else stunt his development as a tragic dramatist. One can only regret that the transfer operated to the prejudice of Molière, whose record in both his professional and personal dealings was impeccable.

The future relations of Racine and Molière were correct but distant. Molière produced a minor author's parody of

Racine's next play, *Andromaque*, which did no harm to the original and was not particularly resented. Racine is reported to have defended *Le Misanthrope*, remarking that it was impossible for Molière to write a bad play; Molière is said, with at least equal generosity, to have praised *Les Plaideurs*. Both these anecdotes are secondhand. The affair of the actress Du Parc had more complicated undertones, which must be left for a later chapter. It cannot, however, be regarded as a matter of direct professional or personal rivalry between the two men. Of France's two greatest dramatic authors, it is best to say that their spheres were in fact very different and that after a brief fortuitous association it was natural that they should part.

At the Hôtel, the acting of Floridor as Alexandre, Montfleury as Porus, the Des Oeillets as Axiane and the Dennebaut as Cléofile ensured the success of Racine's tragedy. It probably ran for over two months, or 25–30 performances, since the next production of which there is any record was the elder Corneille's *Agésilas* which opened on the 25th February.

For Racine, this was an incentive of incalculable value. Subject, as genius often is, to fluctuations between sanguine confidence and despair, he shows in his first Preface to the published play how triumphant was his mood at this time.

"Whatever success my *Alexandre* may have had on the stage," he writes, "and although the greatest personages on earth and the Alexanders of our time have warmly pronounced in its favour, I do not allow myself to be dazzled by such illustrious applause. I willingly believe that their desire was to encourage a young man and to incite me to do even better in the future; but I confess that, small though my confidence in myself may have been, I can hardly help conceiving a certain good opinion of my tragedy when I see the lengths to which certain people go to decry it. So many intrigues were never directed against a valueless work . . ."

The triumph of that private performance before Louis, and no doubt the gracious approval which was expressed at its close, leads him to dedicate his play to the King and, in drawing the parallel between his hero and his sovereign, to silence his critics with a transcendental argument. Alexander too sentimental? The character of the great conqueror false? No.

"And who should judge better of that than a King whose glory spreads abroad as far as did the fame of the ancient conqueror, and before whom it can be said that *all the nations of the earth are silent*, as the Scripture says of Alexander?"

And going on to develop the theme of the grandeur of Louis and of his conquests still to come, he rises to a climax perhaps merely rhetorical, perhaps wishful, but certainly prophetic:

"For then your subjects will be obliged to devote all their vigils to the narration of so many glorious deeds, nor must they tolerate that Your Majesty should have reason to complain, like Alexander, that you had no one in your own time capable of recording for posterity the memory of your virtues."

CHAPTER VI

THE BREAK WITH PORT-ROYAL

A T the moment when Racine was exulting in the success of *Alexandre*, a pamphlet was published which contained this statement: "In the opinion of devout people, the qualities of a novelist and a playwright are not very honourable; indeed, judged by the standards of the Christian religion, they are abominable. A man who writes novels and plays is a public poisoner—not of the bodies but of the souls of the faithful. He must be considered guilty of an infinite number of spiritual homicides, which he has either caused in reality or which he may have caused by his pernicious writings. The more care he takes to cover with a veil of decency the criminal passions which he describes, the more dangerous they become and the more liable to deceive and corrupt simple and innocent souls."

Such strictures were neither new nor exceptional. They were typical of the ever-recurring quarrel between the moralists and the entertainers, between the Church and the Stage. If Molière, in *Tartuffe*, had dared to carry the attack into the enemy's camp, the offensive usually came from the opposite quarter. Though the theatres were never closed in France, as they had been in England under the Commonwealth, the status of the actor was precarious. He was regarded as a moral outcast and was excommunicate by the mere fact of his profession. He could only be buried in consecrated ground if he renounced the stage before dying. All who had to do with the playhouses—down to the very bill-posters—were considered to be tainted with their

traditional immorality. While the Church took no sanc-
tions against dramatic authors, provided they remained
exclusively 'poets' and were not at the same time actors,
they were not free—in the minds of the puritanical—of
the odium which attached to their interpreters. For more
philosophical minds, they were more blameworthy than
these and the great moralists, from Pascal downwards, went
to the root of the matter by attacking the dramatic art
rather than the actor. The theatre was constantly censured
for failing to draw a clear distinction between passion and
vice, or for presenting vice in over-attractive colours.

The general argument was so familiar that, as an argument, it should hardly have moved Racine. It was the source
and the timing of the pamphlet which struck him on the
raw. For it came from Port-Royal, and was the latest of a
series of public letters which his old master, Nicole, was
writing under the title of *Les Visionnaires*. Nicole was then
engaged in one of those polemics which were his life-
blood, this time against Desmarets de Saint-Sorlin, a figure
of some eminence in the world of letters. Desmarets had
been a playwright, novelist, and epic poet before devoting
himself to a theological campaign in which he not only
wrote against Jansenism but conducted a personal vendetta
against the *solitaires* by engaging spies to find out their hiding-
places and denounce them to the authorities. Nicole's
condemnation of the makers of novels and plays was,
therefore, directly inspired by his hatred of Desmarets. If,
in expressing it, his mind dwelt for a moment on the
aberration of Racine, he did not say so and by no open word
included him in his anathema.

But Racine read it in a different light. Here, once again,
was Port-Royal wagging its disapproving finger, deploring,
if not him, at least the glittering profession of the theatre
with which, in his enthusiasm, he felt particularly inclined
to identify himself. His reaction to Nicole's words was
like that of a man galled by domestic nagging. This was
the extension of the real family quarrel which had embittered his first attempts at 'emancipation'.

Some time after his return from Uzès, a letter had reached him from his aunt Agnès. It is undated, but it probably belongs to the latter half of 1663, when he was resuming his relations with the Hôtel de Bourgogne and planning *La Thébaïde*.

"Glory to Jesus Christ and to the most holy Sacrament", Agnès de Sainte-Thècle heads it, and, having done so, goes straight to the point.

"Having heard from Mlle . . . [? Vitart] that you thought of making a journey here with her husband, I had intended to ask our Mother [Superior] for permission to see you, because several persons had assured us that you were minded to think seriously of your future, and I should have been very glad to hear this from your own mouth, so that I could have shown you the joy I should have felt, had it pleased God to touch your heart. But I heard, a few days ago, a piece of news which hurt me deeply. I write you this in the bitterness of my heart with my eyes full of tears, which I wish I could pour out abundantly before God to obtain from him your salvation—the thing I desire more ardently than anything else in the world. But I have learnt with sorrow that you frequent more than ever the company of people whose name is abominable to every person who has even a tinge of piety—and with good reason, since they are cut off from the Church and from the communion of the faithful even at death, unless they recognize the error of their ways."

Here perhaps Racine looked up from the page, despairing at his aunt's invincible bigotry. It was a deadlock. He read on:

"So you can judge, my dear nephew, in what a state of anguish I am, for you must know the affection I have always had for you and that all I have ever desired was to see you serving God in some honest employment. I beseech you, my dear nephew, to take pity on your own soul and to search your own heart, that there you may seriously contemplate the abyss into which you have flung yourself. I will pray to God that He may grant you this grace.

I hope that what I have been told is not true. But if you are so unhappy as not to have broken off an intercourse which dishonours you before God and before men, you must not think of coming to see us, for you know well that I should not be able to speak to you, knowing that you are in a state so deplorable and so contrary to Christianity. Nevertheless, I shall not cease to pray God to have mercy upon you, and upon me in so doing, since your salvation is so dear to me.''

So far as is known, this was the last communication between the two relatives for some fourteen years. Agnès de Sainte-Thècle Racine stood by her ultimatum. Jean Racine accepted it. No compromise was indeed possible. They looked at life from two irreconcilable points of view, were driven forward by two completely divergent motives. For Agnès, whose body and soul had been pledged to Port-Royal since the age of fifteen, the choice before her nephew was simple: either damnation in the world, or salvation away from it. For him, there were finer shades, more complicated distinctions. But if he was challenged in that plain, dogmatic fashion, he must reply as plainly, leaving no doubt as to his choice.

His final answer came in the scathing refutation of Nicole's pamphlet which he wrote at the beginning of 1666. In this, the *Lettre à l'auteur des Hérésies imaginaires et des deux Visionnaires*, Racine deliberately adopts the standpoint of the man of letters, uninterested in theological disputes, concerned only with upholding the honour and tone of his profession.

"I declare that I take no sides as between M. Desmarets and you," he begins icily. "I leave the world to judge which of you two is the *visionary*. Until now I had read your Letters with a limited interest, sometimes with pleasure, sometimes with distaste, according as to whether they struck me as well or badly written."

Maintaining his pose of a detached young critic who happens to have picked up a pamphlet emanating from some hermit whose wrong-headed views he feels it his duty to correct, the pupil of Port-Royal turns to answer Nicole's charges against the immorality of writers:

"But we know all about your own austere morality. We are not at all surprised that you should damn the poets; you damn many others besides them. What does surprise us is that you should seek to prevent men from honouring them. Come, sir, content yourself with ordering the precedence of the next world; do not assign the rewards of this one. You left it some time ago. Leave it to judge of the things which belong to it."

But he cannot maintain this detachment. This, we have seen, is part of a family quarrel. His inside knowledge of Port-Royal leads him to make points which must have struck his old masters as the extreme of treachery. He taunts the Jansenists with their obstinacy and narrowness in theological matters ("Not everyone can write against the Jesuits. There is more than one way of achieving fame"), with their clumsiness in setting the whole world against them at the same time, with their tendency to approve their friends and to condemn their enemies equally blindly, with the heavy facetiousness of their prose style— always excepting Pascal.

Perhaps all this could have been said by an outside adversary, provided he had made a close study of Jansenist methods. But only a deserter from within the citadel could have related the anecdotes which illustrate but disfigure Racine's *Letter*.

You condemn the comedy? he inquires. But one of your shining lights, Le Maître de Sacy, once translated several comedies from the Latin of Terence. Have you grown holier since? Not at all; but that was before Desmarets attacked you. "The crime of the poet has angered you against poetry." You condemn the novel? But have you forgotten that when Mademoiselle de Scudéry drew a flattering portrait of Port-Royal in *Clélie*, this abominable book was eagerly passed round among the *solitaires*. They all wanted to see the passage in which she called them "illustrious". Then how do you explain your treatment

[79]

of M. le Maître? Before renouncing the world he had practised at the bar, had committed the crime of writing verses. When he retired to Port-Royal, you allowed him, in spite of his past, to make translations for you, to compose theological works upholding your doctrines. But, you say, before this he underwent a long and heavy penance. He spent two whole years digging in the garden, mowing in the meadows, washing the crockery. And that, of course, rendered him worthy of the doctrine of St. Augustine.

This sneer at the man who had taken a paternal interest in Racine, and was now dead, was perhaps the most malicious feature of the whole attack. It troubled Port-Royal as much as his anecdote of the Mother Superior Angélique (now also dead) who, according to Racine, had once dispensed the most meagre hospitality to two visiting friars because she suspected them of being enemies of the house. When she discovered her mistake, the grey bread and cider which had been set before them were whisked away and replaced by white bread and vintage wine.

All these respected figures, caught sometimes in homely attitudes, filed past in Racine's taut, stinging prose; until finally not even the Great Arnauld, the house's darling and champion, was spared. For, observed the young writer, returning to his literary standpoint: "The liveliness of M. Pascal has done greater service to you than all the solemnity of M. Arnauld."

Racine did not at first sign his pamphlet, but such was its success that others began to claim, or to let it be understood, that they were the authors. This provocation was more than Racine could endure, and he came into the open. No doubt he had never intended to be truly anonymous, but would have preferred to have his name whispered by the conoscenti rather than displayed openly in print.

Two independent replies were published by supporters of Port-Royal. One was by the Jansenist Du Bois, the other is credibly attributed to the barrister Barbier d'Aucour, who was to pursue Racine again ten years later, in a clumsy satire directed against his character and his plays. Both replies make dull reading beside Racine's brisk and personal assault, but their more solid arguments destroy most of his debating-points. On an impartial view, it is evident that Racine had jumped in rashly and allowed himself to be trapped. Du Bois hit shrewdly on Racine's weakness—his vanity as an author—when he wrote:

"You do not mind being damned, but you cannot bear not to be esteemed. You renounce the communion of the saints for the hope of a share in the heritage of Sophocles and Virgil."

The final achievement of Racine's life was that he managed to have both, but neither he nor the excellent Du Bois could have foreseen this at the time.

Barbier d'Aucour made a more malicious point:

"You will not do much harm [to M. Nicole] nor to the others whom you seek to involve in the quarrel you have picked. You might have looked for some better means of achieving fame."

The innuendo cannot be entirely ignored. In the eyes of the public Racine had indeed descended to the common practice of writers who, in order to arrive, noisily attacked those whom they saw above them. It was the technique which Donneau de Visé and Boursault had followed when they measured themselves against Molière. But Racine's virgin venture appeared more odious than theirs because it was directed against his own people, the men who had educated and befriended him. Ultimately, this explains it. He was in revolt against the restraining influences of his boyhood; now or never he must break finally free, and the indiscriminate sarcasm of his diatribe was part of a desperate struggle to reach the open air. But to the onlooker, as well as to the Port-Royalists themselves, these secret motives were not evident. For them, Jean Racine was a man who in the insolence of his first success had turned on his old masters and hoped to climb to higher notoriety by betraying them.

Circumstances made his action appear worse. Port-Royal was then in the throes of yet another persecution.

The *solitaires* were once again in hiding or in exile. Le Maître de Sacy, whom Racine had cited for his translations of Terence, was soon afterwards caught and imprisoned in the Bastille—thanks precisely to the denunciations of men like Desmarets. The plight of the nuns—Racine's aunt among them—was even worse. Those of the Paris house were dispersed. Those of Port-Royal des Champs, after being forcibly removed from their convent in 1664, had been allowed to return in July of the following year, but in conditions which spelt spiritual bondage. They were refused the sacraments, even on their death-beds. Their religious offices were clipped and controlled by a hostile chaplain appointed by the Archbishop of Paris. A guard of soldiers was quartered in the convent itself with orders to segregate them from the outside world. They tried to appeal to the judicial tribunals. This recourse was denied them by a decree issued in February 1666, at about the date of Racine's attack on Nicole. In their despair they conceived one of those strange stratagems which could only spring from minds mingling absolute faith with pure superstition. A nun died, of necessity unshriven. Before burying her, they placed in her hand a petition signed by the whole community which she was charged to deliver before the highest tribunal of all, that of Christ. If the appeal proved their superstition, it also proved their spirit, for it was no meek document.

"Repulsed by all the judges of the world," it began, "we have appealed to the Sovereign Judge, and so far He has remained silent. He seems to despise our prayers. We are afraid that finally the world will say, insulting our misery: Where then is their God?"

Such was the moral atmosphere of Port-Royal, and it is small wonder that the Racine whose *Alexandre* had just been acted by Montfleury, Floridor, and the Des Oeillets could no longer accept it or sympathize with it. He struck back at his two critics in a second Letter in which he again championed the world against the cloister and ended by washing his hands of the whole pack of theologians.

"I do not refuse to read your *Apologies* or to be a spectator of your disputes, but I will not be involved in them. It would be strange indeed if, for an opinion which I expressed in passing, I should have brought down upon me all the disciples of St. Augustine."

A year later, in a Preface intended to introduce the two Letters, he was a little more conciliatory and affected to consider his attack on Nicole as a humorous remonstrance which had been taken too seriously. Neither this Preface nor the second Letter was published. One supposition is that friends of Racine, and in particular Boileau, dissuaded him from continuing a polemic which "did credit to his wit, but not to his heart", and that he followed their advice not only by withholding the second Letter but by withdrawing from circulation as many copies of the first as he could recover. This is the version given by his son Louis and, at the least, is highly suspect. A second hypothesis, supported by a letter written from Port-Royal to Nicolas Vitart, is that the poet was silenced by pressure which Port-Royal brought to bear on him. Vitart, hearing that Nicole intended to include in a new edition of the *Visionnaires* the two replies by Du Bois and Barbier d'Aucour, had attempted to help his cousin by requesting their exclusion. His Port-Royalist correspondent—conceivably Lancelot—replied that it was too late. The edition was already in print and part of it had been distributed. He went on to threaten Racine with exposure if he persisted in his attacks. Port-Royal, it seemed, possessed a note in Racine's hand disclaiming authorship of the first Letter against Nicole which he had since recognized as his. If he continued the polemic, this note would be published and the young poet would be placed in an impossible position.

If this version of the affair is correct—and there seems no reason to doubt it—it would appear that some minds at Port-Royal were less unworldly than Racine had represented them.

But Port-Royal avoided after all an open personal encounter. Its leaders went their way, unshakably

[83]

convinced of their own rightness, and occupied with greater matters than disputes with an errant pupil. Two years later they entered on a period of respite, thanks to the intervention of a new Pope and the protection of Condé's sister, the powerful Duchesse de Longueville. Racine also had far different preoccupations in the immediate future. He had taken his stand as a dramatic poet and a man of the world and he had no intention of receding from it. Perhaps during the following years, when he was in the midst of the literary mêlée, he regretted not having dealt more serenely with his old teachers. It was always his way to react violently, then gradually to take a more tolerant view of people and events. But if such became his feeling towards Port-Royal, he did not show it for a long time.

Racine's deepest grievance against Port-Royal, which he could feel but never see objectively enough to formulate, was that it wished to separate him from humanity. Already by the loss of his parents and by a certain aloofness in his own nature, he had a tendency to isolate himself which he regretted and struggled to overcome. Far from helping him, the teaching of his Jansenist masters encouraged this tendency. Man turned inward upon himself, they held, is sinful; therefore he must turn towards God. This doctrine of older minds who had renounced or fled from the world omitted the second alternative, which was that he should turn towards his fellow-men. This alone attracted the sensitive young poet—all the more strongly because he mistrusted his ability to do so. At the moments when he felt the pull of Port-Royal towards the solitary life, reinforcing the insidious call of his own nature, he rose in blind, unreasoning revolt. Their prison had an escape-door towards God, but not towards the humanity for which he longed.

In his dealings with his friends and his family Racine was far from being a monster of ingratitude. The faults on their side were at least as great as on his. A letter written to his sister Marie a few months before the quarrel with Nicole

(August 1665) reveals clearly enough his true attitude towards them. After saying that he has not heard from her for at least six months the author of *Alexandre* continues:

"Tell me why you are angry with me and I will try to satisfy you, for you are often inclined to think that things are different from what they are. Whatever may be the matter, tell me what it is that you have against me.

"I have got a few small things to send you, but I shall wait until cousin Du Chesne or cousin de Sacy is going your way. I have returned the lace which she bought for you to the shop and she will buy you a different piece. If you want anything, however small, you have only to let me know—don't stand on ceremony. I am not in such a poor position that I cannot satisfy you, whatever your opinion of me may be! But above all write to me, please write, and I will write more often too. I have heard about all the squabbles between Logeois and Mademoiselle Nanon and between M. de Sacy and the attorney. Send me news of yourself and love me always. *Racine.*"

CHAPTER VII

ANDROMAQUE

TWO years after *Alexandre*, Racine's third tragedy, *Andromaque*, was performed in the Queen's apartments in the Louvre before the Sovereigns and a few privileged members of their Court. This sign of royal approval—which was no more than had been given to *Alexandre*—had been preceded by a more intimate mark of favour. Racine's dedication to Henrietta of England, Duchess of Orleans, shows that she had allowed him to read the play to her while he was composing it, had made suggestions of her own and had "honoured with a few tears" the sorrows of his characters. This collaboration with Madame, renowned as she was for her sensibility and intelligence, was the sweetest possible foretaste of public success. Here, in the person of the twenty-three-year-old daughter of a King of England, was the 'young princess' of his reading and of all his secular plays, from Antigone of *La Thébaïde* to the blonde, tender Aricie of *Phèdre*, still shadowy in the future. More than by the carefully-worded praise of Louis, Racine must have been warmed by the frank sympathy of Henrietta, whose destiny was as terrible as that of any princess immortalized by the Greeks.

On 18th November 1667, the day following the private performance at the Louvre, the play opened at the Hôtel de Bourgogne. It was an immediate success. The only completely contemporary account which we have is in the issue of 26th November of the *Lettre en vers à Madame*, a weekly gazette compiled by Robinet. Robinet—an execrable rhymer but a conscientious reporter—contrives to relate the plot and casting of the tragedy without making a single illuminating remark. Only the length of his notice points to the importance of the occasion. But the triumph of *Andromaque* echoes in letters and memoirs through the rest of the century. Of all Racine's tragedies, it was the most frequently acted in his lifetime. Nearly thirty years later, Charles Perrault, looking back with the detachment of a man whose literary battles were at last over and whose main concern at that moment was to prepare his *Tales of Mother Goose* for the publisher, could declare that the première of *Andromaque* had caused a theatrical sensation comparable to *Le Cid*. Madame de Sévigné, that inveterate disparager of Racine, admitted that a performance of *Andromaque* "made me shed more than six tears". Saint-Evremond received a copy of the play in London soon after publication and admitted after reading it, as though grudgingly taking account of Parisian opinion, that "on the whole, Racine must enjoy a higher reputation than any other dramatist after Corneille".

Six months after the première (in May 1668) Molière produced Subligny's *Folle Querelle*, a skit on *Andromaque* which testifies to the vogue of the original. Subligny shows a pair of lovers divided by their opinions on the merits of Racine's tragedy, and he introduces into his comedy criticisms of Racine's style which were by no means all unjustified.

While *Andromaque* made an immediate appeal to the contemporary public, it also had in it the lasting elements of a work of art. It was unmistakably the work of a dramatist who now possessed his medium. Whereas in *La Thébaïde* he had fumbled and in *Alexandre* he had experimented with a conventional plot fashionably dressed, in *Andromaque* he had found, or rather constructed, a subject perfectly suited to the theatre.

Racine quotes as his main inspiration a short passage from the *Aeneid* which describes the captive Andromache lamenting before Hector's cenotaph. In this not very

[87]

suggestive extract he states that he found the whole subject of his tragedy—scene, action, the four chief actors, "and even their characters"—except for the character of Hermione for which he drew on Euripides. Other features were suggested by the *Iliad* and by Seneca. But if all these ancient sources are brought together (or if any one of them is followed exclusively), the result is still not *Andromaque*. Respecting the literary conventions of his time, Racine is always careful to justify his plays by quoting classical authorities. In fact, no one is deceived. That Pyrrhus occurred in Seneca and Hermione in Euripides is of secondary importance. Before they could participate in the Racinian drama, they had to be re-created.

Stripped of its classical trappings, *Andromaque* is the story of a woman who is in the power of a dominating man who loves her passionately, but whom she cannot love in return. Her affections are set on her dead husband and on the child which she has had by him, and which it is in her captor's power to destroy. Her captor is irked by the desperate love of a younger girl to whom he is betrothed. She in turn is loved, with no less desperation, by a man who believes that she will turn to him if her arranged marriage is frustrated. These four characters constitute a hopeless chain of lovers, each one's face fixed on another who cannot respond. Andromaque is absorbed in her son Astyanax and in the memory of the dead Hector; Pyrrhus pursues Andromaque; Hermione, Pyrrhus; and Oreste, Hermione. Between each of these pairs of characters, morally handcuffed together as they are, lies a relationship supplementary to the simple one of pursuit and avoidance. Pyrrhus can practise emotional blackmail on Andromaque by threatening her child; Hermione is the fiancée to whom Pyrrhus has given his promise and whom reasons of State require him to marry; Oreste is an official envoy, whose mission, if successful, would result in the marriage of Hermione to Pyrrhus, and hence the destruction of his own hopes. The chain finally disintegrates when Oreste, strained beyond endurance, cuts across it in order to murder Pyrrhus. The links are now broken and all the characters, except Andromaque, fall away into death or madness.

Once constructed, the subject of *Andromaque* is an ingenious machine which can hardly fail to be effective in competent hands. It lends itself to a variety of settings, from the magnificent to the sordid. It could furnish, for example, a modern study in total frustration dressed in the language of the psychiatrist's case-book. It could serve for a slum-and-gunman drama filled with overstated emotion and sensational action. Without variation in the basic design, the treatment could be more or less subtle according to the author's talent and his conception of his audience.

Racine's primary achievement was to have built the machine and then to have used it to yield the maximum of dramatic effect, given the resources of the stage of his time. His play is full of tremendous situations, full of scenes of pathos, brutality, or suspense linked together in a sequence which appears inevitable. In fact, the dramatic machinery is so efficient that at times it is a little obtrusive; it then obscures the other virtues of the tragedy. In Racine's later plays, the machine is more carefully covered; the poet and the psychologist occupy the foreground, the necessary play-builder hides behind them. This is the result, on the one hand, of a developing experience in the craft of writing for the stage, on the other of an increased subtlety in the analysis of the passions. But beyond this, it must be remembered that Racine never again employed a plot of such complexity as in *Andromaque*, but chose themes which permitted of simpler dramatic handling.

To many, the obvious 'drama' of *Andromaque*, which ensured its success from the first, is its greatest quality. It would indeed be absurd to blame a work written for the theatre because its theatrical merits are too striking. Nevertheless, it is arguable that Racine, determined to carry his audience with him to the height of a tremendous climax, overwrote the last act with a certain damage to plausibility. The most questionable scene is Scene iii, in which Hermione, having persuaded Oreste to kill Pyrrhus,

suffers a revulsion of feeling at the news of his death and
turns on Oreste with hatred and loathing, as though he
alone were responsible for the crime. Her accusation,
ending with the famous words:

> Pourquoi l'assassiner? Qu'a-t-il fait? A quel titre?
> Qui te l'a dit?

has thrilled many generations of playgoers by its unexpec-
tedness. As an example of strong theatre it is justified, and
in the high key in which the whole scene is played it passes
as the highest, but not a discordant, note. Considered more
coolly outside the theatre, particularly by a critic willing
to see even in the Racine of *Andromaque* the profound
psychologist rather than the proficient young playwright,
Hermione's hysterical question may appear too violent to
ring true. Such a critic may even go on to argue that
Hermione is not really addressing Oreste, to whom she
appears to be speaking, but is questioning herself and her
own motives. Such refinements of interpretation are
typical of much modern critical writing on the Racinian
theme. They deny Racine his strength as a man of the
theatre in order to build him a reputation as a casuist of the
passions who would have been more at home in Madeleine
de Scudéry's salon than in the Hôtel de Bourgogne. Neither
his true reputation nor an understanding of his work is
thereby advanced. Racine is as subtle as his medium will
allow: where too much subtlety would be undramatic, he
boldly sacrifices it, even (though not often) at the risk of
psychological crudity.[1]

---

[1] The same device is used by Webster in *The Duchess of Malfi*, Act IV,
Sc. ii:

FERDINAND: I bade thee, when I was distracted of my wits,
Go kill my dearest friend, and thou hast done't . . .
. . . I hate thee for't.
. . .
By what authority didst thou execute
This bloody sentence?
BOSOLA: By yours—
FERDINAND: Mine? Was I her judge? etc.

The last act of *Andromaque* is an attempt—and a successful attempt—to carry a reasonably critical audience up to a height of horror and excitement at which they will accept the madness of Oreste as a natural dénouement. The machine has been wound up and it runs down in no whimper. If Racine uses a little more force than is necessary, that is an excess which is perceived in reading the play in the study, but hardly in the theatre.

The view of the critic, trained to detect and interpret, but not to create, is often at variance with that of the author, whose main concern is to carry his particular public with him. The opinion of a practising dramatist on this point is interesting. It illustrates aptly the two different approaches.

"No author is perfect," Somerset Maugham once wrote.[1] "You must accept his defects; they are often the necessary complement to his merits; and this may be said in gratitude to posterity, that it is very willing to do this. It takes what is good in a writer and is not troubled by what is bad. It goes so far sometimes, to the confusion of the candid reader, as to claim a profound significance for obvious faults. So you will see the critics (the awe-inspiring voice of posterity) find subtle reasons to explain to his credit something in a play of Shakespeare's that any dramatist could tell them needed no other explanation than haste, indifference, or wilfulness."

Andromaque is a young author's *tour de force*. But the precision and assurance with which it is written should not be allowed to conceal its other, equally important quality. By its poetry it establishes a tone which has come to be considered as peculiarly Racinian, and which appears most clearly in his three plays inspired by the Greeks: *Andromaque*, *Iphigénie*, and *Phèdre*. This verse—rapid, economical, but never realistic—creates for the characters who speak it an atmosphere which is neither sordid nor heroic, neither

[1] Preface to *Altogether*, by W. Somerset Maugham. (London, 1934.) Quoted by permission of the author and Messrs. William Heinemann Ltd.

legendary nor contemporary, neither wholly Greek nor
wholly French. It might be defined as the atmosphere of the
assize court temperately idealized; alternatively, as the
atmosphere of mythology brought within reach of *l'homme
moyen sensuel*. Since the Renaissance attempts have constantly been made to contemporize the Greeks, and in
France more dramatists have been fascinated by the problem
than in any other Western country. A perfect solution is
no doubt impossible, but, on a long view, Racine has come
nearer to it than any other dramatist. His method is not an
adaptation but a fundamental reconstruction in which the
poet is as deeply concerned as the playwright.

2

In the first production of *Andromaque* at the Hôtel de
Bourgogne, Racine was nobly served by his interpreters.
They gave of their utmost to ensure the success of a play
which no doubt fired their enthusiasm by the opportunities
which it provided for virtuoso acting. They were the most
distinguished cast that could have been assembled on the
tragic stage at that date, though more notable for experience
than for youth.

The title role was given to the youngest of them, an
actress aged about thirty-four called Marquise du Parc. She
had come over from Molière's company the previous
Easter and was now playing her first big part at the Hôtel.
Her striking but somewhat passive beauty suited her to the
part of the tragic widow, although on the score of age she
might have expected to be cast as the younger princess,
Hermione. This part went to the Des Oeillets, who at
forty-six was an old and tested member of the company.
The role of Hermione, although about equal in length to
that of Andromaque, demands greater vivacity in an actress
and greater reserves of temperament. The Des Oeillets,
whom contemporaries described as a charming and intelligent actress, seems to have possessed these qualities.

Floridor, now in his sixtieth year, played the stern but

love-stricken Pyrrhus. A veteran of the Marais, he had missed by only a couple of years the experience of acting in the two plays which established the reputation of Corneille and of Racine. But in 1637, the year of the *Cid*, he was still with a travelling company and had just re-crossed the Channel after an unsuccessful season of French plays at two different London theatres. He joined the Marais in 1638, acted in Corneille's other early triumphs, from *Horace* to *Rodogune*, then transferred to the Hôtel. He was thus a very seasoned actor, universally respected and popular, though a less flamboyant personality than his great colleague.

The impetuous Oreste, love-demented and fate-pursued, was played by Montfleury, then sixty-seven, whose corpulence and mannerisms Molière had smiled at. Such was the vehemence of his acting that the audiences forgot his age, ignored his physique and thrilled to the pure fire of his art. He performed with such ardour that it killed him. The emotional expenditure of the part, rising to the climax of madness so written by Racine that it tempts an actor to go beyond his utmost, caused him to burst a blood-vessel. He was carried to his house to die.

"I have set a detestable example," he remarked on his death-bed. "Henceforth no author will rest content until he has killed a comedian."

So perished, in a manner not unworthy of Molière, Molière's bitterest professional enemy. The gazette-writer Robinet rises to a kind of rough poetry when he records how Montfleury

> a, en jouant Oreste,
> Hélas, joué de tout son reste.
> O Rôle tragique et mortel,
> Combien tu fais perdre à l'Hôtel
> En cet Acteur inimitable.

No theatrical taboo attaches to *Andromaque*, though it well might. Of the four actors who created the four chief parts, Montfleury was dead within a month. A year later, the Du Parc had followed him. Two years more, and the

[93]

Des Oeillets was dead. Only the veteran Floridor survived long enough to play in two more of Racine's tragedies. Then he, too, succumbed. Thus, less than four years after the opening performance of *Andromaque*, the king, queen, prince, and princess of the drama had disappeared, and with them the real princess, Henrietta, who had taken the play under her wing and who died at the age of twenty-six in an atmosphere of confusion and suspicion.

Some superstitious client of the fashionable fortune-tellers, or some moralizing puritan, might have been expected to point to this strange death-roll, but none did.

As for the author, his triumph was more lasting. The gazette-writer's first report, as was often the case, had been concerned mainly with the actors. He devoted only a few lines of perfunctory praise to the author, perpetrating for the first time in print the childish pun which was to haunt Racine throughout his career:

> *On ne peut voir assurément*
> *—Ou, du moins, je me l'imagine—*
> *De plus beaux fruits d'une* Racine.

But for more critical minds, Racine was now a dramatist of considerable stature. Actors and actresses might come and go, but to have written *Andromaque* was to have acquired a reputation not lightly to be forgotten. At twenty-eight, he had a name which his friends could admire and which his enemies were eager to attack.

CHAPTER VIII

LIFE AND DEATH OF THE DU PARC

LES PLAIDEURS

I N the course of a conversation at Auteuil thirty-six years after the event, Boileau is reported to have said:

"Monsieur Racine was in love with the Du Parc, who was tall, well made, but not a good actress. He wrote *Andromaque* for her; he taught her the part and made her rehearse it like a schoolgirl."

Before we examine this statement and its far-reaching implications, let us recall what is known of Marquise-Thérèse du Parc.

She was the daughter of an Italian called Giacomo de Gorla (or de Gorle) who had established himself at Lyons as a showman and quack doctor, a combination of professions which went very easily together and remained associated in rural parts of France and Britain at least until the end of the nineteenth century. While de Gorla huckstered his remedies, a drummer played or a girl danced. When he drew teeth or performed rudimentary surgical operations, musicians and mountebanks performed to screen the patient's complaints.

Marquise (a 'show' name in itself) probably made her first public appearances outside her father's booth. Certainly she was a dancer as well as an actress. During one of the visits which Molière's company paid to Lyons, the comedian René Berthelot du Parc, whose stage name was Gros-René, made her acquaintance and married her. She was added to

Molière's precarious pay-roll. This is believed to have taken place in 1653, when she was twenty.

For the next five years, her history was merged in that of the wandering troupe of which, together with Madeleine Béjart and the de Brie, she became one of the chief actresses. In April 1658 the troupe arrived at Rouen on what proved to be the last stage of its pilgrimage before its successful establishment in Paris. Marquise was not at first with it. She had remained behind at Lyons, nursed by her friend the de Brie, to give birth to a daughter who received the name of Marie-Anne at her christening on 1st May. The arrival of the two pretty young actresses was impatiently awaited at Rouen, and expectations were not disappointed when at last they reached the provincial capital. Rouen was the home and literary fief of the Great Corneille, who with declining years and talent was beginning to take as much interest in his female interpreters as in the abstract beauties of the drama. Such at least is the conclusion to be drawn from his comments on the acting of the Beauchâteau (in *Oedipe*). Such is the tenor of his remarks a little later on the Des Oeillets and on the promise shown by the still obscure young actress Mademoiselle Marotte. When Marquise du Parc appears, he turns the solemn gaze of genius upon her and is conquered. His emotion seems to have found only literary expression and to have been purely one-sided, but the clumsiness of Corneille's behaviour shows that he was genuinely affected.

"Marquise," he writes, with touching lack of tact,

> *Marquise, if my face*
> *Bears the mark of the years,*
> *Remember that at my age.*
> *You will hardly look better.*
> *. . . In that future time*
> *I shall not be unhonoured.*
> *You will be counted fair*
> *Only because I said so.*

When, six months later, the company leaves Rouen, and

Corneille's wooing has still had no effect, his farewell madrigal repeats the *motif* of his first:

> *Car vous aimez la gloire et vous savez qu'un roi*
> *Ne vous en peut jamais assurer tant que moi.*
> *Il est plus en ma main qu'en celle d'un monarque*
> *De vous faire égaler l'amante de Pétrarque.*

Self-infatuated, like many an ageing great writer, Corneille achieved nothing by his promises of literary immortality. But episodes like this, preserved in the writings of men of talent, gave Marquise a reputation for coldness towards her admirers. It was said that while she had still been in the south, the poet Sarrazin went mad and eventually died for hopeless love of her, though the cause of his madness cannot be definitely known. A later libellist asserted that Molière was rebuffed by her before turning, first to the de Brie, then to Armande Béjart who became his wife. But this story rests on nothing more than a malicious pen guided by its owner's conventional view of an actor-manager's relationships with the women of his company. It is not impossible that the Du Parc's unresponsiveness to her admirers stemmed at this period from a preference for her husband, the fat and jovial Gros-René, to whom she bore at least four children in seven years. Such an explanation, however, does not seem to have occurred to the majority of biographers who think of her only in her widowhood and who hold that an actress who was undoubtedly beautiful and professionally seductive failed in her duty to biography by not sustaining the character off the stage. All that can be said for certain is that the Du Parc achieved a contemporary reputation for setting hearts aflame without taking fire herself, and with this reputation already advertised by Corneille she came to Paris.

2

Soon after their arrival in the capital, the Du Parc and her husband went over to the Théâtre du Marais, where they remained for a year. They returned to Molière at Easter 1660, in time for Gros-René to step into the shoes of Jodelet, who had just died, and for Marquise to fill a series of comedy and ballet parts which occupied her until the summer of 1664. In the month before the production of *La Thébaïde* she appeared in all her beauty at Versailles in the fêtes of the *Ile enchantée*. On the first night she represented Spring in the Ballet of the Seasons. The official chronicler recorded with admiration her riding of a Spanish horse in the procession which followed the ballet:

"Mademoiselle du Parc, with the sex and advantages of a woman, displayed the skilled horsemanship of a man. Her costume was green with silver embroidery, adorned with natural flowers.

"Summer followed her, represented by the Sieur du Parc riding on an elephant decked with a rich covering."

Autumn, in the person of the actor La Thorillière, came next, mounted on a camel. Winter (Louis Béjart) rode a bear. The procession was closed by a moving mountain, on which sat Molière enthroned as Pan with Armande as Diana.

On the second night, Marquise du Parc appeared as Aglante in *La Princesse d'Elide*. On the third, she was Alcine, mistress of the enchanted palace; sitting languorously on a marine monster, she evolved in company with the de Brie and Armande, who were mounted on lath-and-plaster whales. She acted on subsequent nights in *Les Fâcheux* and *Le Mariage forcé*, but the main impression made by her appearance at Versailles was of her beauty, her grace and her skill as a dancer and horsewoman. These were naturally the qualities which would appeal first to the eyes of the Court and the fact that they alone were recorded speaks neither for nor against her ability as an actress.

Her success in spectacle did not go to her head. Although for a different woman it might have opened up perspectives more alluring than those before a hard-working member of a theatrical company, no scandal attaches to her name. Widowed in the autumn of the year of the *Pleasures of the*

Enchanted Island, she soon had to support alone her children and her stepmother. She remained at the Palais-Royal for two and a half years longer, dancing in ballets devised for the Court, creating the parts of Axiane in Molière's short-lived production of *Alexandre*, of Elvire in *Don Juan* and of the prude Arsinoé in *Le Misanthrope*, and appearing finally in Corneille's *Attila*.

After the short run of this unsuccessful tragedy, the first which Corneille gave to the Palais-Royal in preference to the Hôtel (or had Floridor and Montfleury grown cool towards the great author?) the Du Parc left Molière and joined the *Grands Comédiens*. This was at Easter 1667. Her departure seems to have been effected without ill-will on either side.

3

Such was the woman for whom, according to tradition, Racine wrote *Andromaque*, and with whom, for a short time, his life seems to have been linked.

Let us try to see these matters in their true perspective. On the first point, 'tradition' begins with Boileau, sitting in December 1703 in his house at Auteuil. Racine has been dead for over four years, the Du Parc for thirty-five. Boileau is carefully cementing his reputation as the literary pontiff and mentor of the century which has just ended. He remembers scenes which no one else is in a position to recall, advice which he gave in private to writers now dead, decisive influences which he wielded on the composition of works now famous. Racine's tragedies are an important part of Boileau's retrospective domain, and it is well known that the two were close friends in Racine's later years. It is natural that Boileau should have something exclusive to say about the genesis of *Andromaque*, Racine's first great play. When he speaks, he gives good measure.[1]

To his flat statement that Racine was inspired to write

[1] His remarks, made in conversation with Mathieu Marais, were noted down by Brossette for use in his memoirs on Boileau. (*See* Mesnard: *Notice Biographique* in the *Œuvres de Racine*. Hachette, 1865).

his tragedy by love of the Du Parc and that, having done so, he was obliged to drill her in her part "like a schoolgirl", later writers have added the supposition (it is nothing more) that Racine 'stole' the actress from Molière and placed her in the Hôtel; this as a natural corollary to removing his play *Alexandre* from the Palais-Royal. But the two events were separated by some fifteen months, during which the Du Parc continued as an active and valued member of Molière's company. It could be assumed—though there is not an iota of evidence—that, well after *Alexandre*, Racine helped to persuade her to leave Molière. It is harder to believe that it was his influence working on the Hôtel de Bourgogne that decided that exclusive company to admit her. At the date of her entry into the company, Racine had to his credit one reasonably successful play. In his eagerness to have it produced by the Hôtel, he had violated professional etiquette in a manner which showed what store he set by the *Grands Comédiens*. At the best—all this was before *Andromaque*—he was not more than a young dramatist of considerable promise. He was certainly in no position to impose on Floridor and Montfleury an actress who could not act, simply because she happened to be his mistress.

The more plausible, if less romantic, supposition is that the Hôtel, seeing an actress of talent who was willing to join it, encouraged her to do so—the more readily because Montfleury's gain would be Molière's loss—and that the Du Parc, for her part, was attracted by the higher remuneration at the Hôtel and by the prospect of appearing with the foremost tragic actors of the time. There are indications, based on the parts in which Molière had cast her, that she shone more brightly in tragic than in comic roles. Her physical appearance—her height, beauty, and dignity—gave her natural advantages as a *tragédienne* which would be wasted in comedy. The fact that she was also a good dancer and rider is not incompatible with this view of her talent and does not necessarily type her as a circus-performer—though some prejudice of this kind may have lingered in the mind of the sedentary Boileau. In short, it is fair to suppose that in joining the Hôtel her chief motives were professional. Racine may have added his own arguments and acted as an intermediary, but it is most improbable that he brought her to the Hôtel on his sole initiative.

If this is admitted, the suggestion that he taught her the part of Andromaque line by line and gesture by gesture grows perceptibly weaker. There are inherent improbabilities in the picture of a barely-established dramatist engaged on his third play teaching her business in detail to an actress some six years his senior, with fourteen years of stage experience behind her, including considerable success in major parts. This conception of Racine as a great trainer of actresses was implanted by Boileau and developed with the best intentions by Louis Racine, desirous of vindicating his father's morality during the discreditable period when he was concerned with theatre people. If his interest in them was that of an elocution-master, the relationship would appear in a more respectable light. The same argument is applied in due course to the Champmeslé, with perhaps more plausibility in that Jean Racine may have improved the diction of this finally great actress, but with less than no effect on the belief that the relationship was also erotic.

If we doubt that Racine drilled the Du Parc in the part of Andromaque, we doubt more strongly that he wrote the tragedy for her. This raises an important question concerning Racine's methods of working which is not exhausted by this one instance. A few years later, in the Champmeslé period, Madame de Sévigné declares that Racine "writes plays for his mistresses, not for posterity" and expresses the opinion that "if ever he ceases to be young and in love, it will not be the same thing". Such remarks suggest a writer who (1) needed the stimulus of love in order to do his best work, and (2) conceived his tragedies as vehicles for the actresses whom he loved. Thus, *Andromaque* would have been composed under the impulse of his passion for the Du Parc and intended as a means of raising her, in one generous sweep, to stardom in the company she had just joined.

The balance of probability weighs heavily against this view. In spite of the title, Racine's play has two heroines and he has put more psychological invention into Hermione. If outside the theatre he was drunk with love for Du Parc-Andromaque, inside the theatre he kept a sober professional eye on Des Oeillets-Hermione. A spectator unversed in stage personalities could but conclude that his interest and preference go to the second character. This, of course, was the part in which the Champmeslé later rose to fame and in which, according to a tradition as deep-rooted as the one which we are examining, she first conquered the attention of Racine.

The process of creative writing is hardly capable of exact analysis. The points of departure and the stimuli to execution are too varied and too mingled ever to be precisely defined. But if a simple answer could be given to the simple question raised by Boileau and Madame de Sévigné, it would surely be that Racine loved his creations first and their interpreters second.

4

Yet, as Racine's mistress, the Du Parc may have contributed something to *Andromaque*. In a sense much more general than that which supposes that she was the model for one particular character or that the play was written as a vehicle for her, her relations with Racine may have furnished the raw material of erotic experience which the composition of such a tragedy seems to demand. While it is dangerous to argue from the internal evidence of a work of literature—with sufficient ingenuity, almost anything can be proved by such means—there is so marked an advance from *Alexandre* to *Andromaque* that it is reasonable to seek some of the causes in the author's life. In the two years which separate the two works, he has grown immensely in power, skill, and confidence. While *Andromaque* is still a young man's creation, it is mature in a sense in which

Alexandre is not. The air of maturity proceeds partly from the dramatist's greater skill: the artist has worked hard and has mastered his medium. The apparent development in psychological understanding also proceeds in part from practice in handling the medium, from a better digestion of literary models and from a keener observation of life. But there is a residual flame in *Andromaque* which it is hard to believe was kindled by professional application only. If the Du Parc did not 'inspire' *Andromaque*, it is very possible that her presence added that vital spark which alone enables an author to move his public, and which no amount of contriving can command. She may, too, have sharpened his emotional insight even if her relationship to him was similar to none of the relationships which he put on the stage. The tradition that Racine composed *Andromaque* under the influence of his first profound passion may therefore contain an element of truth, so long as it is added that the artist remained in control of the lover and never relinquished the right to mould his experience into the most effective shape.

That Marquise du Parc was in fact the mistress of Racine has become a commonplace of Racinian biography and one which should be accepted, although the evidence on which it rests is fragile enough. It consists of three items, none of them conclusive in itself.

The first is Boileau's statement, already quoted, that Racine was 'in love' with her. It must be remembered that, when he made it, Boileau was looking back to a period at which it was unlikely that he had known either of the principals intimately.

The second is a genuinely contemporary account of the Du Parc's funeral by the gazette-writer Robinet. He describes the procession of mourners who followed the bier to the cemetery. Among the actors, painters, and 'adorers' walked

> . . . *les poètes du théâtre,*
> *Dont l'un, le plus intéressé,*
> *Etait à demi trépassé.*

[103]

This has always been understood as a reference to Racine, although Robinet does not explicitly name him.

Finally, Catherine Monvoisin, a soothsayer and poisoner, deposed eleven years afterwards that she had heard from the Du Parc's stepmother that Racine had contracted a secret marriage with the actress. She went on to say that he was suspected of having poisoned her. Motive: "He was jealous of everyone." Catherine Monvoisin's evidence will be discussed more fully in a later chapter. Here it need only be said that it was given after torture, was based on hearsay and that the court finally did not judge it strong enough to institute judicial proceedings against Racine.

Beyond those three items nothing remains which even
* approximates to proof of a liaison. If contemporaries knew more, their information died with them. Friends or enemies, they never put their knowledge or suspicions on record in book, diary, letter, satire, or lampoon. Allusions of the type which surrounded the later liaison with the Champmeslé either were not made or have been lost.

Nevertheless, it does not seem necessary to reject the tradition that the pair were lovers. It fills an obvious gap in the story of Racine's life. Given his nervous temperament, the free circumstances in which he now lived and his growing prosperity, it would indeed be strange if he had not taken a mistress before his twenty-eighth year. He is no longer the gauche and mistrustful neophyte of Uzès. After *Alexandre*, he has the means and the opportunity to frequent the town, the theatre, and the Court. It would be abnormal if he did not live as others of his contemporaries in similar positions. Why should he not have attached himself to the Du Parc, who was now as free as he was to follow her inclinations? A genuine deep feeling may have drawn this woman, who had refused other, more tempting advances, towards the man younger than herself, shy, brusque, and ardent, who was also a rising light of her own profession.

5

The sequel was very short. Racine and the Du Parc continued, we assume, to be lovers through most of the year following *Andromaque*. He had no new tragedy in hand. Her theatrical record was blank. In the production which followed *Andromaque* (Thomas Corneille's *Laodice*) the principal female parts went to the Des Oeillets and the Dennebaut. In fact, the silence of the chroniclers and critics makes it uncertain whether, after the run of Racine's tragedy had ended, she ever mounted on the stage again.

During the summer, however, she was in the public eye for another reason. The event was typical of the unsuccessful admirations which she so often provoked and her apparent lack of response proves either her chastity or her devotion to Racine.

The impetuous Chevalier de Rohan, scatterbrained heir of one of the greatest families in France, proclaimed his intention of marrying her, let the world and his relations say what they would. The remarks of Bussy-Rabutin, Madame de Sévigné's cynical cousin, give the best comment on this affair, as they are the best testimony to the reputation of Marquise from a source not suspect of exaggerated chivalry.

"I admire the star of the Du Parc," he writes to a correspondent on 29th July 1668. "She has kindled a thousand passions: a thousand people and not one of them mediocre. The folly of the Chevalier de Rohan will be complete if he marries her. It is an excellent thing for the honour of Love that such extraordinary things should happen from time to time in his domain. They revive our respect for him."

No more was heard of the unthinkable marriage. The key—opposition by the Chevalier's family to the point of using force—probably lies in a gossip-paragraph published the same month in Brussels, although the writer is mistaken in his names:

"The *Chevalier de Genlis* has been given guards to restrain him from marrying the Demoiselle du Parc, play-actress."

The Chevalier de Rohan's next scandalous adventure was of a more dangerous kind. Six years later he was beheaded for plotting against the throne.

The reactions of the actress, and of Racine, to de Rohan's impetuous behaviour can be no more than guessed. It was the last public passion that she was to kindle, for in December of the same year she lay dying. On the evidence of Catherine Monvoisin, already mentioned, it is possible to construct a picture of Racine watching broken-heartedly by her deathbed, jealously forbidding the door to her stepmother and to the other sordid creatures of the underworld—wisewomen, procuresses, and abortionists—with whom one side of her life was linked. It is possible that, nauseated by the human vultures who hovered round his dying mistress, and in a forlorn attempt to salvage her memory, the poet drew a ring from her finger and removed jewels and other effects which he had given her. But this rests on hearsay retailed by an evil, ignorant, and distracted woman. The cause of death is wrapped in equal mystery. Discounting the improbable suggestion of poison, the Du Parc may have died in childbed, or from the consequences of an abortion, or of a natural illness. From that strange atmosphere of medicine, magic, and slander, distorted images rise as though in the steam of a witches' brew. It is impossible to discern the truth.

All that is certain is that she died on 11th December 1668 in her lodging in the Rue de Richelieu, that she was buried on the 13th according to the rites of the Church, and that a huge concourse, assembling most of the theatrical profession as well as a great part of the town, attended the funeral. The facts are given in the Register of Burials of the church of Saint-Roch and by the Robinet. But her best epitaph was written by another hand:

D'abord qu'on la voyait paraître,
Nous sentions dans nos cœurs certaine flamme naître

Que le silence exprime mieux;
Chez nous, nous n'étions plus les maîtres:
Elle savait si bien cet art ingénieux
D'entrer dans le cœur par les yeux
Que cet art paraissait en elle
Comme une chose naturelle,
Et nous nous estimions heureux
D'être brûlés de si beaux feux,
Et de mourir enfin d'une cause si belle.

Racine himself was silent. As might be expected, no mention of the Du Parc written by him survives, if it ever existed. More than this, it is impossible to discern in his published work any trace of the impression made on him by her untimely death. At about the time when that occurred, he was occupied with the publication of his light-hearted comedy *Les Plaideurs*. If he mourned her, it was in his heart.

6

Les Plaideurs is only an interlude, though a pleasant one, in Racine's career as a dramatist. He had first conceived the comedy as a scenario for the Italian Players, who would have improvised their own dialogue and acted the piece on the stage which they shared with Molière in the manner of a broad burlesque. But the departure from Paris of the actor Scaramouche caused Racine to change his design and to write *Les Plaideurs* as a regular three-act comedy for the Hôtel de Bourgogne.

Invoking, as for *Andromaque*, classical authority for his invention, Racine declares that the germ of his comedy was in *The Wasps* of Aristophanes and that its composition was greatly assisted by the encouragement of his friends who were anxious to see whether the wit of the Greek author would be effective on the French stage.

"And so, half urging me on, half trying their own hands at the work, they forced me to begin a play which was not long in being finished."

The result was a broad satire on some of the more extravagant characters of the Parisian legal world. For its
burlesque technicalities Racine drew on his recollections
of "a lawsuit which neither my judges nor myself ever
properly understood". This was no doubt the affair of the
benefice in Anjou which had already been the subject of
legal proceedings in the Uzès days and which Racine acquired later. It is conjectured that he was deprived of it by
new litigation in the summer of 1668, and that he came
fresh from the lawcourts to write his comedy.[1]

In spite of these diverse inspirations, the play which
Racine finally wrote has a unity and a character entirely its
own. The weird actions of the judge and litigants, each
imbued with a fixed idea which suspends him just outside
the margin of the normal world, fill *Les Plaideurs* with a
nonsensical solemnity. The knock-about element—probably better suited to the Italians than to the Hôtel—gives the
piece a youthful irresponsibility. Racine had written a
comedy gay in its conception, comic in its lines and situations and different from anything that his contemporaries
produced. It became an established favourite with Town
and Court and during the last twenty years of his life was
acted more frequently than any one of his tragedies. To-day
it stands in the repertoire of the Théâtre Français on a par
with the most popular of Molière's works. When, however, it was first produced at the Hôtel de Bourgogne,
probably in November 1668, it failed to please and was
withdrawn. Perhaps only Molière's company could have
done it justice.

Shortly afterwards the *Grands Comédiens* were summoned
to entertain the Court at Saint-Germain. After giving a
five-act tragedy, they threw in *Les Plaideurs* as a make-weight.
It was a vast success. "The King thought it no dishonour
to his dignity or his taste to roar with laughter—so loudly
that the Court were astonished." Thoroughly elated, the

---

[1] He describes himself as *prieur d'Epinay* in a document dated 12th
May 1668, but does not use the title in the *privilège* of *Les Plaideurs* dated
5th December 1668. The inference is that he lost it in the interval.

actors crowded into their three coaches, drove back to Paris through the night and hardly stopped until they came to Racine's lodging. They shouted to the happy author to come down and share the story of their triumph and his. No doubt many voices spoke at once. The story would be declaimed rather than related. The Beauchâteau, a little tipsy, would insist on showing them all over again that bit of business where she pushed the judge through the cellar window. It had sent the King into hysterics. In one of the coaches young Brécourt's face was slapped ringingly. The horses jingled their harness and the coachmen, well-wined too, laughed from their boxes.

Windows opened in the quiet, respectable street. Anxious citizens peered out under their night-caps. This disturbance after midnight, centring round the correct, fashionable M. Racine, could mean only one thing. In his comedy against the Law he had overstepped the bounds of prudence and here were the Justices, with three coachloads of officers, come to carry him off to prison.

The next morning Racine may have found it difficult to explain why he was not, as his neighbours believed, confined in the Conciergerie. They would be much less scandalized by a police raid than by the visit of a band of drunken players and he may have found it convenient to let the original rumour stand, adding a few vague references to the protecting influences which had finally saved him.

Had it been necessary, it could have been true. Louis XIV's pleasure in *Les Plaideurs* was expressed on 31st December 1668 by a grant of 1200 *livres* to the poet "in consideration of his application to *belles-lettres* and of the dramatic pieces which he gives to the public".

CHAPTER IX

THE CHALLENGE OF CORNEILLE

NEITHER the excursion of *Les Plaideurs* nor the death of the Du Parc caused Racine to deviate for long from his more serious professional ambitions. *Andromaque* had confirmed his self-confidence and given him a strong taste for fame. There was no measuring the heights to which, as a tragic drama-tist, he might rise. The only doubt—since no writer, however original, works without reference to his contem-porary world—concerned the path which he should take and the exact nature of the reputation to which he should aspire.

Racine reacted, as he himself has pointed out, with ex-treme sensitiveness to criticism. It goaded him first into acid vindications of his own work. Later, he sometimes recognized the validity of the objections raised and adopted the suggestions of his critics on minor points. There was, however, one type of criticism too general to be met by partial refutations or to be appeased by small changes in the published editions of his plays. It concerned the whole writer and the total impression which his work made, and it is best represented by the comments written by Saint-Evremond in the summer of 1668.

It was the year of the *Essay of Dramatic Poesy*, the year after the publication of *Paradise Lost*. As a man of wide cultural sympathies, Saint-Evremond could hardly avoid responding in some measure to the more serious influences current in Restoration London. They did not clash too violently with his own rooted preferences, formed in the days when he was younger and in France. As an exile, he could not help loving the heroic generation of his youth more fondly than if he had remained with it. As a man of letters he could re-live the past in a work of literature. His particular Grecian Urn was Corneille. At twenty-six he had shouted for Rodrigue and thrilled for Chimène. Nothing could obscure the glory which they radiated, for he had left home before the iron-tongued giants who followed them over the stages of the Marais and the Hôtel de Bourgogne had begun to appear outmoded. He knew that Corneille had declined from that early magnificence and that a new taste was growing up across the water. But he was inclined to think it a debased taste. A great poet is always a great poet and if he happens to have moved us in earlier, happier days he is well-nigh unassailable.

Saint-Evremond was a fair-minded man, possessed of no mean critical faculties, so that when his friends in Paris sent him at the same time copies of Corneille's latest tragedy of *Attila* and Racine's *Andromaque*, he read both conscientiously and attempted to compare their merits without prejudice. Nevertheless, his bias for Corneille was stronger than his judgment. *Attila* he found admirable. As for Racine:

"It seems to me that *Andromaque* has every appearance of a fine work; it comes very near to having elements of greatness. Those who do not go deeply into these things will admire it; those who demand unqualified beauties will seek in it a *je ne sais quoi* whose absence will prevent them from being entirely satisfied. You are right in saying that the play has suffered by Montfleury's death; it calls for great actors who can supply by their acting what is not in the text. But, on the whole, it is a fine play, much above the average though a little below greatness."

Saint-Evremond despatches his critique to his friend the Comte de Lionne, who circulates it privately through the salons of Paris. There it meets with the approval of all who, for whatever reason, disliked the young playwright. Some were rivals jealous of his growing reputation. Others were relatively disinterested persons of the generation and mental habits of Saint-Evremond who were glad to see their opinion put with more clarity and authority than they themselves could command. If the exile is out of touch, he enjoys compensating advantages. His remoteness lends weight to his judgments. He is credited with seeing the broad issues in better perspective. Thus Saint-Evremond's measured words, based on an evident desire to be impartial, were more bitter to Racine than the attacks of his immediate contemporaries who challenged him on points of detail sometimes puerile in their pedantry. Saint-Evremond seemed to question, not his historical accuracy or the correctness of his verse, but the quality of his genius.

Wherever he looked—and he looked very high—there was Corneille blocking his sunlight: less the real Corneille, who admittedly was past his best, than Corneille's reputation. Huge and shadowy, it refused to define itself except by catchwords: *great* and *sublime*. How many men of ambition and originality have allowed themselves to be sidetracked by similar catchwords which defy definition because they are synthetic products built from the mass-feeling of a period or a social group. *Honnête*, elegant, sentimental, natural, *spirituel*, proletarian, integrated, civilized, such words must not be scrutinized at the moment of their ascendancy. They must be 'felt' and accepted. The alternative is to overthrow them by revolution, but Racine was not consciously bent on changing the régime: his ambition at that time was to usurp Corneille's reputation and to seat himself on the same throne. Looking back, it is easy to say that his talent traced an alternative road for him. It was less clear at the time. Since *great* and *sublime* were the highest words of praise in the mouths of serious critics, he would have them for himself.

The Racine who meditated this challenge was the fighter rather than the artist.

An admirer of Racine will always think the prestige of Corneille a little overblown. His grandiloquence oppresses and he carves giants out of cardboard. Yet his contemporary achievement is undeniable. Not only did he form French classical tragedy for the stage, but he gave it standing as a literary genre which it would hardly have acquired otherwise. Thirty-three years older than Racine, he established the medium which his young rival was to perfect. It is possible to question his genius, but not to deny him the boldness and energy of a pioneer.

His great plays were all written in his physical prime. At the age of thirty this lawyer from Rouen achieved sudden unqualified fame with his second tragedy, *Le Cid*, which drew the whole town to the Marais and set up a new model for the drama. There followed in succession *Horace*, *Cinna*, *Polyeucte*, and *La Mort de Pompée*—four great tragedies—and one comedy, *Le Menteur*, after which Corneille transferred his allegiance to the Hôtel de Bourgogne. His first tragedy for the Hôtel, *Rodogune*, already showed a considerable decline in power. By his thirty-eighth year his best vein was exhausted. The remainder of his long career as a writer was taken up with unsuccessful attempts to renew himself. He gave half a dozen more plays to the *Grands Comédiens* then, after the plain failure of *Pertharite*, retired to live quietly at Rouen.   *

Seven years later he emerged from his retirement—his interest in the theatre perhaps rekindled by the visit of Molière's company. In 1659, the year of the Spanish Peace, he returned triumphantly to the Hôtel with *Œdipe*. (At that time, Racine, released from Port-Royal, was just beginning to enjoy the greater freedom of Paris.) But if *Œdipe* was a box-office success for Corneille, it was the last. During his formative years, Racine watched the 'great author' groping his way round a world grown unfamiliar, experimenting with a *pièce à machines*, shifting from the Hôtel to the Marais, then back to the Hôtel, and eventually, with *Attila*, betaking himself to Molière at the Palais-Royal.

The sexagenarian Corneille should have been a pathetic figure, but he was not. Contemporaries were too close to see as clearly as the modern historian of the theatre that the Great Corneille by then was stuffed with straw. His reputation was still formidable. A number of men of letters deliberately preferred the static glory of the old giant to the less calculable competition of a younger man. Even in the theatre he remained a force, less because of the new plays which he was writing than thanks to his early triumphs which were constantly revived. They were as good vehicles as ever for a school of acting which had not changed radically in thirty years.

Corneille's own attitude was different. His old plays were his rock, but his new plays were also good. If they failed to please it was the fault of the times, or of the actors, or of a hostile *cabale*. By nature solitary, contemplative rather than observant, pompous rather than insinuating, he strode heavily about the world of letters and on the rare occasions when he noticed mockery, dismissed it as impertinence. "What," he exclaimed, when told that Racine had parodied one of his most famous lines in *Les Plaideurs*, "What business has a young man to go about ridiculing people's finest verses?"

He developed a mild form of persecution-mania, of which the most evident symptom was a jealousy of rising authors.

There is some plausibility in the story that, after hearing a reading of *Alexandre*, Corneille advised Racine not to essay the theatre but to concentrate on other types of poetry. Even if the remark is apocryphal, it fairly represents the attitude which Corneille would necessarily adopt towards the romanced history of which *Alexandre* was an example. If it is debatable which of the two dramatists was the first to attack, there is no doubt that Corneille willingly joined battle when it was offered him and that in his own estimation he was neither pathetic nor outmatched.

3

Others besides Corneille stood in Racine's path. He saw them, for the most part, as sycophants of his chief opponent, members of a hostile faction eager to damage him in the name of their idol. Sometimes, perhaps, he saw the hand of Corneille where it was not and the elusive nature of the adversary then led him to strike harder than circumstances warranted.

How otherwise explain his aversion for the Abbé Boyer, a prolific author who during the 'sixties was producing at the average rate of one play a year? It was true that his old tragedy *Le Grand Alexandre* had been revived by Mont-fleury in competition with Racine's tragedy at the Palais-Royal, but it had been dropped the moment that Racine's play was offered. This had been at most a phantom rivalry. Yet Racine was to exercise his wit at Boyer's expense until the day of the latter's death. He was no doubt exasperated by the sight of Boyer steadily writing his annual play, achieving fair success though never brilliance, enjoying a contemporary reputation which caused Chapelain to describe him to Colbert as " a dramatic poet who comes second only to Corneille in this profession ". Boyer was another reputation cumbering the ground rather than an active rival. For this reason, added to the fact that medio-crity easily irritates genius, Racine did not feel able to disregard him.[1]

In Philippe Quinault, Racine had a more dangerous contemporary. Rather than an obstacle, he was a snare. He was four years older than Racine and, after an apprentice-ship served with the poet Tristan l'Hermite, had produced his first comedy at the age of eighteen. Now he was writing romantic tragedies for the Hôtel de Bourgogne and striking with great skill a note softer than Seneca and the Spaniards, yet less languishing than Ariosto and the

[1] Much later, Boyer was to compete deliberately with Racine as a writer of Biblical plays. But this did not occur until after *Athalie* and was the culmination of a long-standing rivalry, not its source. See p. 283.

pastoral romances, which chimed exactly with public taste. Its ideal hero was Louis XIV, statesman and warrior, putting on golden armour at the close of the day's business to ride in carousel with his 'knights' and, that over, to assume the mantle of a lover. Popular art is always on safe ground when it puts the young executive into fancy dress and this feature of Quinault's tragedies (which Racine had reproduced in *Alexandre*) was hailed with relief after the stern heroics of Corneille. Quinault's *Astrate, Roi de Tyr*, produced at the Hôtel de Bourgogne in the winter of the year which had seen the unimpressive launching of *La Thébaïde*, was a spectacular success, notwithstanding the contempt with which Boileau dismissed it later. The piece was praised for ''containing tenderness everywhere—that delicate tenderness so peculiar to M. Quinault. One notices also several novel observations on politics and love, which are developed to their full extent . . . The situations, astonishing though some of them appear, are unravelled smoothly and without violence''.

This suave, undemanding type of entertainment might well have become characteristic of French tragedy after Corneille and have marked its decadence but for two redeeming factors. The first was the appearance of Racine, in whose character as an artist ''delicate tenderness'' was subservient to a certain polished brutality. (But this brutality might have been eliminated, as it was in *Bérénice*, and its maintenance was due, in some measure, to his preoccupation with Corneille.) The second was the disappearance of Quinault from straight drama to collaborate with Lully in opera. This occurred in 1671, the year after *Bérénice*, and, while it provided Quinault with a more congenial outlet for his talent, it also removed from Racine's path a competitor and a temptation. Racine's bid to out-Corneille Corneille ultimately strengthened his art; had he persisted in attempting to out-Quinault Quinault, he might have succeeded, but at the cost of deserving absolutely to be called the 'tender' Racine. The existence of the pompous, masculine Corneille lessened the risk of his

Photo : Hachette.

AT PORT-ROYAL: A DYING NUN RECEIVES THE LAST SACRAMENTS.

Engraving by Magdeleine Hortemels.

PIERRE CORNEILLE AT THE HEIGHT OF HIS POWERS.
From the 1644 edition of his plays.

becoming a purveyor of delicious trifles and so forestalling Marivaux.

Another author whom Racine saw well established in front of him was Thomas Corneille, but with him Racine never seems to have clashed. Perhaps he could not be jealous of so eclectic and popular a talent. Very different in character and performance from his formidable brother, Corneille de l'Isle—as contemporaries knew him—was the most successful box-office author of his day. In a professional career which spanned Racine's and was over three times as long, he scored at least one triumph in each dramatic genre. His tragi-comedy *Timocrate* ran for six months at the Marais in 1656 and by its eighty-six consecutive performances set up a record run for the century. When, five years later, the Hôtel de Bourgogne gave his tragedy *Camma*, the actors were almost crowded off the stage by the press of spectators; to relieve the congestion Montfleury was obliged to play on Thursday in addition to the regular theatre days of Friday, Sunday, and Tuesday. Thomas Corneille came near to repeating this triumph in tragedy with *Ariane* (1672) and *Le Comte d'Essex* (1678), though the success of both was due largely to the acting of the Champmeslé. Between these two, he collaborated with Donneau de Visé to write *Circé*, a tragedy with *machines* and music which was immensely popular and, but for the intrigues of Lully, might have set up another record in its kind. Having established a monopoly in opera, or anything approaching opera, Lully presently accepted Thomas Corneille's collaboration as a librettist. In this field also he proved to have a pleasing talent, although he did not surpass Quinault. As though to prove his versatility, he wrote popular comedies at intervals throughout his career, ranging from early imitations of the Spanish to a grimly topical skit on the poisoning trials which he composed with Donneau de Visé in the winter of 1679.

Such were the principal writers for the French stage at the time when Racine, having 'arrived' with *Andromaque*, stood looking for fresh fields to conquer. The others—

Gilbert, Subligny, Boursault, de Visé, Le Clerc—might sometimes get in his way, but even at this point he cannot have considered them as serious rival dramatists. They were occasional playwrights, but much more journalists, pamphleteers or satirists. When in these capacities they attacked him, Racine hit back very hard. He saw them not only as critics raising an immediate and limited objection but as satellites of his great predecessor. After the rejection of his first play by the Marais he had suspected a covert motive for the refusal—an intrigue against him, or a personal grudge. Now he can be certain that he has enemies and that behind them all—in spirit, if not always in fact—is the figure of the Great Corneille.

The prospect of building up an independent reputation for himself does not satisfy him. He must first meet Corneille on his own ground and dethrone him. Until he ceases to hear that Corneille is sublime while Racine is merely pleasing, all his triumphs will be incomplete.

CHAPTER X

THE ASSAULT ON CORNEILLE

BRITANNICUS

WO years after *Andromaque* the playbills of the Hôtel de Bourgogne announced Racine's *Britannicus*. He had spent the best part of the year following *Les Plaideurs* in composing and polishing his fourth tragedy. With no one star actress in mind, no passionate attachment to inspire him, he had put all his dramatic skill, all his feeling for psychological and historical truth, into this play which he hoped would lift him to the top of his profession. Seven years later, when all his secular tragedies except *Phèdre* had been written, he observed of *Britannicus* that "of all my tragedies this is the one which I can say I worked on most carefully". He intended it to affirm his mastery in 'political' drama as *Andromaque* had established his reputation in sentimental, and to prove that he was as much at home in a Roman subject as in a Greek.

His theme was the first crime of the youthful Nero, whom he took at the interesting point in his life when his character still appeared undecided and when the *monstre naissant* still had power to choose between a future of good or of evil. By the final curtain he has committed himself. The murder of his innocent rival Britannicus points the way he will follow during the rest of his career. To exteriorize the hesitations in Nero's mind, Racine provides him with two counsellors who sway him alternately towards virtue and vice. Burrhus, the honest man, fights a losing battle against Narcisse, the subtle corruptor, whom some French critics have compared to Iago though he seems to us of considerably lesser stature. Racine himself was content to define his creation as a "Court pest".

The 'political' aspects of the play are strengthened by the scheming of Nero's mother, Agrippine, a domineering woman with a criminal past. Having poisoned her second husband in order to secure the Empire for her son, she now feels that power is slipping from her hands. Nero, whom she has regarded as her puppet, is beginning to assert his own will. In a desperate attempt to redress the balance, she suddenly throws her weight on the side of Britannicus, although her earlier intrigues have excluded him from the throne. But Nero, abetted by Narcisse, is too ingenious for her and in the last-act poisoning of Britannicus she sees her own doom foreshadowed.

The waning fortune of Agrippine, the rise of Nero, the manoeuvres of Narcisse, and the murder of Britannicus provide in themselves the elements of a sufficiently robust plot. Racine, however, weaves in a love-interest by introducing among his characters the princess Junie, betrothed to Britannicus and coveted by Nero. Sexual jealousy (and the opportunity for a superb scene of emotional blackmail) thus reinforces the political rivalry between the two men, though it does not dominate this play as it does *Andromaque*.

Having begun with a conception in the virile Cornelian-Roman vein, Racine may have wondered, when the play was finished and produced, whether he had not over-emphasized the erotic element. He covers his uncertainty by a vigorous justification of Junie whom he champions the more warmly because—unlike the other characters—she was nine-tenths his own creation.

"Junie also has had her critics; they declare that out of an old coquette named Junia Silana I have made a virtuous young girl. How would they answer me if I told them that Junie is an invented character, like Emilie in [Corneille's] *Cinna* or Sabine in *Horace*? But I can tell them that if they had read history properly they would have found a Junia Calvina, of the family of Augustus and the sister of Silanus. . . . This Junie was young, beautiful and, as Seneca says, *festivissima omnium puellarum*—of all maidens the sprightliest. She loved her brother tenderly and their enemies, says Tacitus, accused them both of incest, although they were only guilty of a little indiscretion. If I represent her as being more modest than she was, I have never heard that it was forbidden to amend the morals of a character, particularly when the character is unknown.''

Since *Alexandre* and *Andromaque* it had become impossible for Racine to write a play—and equally impossible for his public to accept one from him—which did not contain a love-interest centred upon a tender but spirited sub-heroine. He created Junie almost by instinct. The rest of his characters and their relationships were the product of careful and ingenious planning. All his conscious effort was directed to the task of making them plausible and dramatic-ally balanced. In this case the effort had been great but, he felt, successful. He had challenged Corneille, yet with-out laying himself open to a charge of imitation. Drawing only on the material he found in Roman history, he had devised a powerful story of which no previous dramatiza-tion existed. Confidently he gave it, with the six promising parts which it contained, to the team of the Hôtel. Despite the loss of Montfleury and the Du Parc, they still possessed considerable acting strength.

2

The première was on Friday, 13th December 1669. On the same unpropitious date the Marquis de Courboyer was executed on the Place de Grève for having slanderously accused another nobleman of high treason, thus providing a rival attraction. Among the thinned audience at the Hôtel the *cabale* of rival authors was busy, pouring poison into their neighbours' ears as Nero poured poison into the cup of Britannicus. One of them was that lively critic and journalist Edme Boursault who, in his *nouvelle*, *Artémise et Poliante*, has left us the only substantial eye-witness account of a Racinian first-night.

"Seven had struck on every clock in Paris when I came out of the Hôtel de Bourgogne after seeing the first performance of M. Racine's *Britannicus*. M. Racine has been threatening with violent death—no less—all others who dare to write for the theatre. Even I, who presumed to do so once—but so little that, luckily, no one remembers it— could scarce avoid trembling like the rest. So with the intention of perishing in a less ignoble way than my colleagues whose only resource would be to go and hang themselves, I took my place in the pit expecting to be honourably crushed to death by the crowd. But the Marquis de Courboyer having chosen this same day to justify his titles of nobility, had drawn off all the merchants of the Rue Saint-Denis who normally attend the premières at the Hôtel, and I found myself with so much room that I decided to ask M. de Corneille, whom I noticed sitting alone in a box, to be so good as to dash himself down upon me as soon as the desire to despair of life should overtake him. But at this moment Agrippine, sometime Empress of Rome, who, for fear of missing Nero to whom she desired to speak, had been waiting at his door since four o'clock in the morning, imposed silence on all who had come with the intention of listening . . .

"Monsieur de X, an admirer of M. Racine's noble verses, did everything that a true author's friend can to contribute to the success of his play, and was too impatient to wait until it began before breaking into joyful applause. His face, which at a pinch might serve as a compendium of the passions, espoused all those expressed in the play one after another and transformed itself like a chameleon as the different actors spoke their parts. The young Britannicus particularly, who had but recently discarded his bib and tucker, affected him so strongly that, having smiled in anticipation of the happiness which seemed to await his idol, the sudden tidings of his death constrained him to weep. I can imagine nothing more obliging than to be able to place at will a fount of joy and a fount of sorrow at the very humble service of M. Racine.[1]

"Meanwhile the authors who uncharitably assemble to decide the fate of new plays and who usually sit together on a bench in the Hôtel de Bourgogne known as the Awful Seat because of the injustices dispensed from it, had dispersed among the audience for fear of being recognized and during the first two acts the fear of death impelled them to deny their glorious avocation. The third act having slightly reassured them, the fourth seemed to destroy their hopes of reprieve, but the fifth—which is usually considered the most deadly of all—was yet so kind as to restore them to life. Some connoisseurs, near whom I stood *incognito* so as to overhear their opinions, found the verse most refined, but they judged Agrippine to be unreasonably proud, Burrhus aimlessly virtuous, Britannicus recklessly enamoured, Narcisse needlessly treacherous, Junie irresolutely constant and Néron wantonly cruel . . .

"Although nothing obliges me to be a well-wisher of M. Racine, who has done me some disservice without my giving him cause, I intend to do justice to his play without considering who is its author. It is agreed that *Britannicus* contains lines as fine as can be written; and this does not surprise me, for it is impossible that M. Racine should compose bad verse. Certainly he has repeated a number of times: *Que fais-je? Que dis-je?* and *Quoi qu'il en soit*—phrases which hardly belong to good poetry; but I regard that as no doubt he regarded it himself, as a natural manner of speaking which might escape from the austerest mind, and figure in a style entirely correct in other respects.

"However, if the play did not have all the success that had been predicted for it, it was not the fault of the actors, all of whom played their parts to perfection. The Des

---

[1] Some eighty years later the Brothers Parfaict identified the obliging Monsieur de X with Boileau. But this conjecture was not logical. The real Boileau, if a friend of Racine's, would certainly have known how the play was going to end.

Oeillets, who opens the play as Nero's mother and who
invariably charms all before whom she appears, did better
than she has ever done before; and if La Fleur, who enters
next as Burrhus, were the original rather than the copy of
that personage, he could hardly be more true to life.
Brécourt, whose intelligence is universally admired, plays
Britannicus better than if he were the authentic son of
Claudia, and Hauteroche acts with such subtlety that he
would deceive a cleverer man than Britannicus. The
Dennebaut, who since her first appearance on the stage has
commanded the applause of all who have seen her, performed the part of Junie so ravishingly well that not a single
spectator failed to share in her sorrow. As for Floridor,
who has no need of praise from me and who is such an
accomplished actor that in his mouth an unpleasant word
no longer seems unpleasing, one can only say that if Nero,
who took such a delight in reciting poetry, had not been
dead these fifteen hundred years or so, he would take a
particular interest in his advancement, or else put him to
death through jealousy.''

3

Britannicus was that tantalizing thing, a half-success. Had
it been an outright failure, Boursault would scarcely have
refrained from saying so.[1] As it was, he made the best copy
he could out of a tepid reception and hinted plainly enough
that the hostility of the "threatened" authors had had much
to do with it. Racine, for his part, was convinced that he
had been the victim of a *cabale*. When, three weeks after
the première, he gave his play to the printers, he was
smarting under the injustice done him.

"In spite of all the care I have taken over this tragedy,"
he cries in his Preface, "it seems that the harder I have
striven to make it good, the harder certain persons have

[1] The statement that the play was withdrawn after eight performances
is not contemporary. It was first made by De Léris, in his *Dictionnaire
portatif des théâtres* (1754).

striven to decry it. There is not an intrigue they have stopped short of, not a criticism that they have failed to make.''

Turning at once to the counter-attack, he defines the aims of a good dramatist and the faults of a bad—who in this context can hardly be other than Corneille:

''What must be done to satisfy such exacting judges? The thing would be easy, if only one were prepared to betray common sense. It would be sufficient to reject the natural and to embrace the extraordinary. In place of a simple plot, not overcharged with incidents—such as a plot which is confined to a single day must be—and which, advancing progressively towards its end, is sustained wholly by the interests, feelings, and passions of the characters, we are asked to cram this same plot with a variety of incidents which would require a month in which to occur, with a mass of stage business as surprising as it would be improbable, and with a vast number of windy speeches in which the actors would be made to say the opposite of what they ought to say.''

In case the allusion is still not clear, Racine quotes several examples of out-of-character behaviour obviously taken from Corneille's plays, though he refrains from naming his great adversary. One more blow, while the spirit of battle is hot in him, and he has finished.

''Nothing is more natural,'' he remarks, ''than to defend oneself when one feels that one is unjustly attacked. Even Terence seems to have written prologues with the sole object of defending himself against the criticisms of an evil-intentioned old poet—*malevoli veteris poetæ*—who used to come and solicit opinions against him even during the performances of his plays.''

A rising author will often defend his youngest work with maternal ferocity and Racine was no doubt right in believing that *Britannicus* had not been condemned on its merits. Proof that this was so gradually reached him. A few months after the first production there came from across the Channel a piece of independent criticism, still qualified, it is true, but containing the word for which he had been vainly waiting:

"I have read *Britannicus* with sufficient attention to notice some excellent things in it. To my mind, it surpasses *Alexandre* and *Andromaque*. Its versification is more magnificent and I should not be surprised if it were found to contain *the sublime*."

This from the pen of Saint-Evremond was a token of capitulation, a sign that even that inveterate admirer of Corneille was willing to admit that the halo might perhaps be shared.

Time confirmed this judgment and Racine's own opinion of his first Roman tragedy. Seven years later he could write: "The criticisms have vanished. The play remains. To-day of all my tragedies it is this which the Court and the public are most willing to see revived."

But in January 1670 the general verdict was still unfavourable. Racine received much praise as a poet, but little as a maker of virile political tragedy. In this domain Corneille still appeared pre-eminent. Racine's disappointment at not having scored an unqualified triumph was deepened by the fact that he had strained his natural talent in order to compose a work for which it was not obviously fitted. The constant restraint and premeditation which must have been entailed by the deviation from *Andromaque* to *Britannicus* enhanced his estimate of the second play—it is natural to think that one's hardest achievement is the finest—and made his immediate reaction the more bitter. His desire for victory over the "evil-intentioned old poet" and his supporters was now reinforced by a desire for revenge.

4

It is impossible to leave *Britannicus* without observing that in this play the character-pattern of Racinian tragedy becomes clearly apparent for the first time. *Britannicus* might be said to establish a convention, if 'convention' were not too rigid a term to apply to an arrangement loose enough to allow of drastic variations within its framework.

The linchpin is the pair of young lovers—the prince and princess—both relatively inexperienced, sympathetic, and at the mercy of other characters, more mature or more evil. This pair is nearly always present, whether it is called Britannicus–Junie, Bajazet–Atalide, Xipharès–Monime, Achille–Iphigénie, or Hippolyte–Aricie. Even in *Andromaque* the pairing was potentially there in Oreste–Hermione but the fact that it was a warring, not a like-minded, couple was one of the features which distinguished that intricate, restless play.

Outside the princely couple stands the king, running in a clear line from Alexandre to Thésée. His influence over the fate of the other characters is ultimately decisive. He has the material power of unleashing or averting the catastrophe, even though the steps which lead up to his action may not lie in his control. In one play, *Bajazet*, he does not appear on the stage; nevertheless, he is a necessary part of the mechanism; it is the intervention of the Sultan Amurat, through his envoy, which provokes disaster. In *Britannicus*, on the other hand, the king—Néron—is the central character of the drama.

The fourth of the basic characters is the queen, who shows wider variations from play to play than any of the others and reflects Racine's most serious attempts at characterization. Preoccupied with this personage, he gave her several different faces and unequal dramatic values. As Andromaque, she is relatively young and plays an essential part in the plot. As Agrippine, she is an elderly, intriguing dowager on the outskirts of the central story. As Roxane, she is a woman in the prime of her beauty whose sex-absorption kindles and finally explodes the play. As Clytemnestre she takes on the graceful figure of a mother entirely concerned with her daughter's happiness and having no influence on the course of events. As Phèdre she is a mature woman whose passion well-nigh constitutes the whole tragedy. In *Mithridate* alone there is no queen, for the single female role of Monime, while nominally that of a queen, belongs to the order of princesses by virtue of her character and her relationship to the prince. As the early sketch of Jocaste in *La Thébaïde* shows, Racine's imagination circled for years round the conception of an experienced or elderly woman to whom he returned in Agrippine and Roxane before giving her final, definitive expression in Phèdre. In a very different setting and dramatic idiom, Athalie came to complete the frustrated sisterhood.

The recurrence of king, queen, prince, and princess, with the frequent addition of a counsellor (Ephestion, Pylade, Burrhus-Narcisse, Acomat, Oenone, and Théramène) does not constitute a mechanical system of characterization, as it might have done in a lesser dramatist. Racine achieves strikingly varied results by making comparatively small alterations in the relationships between his characters. Leaving the mutual inclination of the prince and princess intact, he rings the changes on the king and queen. Three kings—Pyrrhus, Néron, and Mithridate—stand in a love-relationship to the princess, but in each case it is a different relationship and the difference profoundly affects the play. The absent Amurat in *Bajazet* is merely a *deus ex machina* and Thésée in *Phèdre* is little more. Two of the queens—Roxane and Phèdre—are emotionally linked to the prince and are rivals to the princess, so furnishing the mainspring of the action. A third, Agrippine, is concerned not with love, but with power.

The system, which normally provides four big parts, two for women and two for men, with secondary counsellor parts of varying importance, emerges first, as we have seen, in *Britannicus*. Already in *Andromaque*, however, all the type-roles were present, though their relationships were interwoven in a manner which has no parallel in the later plays. Before *Andromaque*, as a glance at the *dramatis personæ* of *La Thébaïde* and *Alexandre* shows, nothing had been settled. In the first play there are only ineffective complications; in the second the scheme is blurred chiefly by the uncertain typing of the two female parts. But from *Britannicus* onward, obeying his growing conviction of the necessity of "a simple plot, not overcharged with incidents", Racine used almost exclusively the character-pattern which we have described. The exception is *Bérénice*, where an excessive desire for simplicity, and perhaps the suggestions of a powerful patroness, caused him to reduce his cast to three characters and to write a play whose data are too austere to conform to any regular system. In five of his great tragedies, however (six, if *Andromaque* is admitted), the main type-roles stand out as easily recognized landmarks.

In adopting this pattern Racine was only following an old tradition of the theatre which went back far enough to be confused perhaps in popular lore with the naming of the court-cards in the card-pack.[1] But without necessarily tracing it so far, it is evident that player kings and player queens were still accepted as stock characters in tragedy in the mid-seventeenth century. "Who plays your kings?"

---

[1] The French court-cards furnish a whole repertory of tragic and romantic parts running from Elizabethan to Augustan times. The modern names are:

Kings: *H*. Charles (Charlemagne). *Sp*. David (Bible). *D*. Caesar. *Cl*. Alexander.

Queens: *H*. Judith (Slayer of Holophernes). *Sp*. Pallas. *D*. Rachel. *Cl*. Argine (Anagram of Regina).

Knaves: *H*. La Hire (Joan of Arc's companion). *Sp*. Ogier (from the romances of chivalry). *D*. Hector. *Cl*. Lancelot.

In the sixteenth and seventeenth centuries, before standardization, alternate names found in some packs were:

Kings: Solomon, Augustus, Menelaus, Clovis, Arthur, Hannibal.

Queens: Helen, Juno, Elizabeth (of England), Dido, Hecuba, Roxane (not Racine's), La Pucelle, Venus, Semiramis, Cleopatra, Pentesilea (Queen of the Amazons), Bathsheba.

Knaves: Paris, Rinaldo, Roland, Roger.

The card 'court' is not complete, for there is no Princess. She seems to have been absorbed by the Queen, who has perhaps disposed of her rival in some forgotten tragedy. The Counsellor has become the Joker and wandered out of the pack. But without straining for too close a parallel, it is easy to see the family likeness in stage and pasteboard characters. This may explain the aversion of the Puritans to both of them.

Molière had asked in *L'Impromptu de Versailles*, as though referring to a traditional role which needed no explanation. Unwisely, when it came to *Andromaque*, Montfleury had preferred to play the prince and had paid the penalty which such a part exacted from age and high blood pressure.

The pair of young lovers derived rather from comedy and the *pastorale*, but it could easily be translated into a tragic setting, as, in a famous instance, Corneille had done in *Le Cid*. The secondary but sometimes important counsellor was the Chamberlain or Vizir of tragic tradition, the fool or the rogue-valet of comedy. Shakespeare had blended the two in Polonius. With the instinct of a dramatic craftsman—and influenced more consciously by the desirability of writing parts corresponding to the range of his particular actors—Racine easily conformed with the accepted custom.

His poetic art and the subtlety of his psychology enabled him, however, to transform the rudimentary framework round which his plays were built. Beginning with a simple system which uncouth audiences at country fairs could grasp without difficulty, he constructed a world of emotional interactions so complex that it satisfied the most sophisticated minds of his day and can still be explored in no patronizing spirit by the Freudian-trained critic of the twentieth century.

CHAPTER XI

THE DEFEAT OF CORNEILLE

BÉRÉNICE

H ENRIETTA of England, Duchess of Orleans, was unhappy in her upbringing, her marriage, and her destiny. The weakly daughter of the exiled Stuart family, she spent her childhood on the fringes of the French Court, exposed to a respectful pity and realizing, as she grew older, that a brilliant match was needed to restore the fortunes of her line. So long as the Commonwealth lasted, however, prospective royal husbands fought shy of her. The highest prospect of all—Louis XIV—eluded her. With the restoration of her brother Charles to the throne of England, she became politically important as the sister of a reigning king and, as a tardy consolation, was married at seventeen to Louis XIV's brother, Monsieur, a notorious homosexual. Secure now in her title of Madame, sister-in-law of the King, the unhappy girl wielded her immense social influence with diffidence. Through a habit implanted in her outcast years, she continually looked to those who surrounded her for reassurance and received it too rarely in a disinterested form. Of a delicate, appealing beauty set off by the highest rank, she inevitably attracted homages which further complicated her difficult life. Among them was that of Louis, who, having refused to consider her as a wife, returned to her for a time as her probably Platonic lover. Her life was full of pitfalls, outward triumphs, inward disappointments and regrets. Too sweet-natured to be cynical, she nursed a romantic spirit which left her sentimentally vulnerable to the end. Sensitive and enlightened, she admitted men of letters to her society and had befriended Molière at the height of the quarrel of *Tartuffe*. With Racine she had discussed *Andromaque* before he cast in its final form that moving exercise on a passionate theme. Now, watching with interest the young dramatist's battle with Corneille, she called Racine to her again and suggested to him the subject of a new tragedy. The heroine was to be Berenice, Queen of Judea, in love with the Emperor Titus, who, for reasons of State, is obliged to renounce his intention of marrying her and to send her back broken-hearted to her dominions. At the same time (this no doubt occurred early in 1670, after the production of *Britannicus* and before the journey of the Princess to England in May), Madame communicated the subject independently to Corneille, who set to work, like Racine, in ignorance of his rival's plans.

Later, when the two plays began to take form, when progress on them was discussed by the friends of the two authors, when casting, rehearsals, and production dates were considered, news of the clash must inevitably have leaked out. A race would develop between the Hôtel de Bourgogne and Molière's theatre. The *Grands Comédiens* won by a week, presenting Racine's *Bérénice* on 21st November 1670. Corneille's *Tite et Bérénice* followed at the Palais-Royal on 28th November.

Henrietta saw neither of them. She had died with tragic suddenness on the night of 30th June and her funeral had been celebrated to the thunder-roll of Bossuet's oratory.

Here we must interrupt the narrative to say that this version of the genesis of the two *Bérénices*, which stood unquestioned since the early eighteenth century, was 'destroyed' in the early twentieth by the persuasively-reasoned book of Gustave Michaut.[1] Later French critics have tended to conclude, as we do, that Michaut exploded the 'legend' with unnecessary violence and that it does

[1] *La Bérénice de Racine*. Paris, 1907.

represent, in all essentials, what actually happened. Michaut used four main arguments. He pointed out that in the Preface and Dedication of *Bérénice*—the Dedication is to Colbert—Racine made no reference to Madame or to a contest with Corneille; that contemporaries made no mention of an arranged 'duel' and in fact remarked that the encounter was a coincidence; that if, as one version had it, *Bérénice* was Madame's own story, it is curious that she should have wished to see these painful memories revived on the public stage; finally Michaut quotes a long list of parallel plays as evidence of similar *rencontres* during the middle decades of the century.

None of these arguments is conclusive. The failure of both authors to mention Henrietta is fully explained on the grounds of delicacy and of prudence. The death of the Princess, occurring less than five months before the plays were produced, had profoundly shocked public opinion. She was generally believed to have been poisoned by two of her husband's favourites, perhaps with her husband's connivance.[1] The highest name in the kingdom, next to Louis, was thus under suspicion. The matter had been glossed over under a crushing display of official sympathy, but Madame was dead and the sooner the scandal of her death was forgotten, the better. In those circumstances, it would have been folly for a playwright to invoke her name in connexion with anything so frivolous as a play—and more than folly if the play could be construed as an allusion to her private life. In dedicating his tragedy to Colbert, the most respectable patron he could have chosen, and in omitting to mention the Princess in his Preface, Racine was

[1] Later research (by Littré and Funck-Brentano) showed that the cause of death was probably acute peritonitis. But here we are concerned with the opinion of immediate contemporaries, who knew nothing of this nineteenth-century diagnosis. Madame herself believed she had been poisoned. The Paris police authorities, while forbidden to take open action, shared that belief. In the dossier of the case, they named as the poisoners the two *mignons* of Monsieur, the Comte de Beuvron and the Chevalier de Lorraine. (*See* J. Peuchet: *Les Secrets de la police, de Louis XIV à Louis-Philippe*. Paris, 1934.)

thus obeying the elementary dictates of caution. Corneille, whose tragedy was published without a preface, had the same reason for silence, with the additional one that the 'duel' had ended in his defeat.

As for their contemporaries, the same diplomatic considerations would close their mouths, even—which is doubtful—if they were aware that Madame had played a part in the encounter. The remark made seven years later by Donneau de Visé that "everyone knows that the two *Bérénices* were written at the same time as a result of chance" is by no means the straightforward testimony that it appears. Coming from that particular source it is most likely to be ironic, or else an example of the gossip-writer's technique of hinting at the truth by denying it. If taken literally, it states more than any reasonable person can accept. Certainly, as Michaut pointed out, the century was full of plays on the same subjects by different authors. In most instances, the explanation is plagiarism or adaptation of an older play. But here two new plays on the same theme are composed simultaneously by two authors at the peak of their rivalry and produced within a week of each other by companies whose rivalry is also in a period of climax. In order to be ready by that vital date in November, Racine had composed at the rhythm of one play a year which was becoming normal to him. Corneille, on the contrary, had roused himself from a silence of nearly four years in order to come to the rendezvous—after the relative failure of *Attila* in March 1667, it had looked as though he might write no more plays. That the duel was "a result of chance" seems impossible to credit.

But perhaps Henrietta's responsibility is still not proved. If it is denied, it must be supposed either that one of the authors got wind of the other's plans and set out wilfully to write in competition, or that some person unknown occupied the position of the Muse at the apex of this literary triangle. Who was that person? We refuse to go out into the desert of conjecture which such a question opens up. If *Bérénice* was inspired, it was by Henrietta, as the retrospective accounts written by the Abbé du Bos, by Corneille's nephew, Fontenelle, and by Racine's son, Louis, all state that it was. The first wrote forty-nine years after the event, the last seventy-seven years. Any one might have been misled or wilfully misleading, but the three together make a formidable body of witnesses.

A final consideration seems to tip the scale. The story of *Bérénice*, as Racine wrote it, was precisely the type of romantic tragi-comedy which would appeal to a woman of Henrietta's character. It was full of pathos, yet urbane. In order to compose it, Racine had taken the elements which in *Andromaque* had already drawn from Madame '*quelques larmes*', had removed their sting, their power and what an over-fastidious taste might call their vulgarity, and had presented them in the nostalgic, non-violent form of a pastoral. All this may merely have been part of his search for simplicity, but if at the same time he was aiming to please the fragile Duchess of Orleans he would hardly have written otherwise.

It is not necessary to see in the play an exact allusion to Henrietta's own life. The eighteenth-century 'keys' to the play see in Titus, Louis XIV, and in Bérénice, whom he renounces for the sake of Rome, either Henrietta or Marie Mancini. These parallels are too precise. Without having one particular situation in mind, Madame, whose life had been full of renunciations, may well have desired to see herself reflected in the character of an antique queen. Bérénice, a gentle, tender, and finally resigned figure, surrounded by her author with every guarantee of propriety, was in all probability Racine's answer to the Princess's wistful command.

Corneille also treated the subject as a romance, but the consequences were disastrous. Adopting a different disposition, with more characters and a richer 'political' plot, he nevertheless fell constantly into bathos. Better by far Racine's stiff but gentlemanly Antiochus than Corneille's second pair of lovers, Domitian and Domitie, who reduce to unintended comedy most of the scenes in which they appear. The old poet's touch, too, had grown unsure and he wrote lines which were the despair of the actors who had to speak them.

> *J'en eus un long chagrin. Tite fit tôt après*
> *De Bérénice à Rome admirer les attraits.*

His tragedy is said to have prompted Boileau to establish the two categories of *galimatias simple* (simple balderdash) and *galimatias double* (compound balderdash). In *galimatias simple* the author is intelligible to himself but not to his audience; in *galimatias double* he is intelligible to neither.

In spite of this, *Tite et Bérénice* was by no means an instant failure. It ran for twenty-two performances at the Palais-Royal, alternating with Molière's new comedy *Le Bourgeois gentilhomme*. The first fifteen performances were well followed, but takings fell off badly towards the end. The last night brought in only 206 *livres*, 10 *sous*, compared to 1913 *livres*, 10 *sous*, for the first.[1] As Corneille had received an advance payment of 2,000 *livres* from Molière, he could not complain of a financial disappointment. But when he looked at the progress of his rival, he realized how far behind he had fallen in prestige.

Racine's *Bérénice* must have come very near to repeating the success of *Andromaque*. Its author records that the house at the thirtieth performance was as crowded as at the first. Long after *Tite et Bérénice* had begun to languish, *Bérénice* was still drawing full houses at the Hôtel and—equally galling to Corneille—earning passionately enthusiastic opinions. When an entertainment was required for the marriage of the Duc de Nevers to Mademoiselle de Thianges, Madame de Montespan's niece, the play chosen was Racine's, not Corneille's. The King and Monsieur, Henrietta's bereaved husband, were present on that occasion.

---

[1] The true ratio of the fall is about five to one—not ten to one as the figures seem to indicate. For the first performances of any important play the prices of seats were doubled. They were reduced to normal as soon as there was a slight slackening of demand.

2

Bérénice is not a 'strong' play. The passion in it never gets out of control. Its situations do not require the ultimate solution of death; a poignant farewell makes a sufficient ending. Nor, in spite of having a Roman theme, is it a political play. The reason of State is not discussed or explored far enough to make it more than a conventional obstacle to love. Any other counter-force would have served as well. Because the dramatic conflict is too delicate and the dénouement not sufficiently terrible, the play has been described as an ' elegy '. This view is summed up in the popular rhyme which is said to have caused Racine great annoyance when a critic applied it to *Bérénice*:

> *Marion pleure, Marion crie,*
> *Marion veut qu'on la marie.*

On the other hand, the play can be regarded as a tragedy of feeling in its most concentrated form. Apart from the confidants, there are only three characters. Of these, only two count. The whole drama consists of a study of their reactions towards a single situation and towards each other. So perfect is the psychological machinery in itself that no physical action is necessary, either in the development of the tragedy or at its close. *Bérénice* is thus a model tragedy, stripped of every non-essential and reduced to the terms of an emotional equation.

This view of the play is a legitimate one to take, but it is more easily arrived at from an academic position than from a seat in the theatre. There, the lack of external action, the absence of considerable surprises, the small number of characters, the pacific dénouement, seem so many refusals to use the opportunities which the theatre offers. The fact that, given virtuoso acting and speaking, the play can still move an audience and that, when first produced, it moved audiences very profoundly, does not prove that we are in the presence of a great tragedy; it does, however, finally establish the reputation of Racine as a brilliant dramatic craftsman.

In adopting the subject of *Bérénice*, he set out deliberately to solve two problems. The first was to take a Cornelian theme—the victory of will over passion—and to treat it in the antithesis of the Cornelian manner. This time, with increasing boldness and experience, he had decided not to repeat the manoeuvre of *Britannicus*, when he had entered partly on Corneille's territory, but to conquer on his own ground. He aimed not merely at a victory of Racine over Corneille but at a victory of the Racinian system over the Cornelian. At least a year earlier he had begun to be conscious of the theoretical difference between them, when, in the Preface to *Britannicus*, he had prescribed "the avoidance of a great multiplicity of incidents". In the Preface to *Bérénice*, he defines his own system still more clearly and extols 'simplicity' as the highest virtue of the tragic dramatist:

"Some people think that simplicity is the sign of a barren imagination. They do not reflect that, on the contrary, imagination consists of making something out of nothing and that the multiplying of incidents has always been the resource of writers who did not feel that their talent was sufficiently fertile or powerful to hold their audience for five acts by means of a simple plot, sustained by the violence of the passions, the beauty of the sentiments and the elegance of the language."

It would appear that Racine, when contemplating his task, deliberately chose it in its hardest form. In order to simplify to the maximum, he temporarily abandoned his king-queen-prince-princess disposition. As we have noted, *Bérénice* is the only one of his mature secular plays which lacks that useful framework; for if Titus is the king, Bérénice is both queen and princess in one and Antiochus can hardly be admitted to the princely brotherhood of Oreste, Bajazet, Hippolyte, and the others. The intentional economy in the design of *Bérénice* becomes still more apparent when it is compared to *Andromaque*. From that play remove entirely the character of Andromaque, with all the reactions she provokes in the other characters. Shear Pyrrhus not only of the violence of his passion but of his brutality and of his possibility of choosing between two women—and then call him Titus. Strip Hermione of her desperate nature and of all her hunted expedients—and call her Bérénice. Finally make Oreste into a chivalrous courtier who would never dream of committing a disloyal act even if Bérénice could dream of inciting him to one, and what is left is Antiochus, who thus becomes an almost mechanical character.

Such were the data of Racine's exercise in Racinian tragedy, his demonstration of how to build something out of nothing and so affirm the superiority of his own theatre over that of a rival whose reputation was still considerable. Having discarded so much that might have enriched his play, he retained as his only assets "the violence of the passions, the beauty of the sentiments and the elegance of the language".

With these, he proposed to conquer the public which had failed to respond with sufficient warmth to *Britannicus*. This second task was even more urgent than the first. Had Corneille not existed, Racine would still have felt in need of a resounding success at this period. It was three years since *Andromaque* had suddenly earned him a name as the most promising of the younger dramatists. Since then neither *Les Plaideurs* nor *Britannicus* seemed to have fulfilled that promise. Could he ever repeat his early triumph? *Bérénice* was designed to convince the public that he could. Without violating the canons of good taste which prevailed among the lettered aristocracy or his own fastidious aesthetic sense, Racine set out with deliberation to make his audiences weep. They were to be "pleased and touched"—but neither amused nor embarrassed, for that would ruin everything. It was a difficult stipulation. To be 'tender' in the vein of the Court and of the Town, of women highly versed in the analysis of the sentiments, of men whose lives were based on their sense of etiquette, of other men ready to cover with derision any trace of naïveté or of what might seem to them unreal fantasy, was as delicate an affair as Molière's parallel problem in comedy. *Faire rire les honnêtes gens* was no more tricky a business than to make them weep.

Racine succeeded by a narrow margin and thanks to his skill of execution rather than to any perspicacity in the choice of subject. Through most of the five acts, he is writing a finger's breadth above the level of the sentimental novelette. Again and again, to the anxious reader, it seems that he cannot keep it up. Breathlessly near, he skims the abyss. He must fall in, as Corneille did. But no. By an immense effort of virtuosity he succeeds in maintaining just the necessary height and when all is safely over and our suspense has given way to admiration, we are reminded of the remark which he made on a later occasion: "The difference between Monsieur Pradon and myself is that I know how to write."

As a result, *Bérénice* contains some of the most admired lines in French poetry. Of their type, they have scarcely been surpassed and they succeed entirely in achieving the end which their author had in view:

> *Je n'écoute plus rien : et pour jamais, adieu . . .*
> *Pour jamais! Ah, seigneur! songez-vous en vous-même*
> *Combien ce mot cruel est affreux quand on aime?*
> *Dans un mois, dans un an, comment souffrirons-nous,*
> *Seigneur, que tant de mers me séparent de vous,*
> *Que le jour recommence, et que le jour finisse,*
> *Sans que jamais Titus puisse voir Bérénice,*
> *Sans que, de tout le jour, je puisse voir Titus?*

Such sinuously insinuating verse did more than bring out the lace handkerchiefs in a seventeenth-century theatre. It set an example which was to be followed a hundred and fifty years later by another poet, Lamartine, who by writing in the same tender, simple, and harmonious key unlocked the floodgates of French Romantic sentiment and opened what seemed to be a new world to his parched contemporaries.

But Racine was not by nature a sentimentalist. The man who had failed to attach much importance to the suicide of the girl at Uzès could indulge in only an occasional orgy of tears. Having played on the emotions of his audience as much as he dared, having perhaps been caught once or twice in his own net, he recovered his balance and conducted his tragedy to a firm and dignified finish. Even Saint-Evremond, when the play reached him in London, only remarked that it contained despair where grief would have been sufficient —a restrained judgment by a man who would readily have uttered an outright condemnation for excessive pathos had he thought it justified. As for Chapelle's verdict on *Bérénice* in the terms of *Marion pleure, Marion crie . . .*, it is all the more unfair because it so barely misses the mark.

3

While *Bérénice* was a contemporary triumph, it has nevertheless, on a longer view, done some injustice to its author's reputation. It is chiefly upon this play—an exception in his dramatic output—that the legend of the 'tender' Racine, in opposition to the 'stern' Corneille, is based. Forgetting his more brutal characters and his stronger situations, the admirers of *Bérénice* early began to look upon him as the poet of poignant farewells. The play soon became (and has remained) a touchstone by which men, or more often women, of feeling recognize a kindred spirit. Six months after its appearance, Madame Bossuet, the sister-in-law of the preacher, writing (as so many women did) to Bussy-Rabutin, exclaimed:

"I am very sorry not to be able to send you Racine's *Bérénice* which I am still expecting from Paris. I am convinced that you will like it. But, to do so, you must be in a vein of *tendresse*—and *tendresse* of the most exquisite kind—for no woman has ever carried love and delicacy so far as *Bérénice*. Lord, what a sweet mistress, and what a pity that a single character does not make a good play!"

Eventually the volume reaches Bussy-Rabutin. A person of less ethereal temper than his correspondent, he writes back:

"You had prepared me for so much *tendresse* that I found less than I expected. In the days when I was inclined to *tendresse* myself, I believe that I should only have given the remnants of it to Bérénice."

But although blunter and more masculine minds (among them in due course was Henrietta's successor, the gross and rustic Princess Palatine, second Duchess of Orleans), have remained unmoved by *Bérénice*, the sensitive have always regarded it as *their* play and therefore Racine as *their* poet. Nearly two hundred years later, the young Taine, an impressionable student reading Racine for his degree, wrote in his notebook:

"Magnificent! Whoever does not admire this manner, is not enraptured by it, is without true taste. But vulgar minds will never understand these delicate touches."

This was the type of sensibility for which Racine composed *Bérénice* and since such men and women are in the main writers, or at least diarists or prolific correspondents, they have very often placed their admiration upon record. Inevitably the element of *tendresse* has received applause disproportionate to its true place in Racine's work. Had she lived to see the finished play, Henriette d'Angleterre would no doubt have applauded too.

Racine's satisfaction with *Bérénice* was almost complete. To one who had criticized him on academic grounds, the Abbé de Villars, he replied in his Preface—all the more convincingly by distorting the Abbé's argument. But on the whole, the Preface is calm, even condescending. It reveals the confidence of the 'arrived' author who, instead of refuting rival points of view, can now afford to speak as an authority on the true nature of tragedy. There is a magnificent assurance in his tone as he replies to certain persons of quality who had wondered whether the play was constructed according to Aristotle's Rules about which they had heard so much:

"I inquired whether they complained that it had bored them. I was told that they all admitted that it was by no means boring, that it even touched them in many scenes, and that they would see it again with pleasure. What more do they ask? I beg them to have a sufficient opinion of themselves to believe that a play which touches them and gives them pleasure cannot be entirely contrary to the rules. The first rule is to please and to touch the heart: all the others exist only as means to achieving the first. But these other rules are long and intricate and I do not advise them to trouble their heads about them: they have more important occupations. Let them discharge on us the fatigue of interpreting Aristotle's *Poetics*; let them reserve themselves for the pleasures of weeping and being moved."

Nothing could show more clearly the degree to which Racine, in his own estimate, had succeeded. Nothing could be more significant than the silence in which he passes over Corneille's unhappy attempt to outbid him. In *Bérénice* Racine's ambition is satisfied for the first time.

CHAPTER XII

PATRONS, FRIENDS AND LOVERS

WHEN *Bérénice* had been running for a month, Racine reached the age of thirty-one. The disappearance—hardly accidental—of his correspondence and of any other personal documents relating to this period has thrown into greater relief the interesting portrait attributed to François de Troy. It shows a young man of strikingly handsome features: the delicate oval of the face frames intelligent, meditative eyes, a fastidious nose and chin, a mouth both supercilious and sensual. The portrait was held for nearly a hundred years to represent the poet in his late twenties or early thirties and its popularity is easily explained on the grounds that it satisfied almost equally his admirers and his detractors. The first saw in it the sensitive young man— poet, lover, and courtier—which they believed Racine to have been at this age. The second, by a slight exaggeration of the same pictorial suggestions, read hardness and a tendency to debauch in the clean-cut features. The portrait has been used as a central argument in elaborating an 'immoral' Racine as distinct from the 'tender' Racine or the 'pious' Racine of the majority of biographers.

It is now, however, established with reasonable certainty that the Langres portrait cannot be of Racine. If it were, his facial structure and the colour of his eyes changed between this portrait and the certainly authentic portrait by Santerre painted in his late fifties. Instead, the oval painting recently rediscovered in the Musée de Versailles by its Curator, M. Mauricheau-Beaupré, and which serves as

the frontispiece to this book, takes its place.[1]   But not *
entirely, for, although no exact date can be assigned to the
Versailles portrait, it would seem to represent Racine in
his middle or late thirties, filled with the assurance and
prosperity that had come to him by then.   This would be
the poet of *Mithridate* and *Iphigénie*, Member of the Academy
and *Trésorier de France*, who could very naturally have sat
for a portrait in the Mignard manner—perhaps even by
Pierre Mignard himself.

If this interpretation is right, we are still without a
likeness of the poet of *Bérénice*.   Discarding the Langres
portrait as a likeness, we may perhaps retain it as a text.
As such, it still has some value.   The qualities most easily
deduced from it are: intelligence, worldliness with a dash
of arrogance, sensuality with a tinge of sentimentality.   To
indicate Racine's character in the phase of life which he was
now entering, it would be hard to find a better set of
generalizations.

Racine's thirties corresponded to that enchanted decade
in the history of France when her Court was accepted
without question as the social and cultural centre of Europe
and when her political power became supreme.   The two
forms of predominance walked more exactly in step than
at any time before or since.   The 'sixties had established
Louis and his conception of monarchy within the kingdom;
the 'seventies saw the exploitation of his prestige at home
and its extension abroad.   They were the flowering of a
lusty plant tended for the most part by sober men or rough
men—the Secretaries of State and the great captains—
whose work would have appeared crude had it not been
crowned by a society frivolous in appearance but necessary
to call forth the full energy of the French character.
The Court was not a parasite, but a reservoir of *moral*.
Though military campaigns might have been won without
it, they would have made of France little more than an
earlier Prussia and of Versailles a Potsdam—whose chief

[1] *See l'Illustration*, 26 February, 1949; F. Calot: *Les Portraits de Racine*,
Paris, 1941; also *Le Figaro littéraire*, 24 September 1949.

interest now is that a brilliant Frenchman once resided there.

At the Court were gathered people whose presence was, in the first place, a tribute to France's political power: Louis's Queen Marie-Thérèse, a Princess of Spain; Henrietta, a Princess of England; after her, the Princess Palatine— Liselotte, as the astonished courtiers called her. Ambassadors from distant Siam visited the Sun King. The Pope and the Sultan sent their envoys to cultivate his favour. Such figures reflected his glory. They did not, however, set the tone of the Court. For that we must look to the native French, and no one person could better typify the society of the *grand siècle* in its most brilliant decade than the unscrupulous Madame de Montespan. She was the mistress of Louis's thirties, in succession to La Vallière, the frail and modest mistress of his twenties. The Montespan established her ascendancy in the year of *Andromaque* and saw it finally wane three years after *Phèdre*. Her reign thus coincided very nearly with Racine's most productive period. While he was waiting on tenterhooks for Molière to return to Paris and produce *La Thébaïde*, she stood at Versailles, hardly remarked among the other Maids of Honour of the Queen, watching the *Plaisirs de l'Ile enchantée*. These, as she knew, were a subtle homage to La Vallière and her purpose to supplant her was already formed. Two years later she was dancing in the winter ballet at Saint-Germain as one of an exclusive group of six which included her rival, the King, and Henrietta of England. At about this time she entered into relations with the sorcerers who wove in and out of the half-tamed century—always ready to supply a love-potion or an incantation, to suppress an unwanted child or concoct a poisoned draught. Through a sinister adventurer called Vanens she met the infamous Catherine Monvoisin who later claimed to have been the 'good friend' of Marquise du Parc. In 1667 she attended the travesty of a religious ceremony—not yet a Black Mass[1]—

[1] The Black Mass proper was said over the naked body of the postulant, which simulated the altar. At the moment of the elevation the throat

where, after intoning a litany of imprecations against La
Vallière, she recited this dreadful prayer:

"I desire the friendship of the King and of My Lord the
Dauphin (Monsieur), may it be lasting towards me, may
the Queen be barren, may the King leave her bed and her
table for me, may I obtain from him all that I ask for
myself and my family; may my servants and followers find
favour in his sight; beloved and respected by the great
lords, may I be called to the councils of the King and know
what goes on at them and, his friendship towards me ever
increasing, may the King leave and forget La Vallière and,
the Queen being repudiated, let me be married to the
King."

Although the security of the throne was never hers, she
attained the majority of her objectives quite quickly. By
the summer of 1668 she had replaced La Vallière who was,
however, forced to remain at Court some six years longer,
tormented by jealousy and remorse and fully satisfying the
vengeance of the Montespan before she was finally allowed
to retire to a convent. As for the Queen, Louis had far too
keen a political sense ever to repudiate her, but he did not
scruple to appear in public seated between her and his
mistress. At the height of her favour, the Montespan
occupied an apartment in the new château of Versailles
much superior to that of Marie-Thérèse. If she did not
attend the Councils of State, she was present in all her glory
at the receptions of foreign ambassadors, a "triumphant
beauty" for Louis to display to the world.

This woman befriended Racine, who no doubt turned to
her after the death of Henriette d'Angleterre. How
sincerely he admired her and how close their relationship
was, it is impossible to say. But a man as ambitious as
Racine and—at this period—as materialistic, must have
felt the attraction of this vital and brilliant personality.

---

of a new-born child was cut, and the blood used in the composition of a
diabolical wafer. Madame de Montespan was the principal in such a
ceremony in 1673. (*See* F. Funck-Brentano: *Le Drame des poisons*. Paris,
1878.)

She represented a world remote from his origins with which his imagination eagerly played. While many paid court to her for her influence over the King, she exercised an independent fascination on those with whom she came into contact and, years after she had ceased to be a social force, the 'Montespan manner' remained imprinted on the intimates of her household. She 'ordered' none of Racine's great plays, as Madame de Maintenon did later for *Esther* and *Athalie*, but she set him at one time to writing an opera. She was probably instrumental in securing for him the post of Historiographer Royal. Throughout his years of success and during the first stage of his activity as an official, she stood in the background, linking him to the King in a more personal way than his other patrons could have done.

These, in contrast, belonged to the 'sober' faction. Foremost among them was Colbert, with whom Racine had stronger bonds than those of an ordinary literary pensioner. He knew him through his connection with the Hôtel de Luynes and, in dedicating *Bérénice* to the Minister, he had performed an act of personal homage to a man whom he might presume to look upon as a friend. De Luynes's son, the young Duc de Chevreuse—in 1671, he was twenty-five—was also on much closer terms with Racine than a formal patron. He must have watched with interest the career of the man whom he had first known as a clerk in his father's household and for whom his regard was always warm. Saint-Aignan also remained well-disposed towards the dramatist, and with his son Beauvilliers completed the circle of level-minded patrons who derived from the Hôtel de Luynes. More intoxicating, if perhaps less dependable, was the favour of the collateral branch of the royal family— the great house of Condé-Conti. Its eldest representative, *le grand Condé*, a blunt-speaking eccentric and perhaps the most authentic lion of his time, took a keen interest in the theatre and loved to surround himself with men of ready wit. If he regarded Racine, as he regarded nearly everyone, with a certain amusement, he was nevertheless a sincere admirer of his literary skill. His admiration was shared by his son, Enghien, and, in due course, by his nephew François-Louis de Bourbon, Prince de Conti.

Protections so near the throne did not exclude the throne itself. The King was two years older than Racine, to whom he bore a certain facial resemblance. During his childhood and boyhood he had been the plaything of events, uncertain of his position, rebelliously dependent on others. When his chance of domination came, he grasped it avidly and arrogantly. In his twenties he experimented with love and war. In his thirties he enjoyed success and increased it. In his forties he heard at last the voice of the preachers who had long been haranguing him on his evil ways, turned to a more sober life and married a modest, pious woman. How far should the parallel be maintained? Certainly it must not be drawn too close, for the characters, even more than the material circumstances of the two men, were very different. But it helps us to understand Racine's outlook during an interesting and crucial period. The King, who was the admired centre of his generation, served in part as its example, in part as a symbol of its vigorous confidence, its pride of achievement, its intelligent worldliness. The mood of the years which saw the crossing of the Rhine, the exaltation of the Montespan and the beginning of the final enlargement of Versailles, was the mood of a whole society. It is not surprising to find that Racine was infected by it.

2

The Marquise de Sévigné did not normally concern herself with the private lives of players and poets. She had, however, a particular reason for writing on 1st April 1671: "There is, besides, a little actress and the Despréaux and the Racines with her; they have delicious *supper-parties*—in other words, wild goings-on."

Her scapegrace son Charles had become entangled with these people and had conceived a violent passion for the little actress who on the stage was Bérénice, off it the Champmeslé. Their affection was at first mutual and she granted him an assignation. But Charles proved less ardent a lover than his declarations had led her to expect, and the actress decided to terminate the affair. She returned his letters, which he showed proudly to his amused mother. "Never have I seen anything warmer or more impassioned. He wept, he died in them. He believes it all while he is writing, but the moment after he thinks it all a joke. I tell you he is worth his weight in gold."

As though to prove his volatile nature, Charles de Sévigné did not return the Champmeslé's letters as she had returned his, but sent them instead to a third party who had much influence over him, the courtesan Ninon de Lenclos. Ninon wished to show them to another of the Champmeslé's lovers, who so far had believed himself to be uniquely favoured. The episode, which must be read in its seventeenth-century context, was intended as part of a robust joke. Ninon hoped that the second lover, who appears to have been a man of quality, would have his mistress horsewhipped for deceiving him. At the eleventh hour, Madame de Sévigné saw that things had gone far enough and persuaded her son to beg the letters back before Ninon could use them.

Amid the chorus of praise which for the next twenty-five years surrounded the Champmeslé's acting, and the chorus of gossip which commented her morals, Madame de Sévigné's mezzo-soprano was often in evidence. She became a sincere admirer of the actress whom henceforth she called "my daughter-in-law".

The Champmeslé was twenty-eight when she created the part of Bérénice. As Marie Desmares, she had made her stage début in her native town of Rouen, then had married *en secondes noces* the actor Charles Chevillet, Sieur de Champmeslé, and had accompanied him to Paris. First he, then she, joined the company of the Marais. Her first part on the Parisian Stage was Venus in a *pastorale* by Boyer. A few months later the good Robinet—rhyming busily so as to have his weekly letter ready in time for the printers—was chanting:

On se sent le sang tout meslé,
Voyant la belle Champmeslé.

She stayed at the Marais for only a year. Her last part, like her first, was that of Venus, which she played opposite her husband's Mars in a tragedy with *machines* by the versatile Donneau de Visé. When the run of this play finished, the Sieur de Champmeslé was released to join the Hôtel de Bourgogne where his wife followed him a few weeks later. At Easter 1670 she made her first appearance at the Hôtel as Hermione in a revival of *Andromaque*. Tradition has it that Racine, expecting that the performance by an inexperienced actress in the part which he had written with such care would be too painful to witness, had intended to stay away; but, persuaded by his friends to change his mind, he had watched with growing enthusiasm and, when the curtain fell, had rushed to the Champmeslé's dressing-room to fling himself in admiration at her feet. Meanwhile the Des Oeillets, tired and ill and a few months only from her deathbed, had watched the performance from the wings and remarked sadly: "The Des Oeillets is no more."[1]

Such anecdotes are perhaps too apt to be literally true, but they are good symbols of the Champmeslé's sudden rise and her future greatness, as well as of her relations with the poet. From now on, she was the chief tragic actress of the Hôtel, overshadowing the Dennebaut who was of the same age and who, after at least five years' successful work with the company, must have been hoping to assume the mantle of the Des Oeillets (there could be no question of the now ageing Beauchâteau, who was to retire on a pension in 1676). But instead of the Dennebaut, the Champmeslé stepped in to create the chief female parts in Racine's five remaining tragedies—with the debatable exception of *Bajazet*. She played (at revivals) all the great Racinian and Cornelian heroines and her reputation, quickly established,

---

[1] "*Il n'y a plus de Des Oeillets.*" A French critic has pointed out that this could also mean: "There are no more Des Oeillets now", i.e. "No one up to my standard".

grew and remained until her death near the close of the century.

To judge by the descriptions of contemporaries, she was not strikingly beautiful. She had dark skin which was considered a defect in the seventeenth century—Racine at Uzès had echoed the common prejudice against it. Her eyes were small and birdlike. Her charm lay in her 'temperament' and in her voice which she used so skilfully that it moved the stoniest hearts. A comment made some ten years after Bérénice[1] analyses her appeal for the audiences of the time:

"The speech of actors is a kind of chant, and you will agree that the Champmeslé would not please us so much if she had a less agreeable voice. But she knows how to use it with so much skill and she introduces aptly such natural inflexions, that it appears as though she really felt in her heart a passion which is only on her lips."

Here, incidentally, is direct evidence that the 'chanting' style of verse-speaking had persisted through Racine's heyday at the Hôtel, and, although the worst excesses of the Montfleury school were perhaps concealed under "a cloak of naturalness", the difference was one of degree rather than of doctrine. Turning his back on natural diction in the full sense that Molière gave to it, and as it was possible in comedy, Racine wrote plays containing passages meant to be treated as incantations.[2] By the beauty and subtle variations of her 'chant' the Champmeslé became his most successful interpreter.

How much Racine the dramatist owed to the Champmeslé and how much she as an actress owed to him it is hardly

[1] In the Entretiens Galants, 1681.

[2] The question of Racine's own views on verse-speaking has of course been discussed continually but inconclusively by French producers, actors, and poets. The style used in the French theatre has varied from period to period, as with Shakespeare in England. The present technique at the Comédie Française is relatively naturalistic, though less so than the modern rendering of Shakespeare's verse by English actors. We believe, however, that it goes considerably beyond Racine's intentions. This does not necessarily condemn it.

possible to determine. No doubt he was stimulated by the knowledge that there was now in the company an actress capable of playing the most exacting female parts, but, as we have already seen, there is no justification for the view that he built his plays round her or even that he altered their character-balance with her in mind. The single-actress design of *Bérénice* is accounted for on quite different grounds. If Henrietta's influence and a doctrinal experiment in 'simplification' are admitted, there is no room for the Champmeslé. When at last in *Phèdre* Racine created a character who clearly outweighed all the others, it was one which was outside the Champmeslé's habitual range and one, moreover, not likely to have been suggested by her personality.

Her debt to him? He may well have rehearsed and produced her very carefully, but it is hard to believe that, as an actress, she was his creation. If she was so dependent on him, it is curious that she continued to triumph for twenty years after all connection between them had been severed—and not only in Racinian parts; it is still more curious that, at the period when they were working together, she was already achieving fame in plays by other authors, for which assuredly he would not have helped her. And what of the remaining actors, some of whom had parts of equal importance to play? Did Racine take no interest in their performances, or did he take equal pains to coach them too?

We are faced with an allegation similar to that made in the case of the Du Parc and originating from the same source. Boileau, reported this time directly by Brossette, first launches a statement disparaging the Champmeslé in order to show that Racine did not depend on his inter-preters for his success. Racine's son Louis takes it up, expands it, and draws a new conclusion from it. He writes: "As he had formed Baron (this was hardly exact), he had formed the Champmeslé, but with much greater pains. First he made her understand the lines which she had to speak, showed her the gestures and dictated the tones (*les tons*) which he even noted down.[1] The pupil, faithful to her lessons, and an actress by artifice, seemed on the stage to be inspired by nature; and since for this reason she acted much better in the plays of her master than in others, people said that they were written for her and deduced that the author was in love with the actress.''

Louis Racine's laudable aim was to whitewash his father, but in order to do this he was forced to attack the talent of an actress whom he had certainly never seen and who had been dead for fifty years at the date he wrote. He does not carry conviction in the face of so many contemporary witnesses to her professional excellence. As for her morality, unlike the Du Parc's, there seems no possibility of defending it. The affair with Charles de Sévigné is only one example of her promiscuity among many. Of her numerous lovers, Racine was undoubtedly one, but since nothing that he or his close friends wrote touching his personal affairs during his greatest creative period has been preserved, it is difficult to judge the exact nature of the liaison. It was probably stormy and lasted intermittently from the time of *Bérénice* to the time of *Phèdre* when, on the evidence of a lampoon, Racine was *déraciné* by the Comte de Clermont-Tonnerre. During those seven years he would be the most constant, if not the happiest of her lovers. The remarks which he made about her when she was dying show that no retrospective *tendresse* for her had lingered in his heart. No trace remains of a great passion. She seems to have been an episode, though a long and important one, in his life and to have left him somewhat bitterly inclined towards her. This argues a predominantly sensual attraction in which vanity also played a part; for the Champmeslé was a celebrity in her way and her favours might be considered a trophy.

---

[1] This statement, for what it is worth, supports the view that Racine intended his lines to be ''chanted''. Some have inferred from it that he even employed some system resembling musical notation. On the other hand, Louis Racine may simply have meant that his father made notes on intonation, pause, stress and other usual aspects of the art of verse-speaking. Whatever their nature, these notes have been lost.

If we look at matters from the Champmeslé's side, the riddle becomes a little clearer. She too seems to have kept her head. She allowed herself to be guided in all professional matters by her husband, whom she followed to Paris and the Marais, then to the Hôtel—where he probably secured a place for her—and with whom she eventually went over to the new Théâtre Guénégaud when the break-up of the Hôtel appeared imminent. In each of these changes he seems to have taken the initiative. They acted opposite each other in most of Racine's tragedies from *Bérénice* to *Phèdre* and continued long after in double harness.[1] The two, in fact, formed a most successful stage partnership, and although maritally he was as inconstant as she was, professionally they stood by one another and prospered together. The rumour inevitably spread that Champmeslé prospered thanks to his wife's influence—a rumour put into song in a famous lampoon of 1672:

> *Champmeslé, cet heureux mortel,*
> *Ne quittera jamais l'Hôtel.*
> *Sa femme a pris Racine là.*
> *Alléluia!*

But a study of their careers suggests that his theatrical position was at least as strong as hers. From their early days, he was her mentor and manager, besides being a reliable actor who could serve as a foil for her own acting. Their relationship is illustrated by a deed of mutual gift which they drew up in January 1678, one year after *Phèdre*. In this document it is stated that, as they have no children, they wish the survivor of the marriage to inherit the whole of their common resources so that he or she may continue to live as comfortably as possible on their joint professional gains.

In his dealings with these hard-headed, light-living people, Racine may have taken matters equally lightly,

---

[1] The Sieur de Champmeslé created Antiochus in *Bérénice*, Bajazet in *Bajazet* and either Xipharès or Pharnace in *Mithridate*. The complete casting of *Iphigénie* and *Phèdre* is not known.

separating his emotions from his career and accepting whatever pleasures came his way. This would seem to be the natural conclusion and no amount of probing is likely to take us much further. It accords with the conception of Racine as a lucid, businesslike man of the world endowed with the sensuality and panache of his generation. It is a not incongruous development of the self-depicted Racine of the Uzès period. And it seems impossible to construe the available evidence in any other light.

Such a portrait of the poet will, however, always be rejected by some who have been deeply moved by his plays and who believe that the passion which they contain must all have been based on personal experience. They cannot accept the apparent contradiction of an author who is ardent in his works but calculating in his life. So arid a personality, they argue, could not have been the creator of Andromaque, Bérénice, and Phèdre. They may be right. Racine in his thirties may have experienced some deep passion which escapes us, and which left no visible mark on his later life. This passion may, in spite of all appearances, have been for the Champmeslé. Or, as M. François Mauriac has suggested, Racine may have had other mistresses besides the Du Parc and the Champmeslé of whom nothing is known. These attachments, more secret, may also have been deeper. But all this is surmise or, at the best, a psychological reconstruction which can be debated endlessly. We do not feel entitled to write a romanced section into the life of a man who in other respects stands before us in so complete and real a form. If we are then driven to conclude that his emotional needs were superficial, we must accept the conclusion. We are still left, if we wish, with the alternative of a Racine whose eroticism was too fastidious to be satisfied by any human relationship, and who projected his desires in his 'young princesses'. But between the two extremes of a cerebral Racine and a sentimental Racine, we believe the former to be nearer the truth.

Meanwhile, it is the spring of 1671. Bérénice has come

to a triumphant close and has been succeeded at the Hôtel by Quinault's *Bellérophon*—the last tragedy which the competitor of the 'tender' Racine will write before devoting himself entirely to opera. A wild supper-party has been enjoyed by the Champmeslé, Charles de Sévigné and also by Racine and Boileau.

3

Boileau-Despréaux is an unexpected figure to find in such company. The fact that Madame de Sévigné speaks in the plural of "the Despréaux and the Racines"—as though, more than individuals, they were symbols of dissipation, makes the affair stranger still. However, the occasion has a historic importance, for it provides the first unimpeachable reference to the presence of Nicolas Boileau at Racine's side.

For long it was universally held that the two men had been close friends since the beginning of Racine's career as a dramatist. It was supposed, on the evidence of an obscure paragraph in one of Racine's letters to Le Vasseur, that they became acquainted soon after December 1663 and that Boileau was thus in a position to influence the other's literary development from *La Thébaïde* on. The flaws in this theory were revealed in a group of articles published in 1928–9 by M. J. Demeure, who was the first to make a critical reassessment of the whole relationship. He went further than it seems necessary to follow him in seeing a positive hostility between the early Boileau and the early Racine, but his main arguments were convincing enough to discredit a tradition which had stood firmly for some two hundred years and which was adopted by every biographer until comparatively recent times.

It is not surprising that they were misled, for the 'tradition' sprang fully armed with anecdotes and precise details from the pen of Louis Racine, the poet's younger son. Louis was writing forty-eight years after his father's death—which had occurred when he himself was a child of six—but he was thought to be in possession of papers and of family lore which made it difficult to disregard his authority. Even now, we cannot simply dismiss him as untrustworthy, but must inquire how and why he was led into error. For this is error and—unlike his comments on the Du Parc and the Champmeslé—not advocacy. In that case he was deliberately defending his father's reputation against what he believed to be slander and, in order to do so, using the arguments which reflexion suggested to him. In the matter of Boileau, however, the family honour was not in question. He was not arguing, but merely expressing a conviction implanted in his earliest years. From childhood he had known Boileau as an intimate friend of the family; after his father's death he came to look upon him almost as a second father, or at least as a precious link with his real father's past—which interested him increasingly as he grew older. At the most, he might be accused of having taken too much on trust, of having neglected to produce a single word or document from the Racine side, in spite of the evident opportunities he had of doing so. Everything that he says derives from Boileau, usually by way of Boileau's reporters and commentators. But why should he be on his guard? Here was a man of the highest integrity, whom, as he had seen with his own eyes, his father respected and trusted, and to whom he naturally went for information about the past.

Boileau or his commentators gave it to him—in the rough, no doubt, for Louis Racine spent many years revolving and arranging it in his own mind before he committed it to paper. But long before that the seed had been sown, from which two various plants were to grow. One was the most readable, most misleading biography of Jean Racine. The other was the reputation of Nicolas Boileau as the guiding-light of French classical literature.

By 1700, Molière, Corneille, La Fontaine, La Bruyère, Racine were all dead. Boileau remained, with eleven years of life before him in which to prepare new editions of his collected works, chat to his admirers and sort and polish his memories. What part, he was asked, and no doubt asked himself, did he play in the glorious age just ended? He attacked in his satires feeble or extravagant authors and destroyed them in the name of Reason. So far this was excellent: but constructively? Like Horace he wrote an *Ars Poetica*, in which he laid down the rules for composing nearly every known genre of poetry. He had omitted the Fable, in spite of La Fontaine's notable handling of it, but had written dogmatically on Tragedy, Comedy, and the Epic, though he touched none of them himself. *But he knew how they should be composed.* To write with such authority he must have had immense experience of the world of letters. With taste and critical acumen such as his, he must have played a decisive part behind the scenes in influencing other writers: men with perhaps more fertile minds, but whose taste was less sure.

This was where the ageing Boileau fell into temptation, for there was no great writer of the Classic Age whose works he could claim to have influenced with any semblance of plausibility except Racine. And Racine, as everyone was aware, had been his close friend for twenty years. From that point, the descent was easy. It was merely a matter of confusing dates, of transposing an anecdote from one occasion to another, of trying too hard to clarify a hazy recollection. Anyone who has written of his personal experiences, or has watched another writing of his, will understand what went on in Boileau's mind. He was doing what every writer does, consciously or unconsciously: he was giving shape to the inconsequent happenings of life, turning the rough and fragmentary material into a coherent, finished product. At the same time, he was buttressing his own position as a high priest of literature and was doing no harm, he believed, to his dead friend. In fact, at that stage of his life and mental evolution (he was now in his seventies) he probably felt that he was doing him a service by associating him with his own prestige.

So the legend of a Boileau-inspired Racine began to take form and so, after being further worked by Brossette and

others, it was passed into the hands of Louis Racine for its
final shaping.

To his account of the early Boileau-Racine relationship
nothing material has ever been added, though, following
his lead, other critics and biographers often discerned the
finger of Boileau where it was not. But all the later additions
to the legend are invention or conjecture.

Only two pieces of evidence might seem, to a conscientious investigator, to be independent of Louis Racine's
preconceptions. The first concerns a scene from *Britannicus*
which did not appear in the published editions of the play
and which Louis Racine printed for the first time in his
Mémoires. He explains that he had had it from Boileau, on
whose advice his father had cut the scene before production.
This would mean that at some date prior to December 1669
Racine was willing to follow his friend's advice on so important a point as the final form of one of his tragedies.
Even if the implication is accepted, the date is a relatively
late one and we are still far from any proof of an intimate
friendship going back to 1663. But it is not indispensable
to accept it. The fact that Boileau was in possession of some
of his friend's papers after his death in no way proves that
he had been responsible for the suppression of the scene.

Secondly, there is an interesting letter written by the
Marquis de Pomponne to his father Arnauld d'Andilly on
"Wednesday, 4th February 1665". This, it will be recalled,
was the year which closed with the production of *Alexandre*.
Pomponne writes:

"After that, M. Ladvocat took me to the Hôtel de Nevers.
There I found only Madame and Mademoiselle de Sévigné,
Madame de Feuquières and Madame de Lafayette, Monsieur
de la Rochefoucauld . . . and a few others; and besides all
these Boileau, whom you know, who had come to recite
his satires, which I thought admirable, and Racine, who
also recited three and a half acts of a play about Porus, so
famous against Alexander, which is assuredly of a very
great beauty."

The letter, which does not survive in manuscript, has

been suspected of being a fabrication.[1] Indeed, if any literary forger had set out to manufacture a show-piece, he could hardly have done better. The only concrete objection against it is that Nicolas Boileau was normally known as Despréaux at that time: the family name was reserved for his elder brother Gilles. But even if the letter is genuine, and if Despréaux was intended, nothing more is proved than that he and Racine were invited to the same salon in 1665 to read their compositions. The evidence of a closer relationship is still lacking.

Nothing, in fact, except the anecdotes of Louis Racine indicates that the two men were more than casual acquaintances until about the date when they supped together with Charles de Sévigné. This accords with the date given by Boileau himself when, at the beginning of 1696, he signed a legal document stating that he had known the dramatist well "for twenty-five years". The figure might be an approximation, but so is "thirty"; when Boileau was virtually on oath he chose the former. It is also consistent with the scant mention that Boileau makes of Racine's works in his earlier writings. Before the *Art Poétique*, which he published in 1674, he mentions his friend's plays only twice and on neither occasion in terms of unequivocal praise.[2] In the *Art Poétique* itself, having recently received a pension of 2,000 *livres* from Louis XIV, he calls in Canto IV upon Racine—but also upon Corneille, Benserade, and Segrais—to devote all his skill to chanting the praises of the Monarch. It is true that Canto III, part of which deals with the art of writing tragedy, has been construed as special pleading in favour of Racine's doctrine of simplicity. But it is sketchy stuff, names neither Racine nor Corneille, and is certainly not an open attack on the latter. In fact, in all that he wrote Boileau never wavered in his admiration for the plays of the older dramatist's prime and even

[1] It first appeared in the *Mémoires de M. de Coulanges*, published by Montmerqué in 1820.

[2] His *Satire III* (1665) contains an equivocal compliment to *Alexandre*; his *Epître I* (1669) a non-committal allusion to *Andromaque*.

treated the works of his dotage with considerable leniency.[1]
Not until 1677, when Racine had written his last and
greatest secular tragedy, when it was settled that the two
of them were to work in partnership as Royal Historians,
did Boileau commit himself to words of open praise. And
* even then he hailed Racine, not as the superior, but as the
successor of the great Corneille, the man who, walking in
his footsteps,

De Corneille vieilli sait consoler Paris.

If Boileau had really been the friend and mentor of the
early Racine cutting his way to recognition through a host
of rivals, his support would have seemed meagre indeed.
It is better for the honour of Boileau to accept his own
statement, in the legal document we have mentioned, that
the friendship began in about 1670-1.

From that time their intimacy grew steadily, until by
the year of *Phèdre* Boileau was a personal friend as well as
a literary ally and was ready, together with the faithful
Nicolas Vitart, to stand sponsor to Jean Racine at his
wedding.

4

At first sight it might not seem to matter greatly whether
a friendship destined to last so long and to become so close
began a few years earlier or later. But the consequence of
accepting the earlier date goes far beyond the small point
of factual accuracy. It corroborates Boileau's hints or
delusions in his old age that Racine had been, in a large
measure, his protégé, and so presents their relationship in
an entirely false light. From the day they met, Racine, not
Boileau, was the leading spirit. In the early 'seventies

[1] The one exception was the famous clerihew of 1667, which may
well have been a momentary sally not intended for publication:

Après *Agésilas*,
Hélas!
Mais après *Attila*,
Holà!

[162]

Racine, with his position as a dramatist at last established, his social connections widespread and powerful, the fulfilment of his material ambitions coinciding with his maturity as an artist and his prime as a man, was a figure more important in every way than the prickly satirist. Frequenting the Court in 1663, dedicating his *Alexandre* to Louis in 1665 and his *Andromaque* to Madame in 1667, he was well ahead of his friend of later years in the race for official favour. Boileau was not received into the royal presence until 1669, to read his then unpublished poem *Le Lutrin*. Racine was elected to the Academy in 1673, where Boileau did not join him until eleven years later. Although the delay can be ascribed partly to the hostility of writers whom he had satirized, this is hardly a sufficient explanation in itself. If his attacks brought him enemies, they also brought him friends in the opposite camp whose influence should have been sufficient to secure his earlier election had his reputation been as considerable then as it later became. Racine's enemies were no less powerful, yet he was elected. The royal pensions-lists are not complete enough to establish any exact comparisons, but, while certain of the sums received by Boileau were greater, the bounty paid to Racine appears to have been more regular and to have begun earlier. Altogether, Racine was in a stronger position than Boileau, and if a helping hand was stretched out it seems more likely to have been the dramatist's.

The relative positions of the two men remained unchanged as long as Racine lived. They are perfectly illustrated by letters which they exchanged in April 1692. Racine, the active partner, in intimate touch with the highest powers at Court, writes with all the tact at his command to Boileau, whose deafness retains him at home:

"Madame de Maintenon told me this morning that the King has fixed our pensions (as Historiographers Royal) at 4,000 *livres* for me and 2,000 *livres* for you: this of course exclusive of our pensions as men of letters. I thanked her warmly both for you and for myself. I have also just been thanking the King . . . So you see that things have been settled as you yourself wished. I cannot help feeling a real sorrow in that I seem to gain by this more than you do; but, apart from the expenses and fatigue of travelling, from which I am glad that you are spared, I know that you are so generous and full of friendship that you would sincerely wish me to be even better remunerated . . . I advise you to write a few lines to the King and the same to Madame de Maintenon . . . Send your letters by the post or by your gardener, as you judge best."

Boileau replies somewhat testily, but within twelve hours:

"Are you mad with your compliments? Do you not know quite well that it was I who, in a manner of speaking, arranged things in the way they have fallen out? And can you doubt that I am perfectly satisfied with an affair in which I am granted all that I ask? . . . I send you two letters which I have written, as you advised, one for the King, one for Madame de Maintenon. I wrote them without making a rough draft, and I ask you to see if you think they are fit to be presented, so that I can revise them if you do not find them suitable . . . "

Racine waits for two days before he returns the letters to Boileau with still tactful, but firm, suggestions for their improvement and a demand to send them back the same afternoon. Boileau complies.

As in material affairs Racine took the lead, so in literary matters he at least preserved his independence. He may have consulted his friend on the versification of his later plays and adopted his suggestions on minor points—just as he emended the text of *Andromaque* to meet the objections of a Subligny—but it is impossible to admit that the consummate poet and dramatist who was Racine was seriously influenced by Boileau, who was neither a dramatist nor a poet. That would indeed be an instance of the thoroughbred taking lessons from the cart-horse. It is for a Frenchman to decide whether or no Boileau was trite, platitudinous, and pedantic, whether his dreary and obvious grandiloquence did not do incalculable damage to imaginative writing and particularly to lyric poetry in France, and whether among the libertine poets of his own time whom he helped to inter there were not several with a prettier wit than he. This is not an Englishman's quarrel; not having possessed a poet slower and shallower by half than Alexander Pope and set him up in authority above the critic's desk and the lecturer's table, we can afford to be self-righteous in this matter. But it is obvious that if Boileau was right in his conception of poetry, then Racine was hopelessly wrong. It needs a strange opacity of taste to suppose that the latter went to school with the former.

This blindness was the real crime of Louis Racine. That he should have glossed over certain passages of his father's life and allowed himself to be misled over others is nothing. He was acting from true filial piety and as his father, in his last years, might well have wished him to act. But that he should have so misjudged Jean Racine's poetic genius and, in his admiration for Boileau, have so completely accepted Boileau's patronizing estimate of Racine the writer, is harder to forgive. The pious, timid son believes that he is giving his father the highest possible praise in pointing out that certain passages of *Britannicus* were "happily imitated" from Tacitus and Seneca. Wherever his work can be construed as solid, respectable, traditional—as Boileau conceived those qualities—he so construes it. But the true originality of Racine—his lightness of touch, his speed, his concentration of emotion, his perfect marriages of words and rhythm to character and situation—this always escapes him.[1]

5

No doubt there is a Classic mentality and a Classic manner, but the Classic 'school' of the sixteen-sixties

[1] "Finally he acquired the esteem of the ladies of Saint-Cyr, who spoke to me of him with such enthusiasm that their words taught me to admire him more than his works had ever done." Louis Racine: *Mémoires*.

was a convenient fiction invented by orderly minds at a
later date. This obsession with 'schools' of literature
combined with a pleasant sentimentality about the habits
of literary men gave rise in the early nineteenth century
to the legend of the Four Friends. It would be fitting if
four of the greatest names of the Age of Louis XIV—say
Racine, Molière, Boileau, and La Fontaine—could be
linked together in some social group. It happened that La
Fontaine had described, in the Prologue of his *Amours de
Psyché*, the literary conversations of four men as they
walked together in a garden. He called them Poliphile,
Acanthe, Ariste, and Gelaste; the nineteenth century at
first identified these with La Fontaine, Racine, Boileau,
and Molière respectively. Later the difficulty, and then
the impossibility of any such identification was realized
and the rustic picture fell apart in confusion. There
remained, however, the tavern. Why should not the four
have sat drinking round the same table? There was a
choice of picturesque names: *Le Mouton Blanc*, *La Croix
de Lorraine*, *La Pomme de Pin*. This legend was destroyed,
not by vagueness, but by too precise a thirst for knowledge
on the part of the investigators. They set out to ascertain
the exact location of *La Pomme de Pin* in the streets of
seventeenth-century Paris. M. J. Demeure, to whose
work on the Boileau legend we are already indebted,
comments drily on their researches:

"This, then, is the information brought back by the
nineteenth-century *érudits*: the Pont Notre-Dame, the
Rue de la Lanterne, the Rue Aufèvre, the Rue de la Licorne
and the Rue Notre-Dame all constituted, opposite the
Madeleine and near to the Palais de Justice and to Notre-
Dame, a single street—the street which Rémy de Gourmont
has baptized the Rue du Pont Notre-Dame. From one end
to the other, on the right and the left of this royal road,
stretched the saloons of that noted establishment *La Pomme
de Pin*."

It seems certain that if Molière, La Fontaine, Racine,
and Boileau did all foregather in the same place, it was in

no earthly Mermaid Tavern but in an Elysium built from the fancies of not-too-inquiring minds.[1]

Racine's circle can in reality have included but few men of letters. La Fontaine he had frequented in his early days, but as a family friend rather than as a fellow writer. The link with Boileau was distinct from this: Boileau does not appear to have associated closely with La Fontaine. There is no sign here of a literary fraternity, nor did any coterie of younger writers form round Racine. This second fact is a little unexpected, until we notice the general absence of cohesion among all the writers of Racine's own generation. The older men grouped themselves on salons, but the men born about 1640 tended to be independents. Their one focal point was the Court, which attracted them by its rich pickings and its glitter, but it was too large and too impersonal an entity to serve as a literary centre. If Racine headed no coterie, it was due as much to contemporary conditions as to the jealousy of his brother-writers and his own mordant tongue.

The Court, which he frequented largely as a matter of business, and the theatre, where his work and his pleasures lay, were the two centres of his social life. His private life was still closely bound to the Vitarts, with or near whom he lived through all these years. Nicolas had become the Intendant of the young Duke and was living at the Hôtel de Chevreuse, in the Rue Saint-Dominique, from 1667 to 1672. In 1671-2 at least Racine also lived in the Rue Saint-Dominique, though whether he lodged at the Hôtel or nearby is not known. Two years later he was at the Hôtel des Ursins, a building in the Ile de la Cité which was let off in private apartments, and here Vitart is also found in 1675-6. Our knowledge of the changing addresses of the two men is incomplete, since it depends upon the fragmentary evidence of legal documents which they happened to sign or witness at various dates, but they are never found far from each other during the whole of Racine's career as

[1] *La Pomme de Pin* is an evocative name in French literature. Villon frequented a tavern with that sign. So did Ronsard. So did Régnier.

a playwright and after his marriage they remain near neighbours. Amid all his triumphs and dissipations, the friendly
atmosphere of the Hôtel de Luynes which had humanized
his adolescence still exerts its influence over him. If he is
a greater man now than Nicolas Vitart, he does not turn
his back on him. On the contrary, having long since paid
back the trifling debts of his youth, he is able to accommo-
date his cousin with a loan of 8,000 *livres*, on which he
receives interest at the rate of five per cent.[1] Marguerite
Vitart, unawed by his literary achievements, no doubt
begins to look at him with the calculating eye of the matron
whose own marriage has been successful. Meanwhile she
and Jean Racine appear together[2] as the god-parents of
Constance-Eugénie, daughter of her young brother-in-law
Antoine (Racine's fellow-pupil at the Collège d'Harcourt)
who has married a Sconin. Her mother-in-law Madame
Claude has died at a ripe old age in 1668. In the same year
peace came temporarily to Port-Royal des Champs. The
nuns—"as pure as angels and as stubborn as devils", as
their exasperated Archbishop described them—were persuaded to sign the new formulary devised by Pope Clement
IX. Agnès de Sainte-Thècle Racine, whose spirit has grown
still stronger through the years of persecution, now serves
the convent as its cellaress. Whatever the half-worldly
Vitarts may do in Paris, it is certain that she has no dealings
with her nephew. No concession could ever come from
her side. And it is better that the two should remain
entirely separated. Her fiery remonstrances could only
madden Racine now. What he needs is not dogma, but the
warmth and tolerance of the Vitarts to relieve the nervous
tensions of the life which he is living. He experiences the
intermittent fever of the creative artist. In his relations
with the Court he must be continually watchful. The life
of the theatre is even more exacting: the rush and apparent
chaos of preparation and rehearsal lead up to the maximum

[1] On 22nd March 1675. *See* E. H. de Grouchy: *Documents inédits relatifs à Jean Racine et à sa famille.* Paris, 1892.
[2] On 12th November 1673.

nervous effort of the first night and are succeeded by uneasy relaxation—the trough of the wave as stormy as its crest. He disputes the Champmeslé with her aristocratic admirers and seems at least to hold his own. He orders bottles of champagne for the Sieur de Champmeslé, who drinks them in all good-fellowship. The lover, courtier, and poet is less than ever in a mood to listen to his rustic aunt.

As for the Du Parc, who has been dead a little over two years, he seems to have lost all touch with her family and *milieu*. Her two daughters Marie-Anne and Catherine have entered the great household of the Countess of Soissons, Mazarin's niece, Nevers's sister. They whisper dark gossip, led on perhaps by Marquise's stepmother, Benoîte Lamarre.

In Racine's mind, purged of *Bérénice*, a new play is taking shape. It will be violent, complicated, exotic.

CHAPTER XIII

A TURKISH INTERLUDE

BAJAZET

THE audiences which filled the Hôtel de Bourgogne in the first week of January 1672, saw yet another aspect of Racine's talent, or perhaps, if their recollections carried them back to *Andromaque*, they perceived the revival of an old aspect. The play offered to them was melodramatic in its rapid changes of situation, violent feelings were violently contrasted, the curtain fell on a welter of carnage. Superficially, however, it was a complete novelty, for the action took place in a harem and, instead of ancient Greeks or Romans, the characters were modern Turks. In order to exploit the latest fashion of *turquerie* (which Molière and Lully had also reflected in the ballet of the *Bourgeois gentilhomme* the previous winter), Racine had temporarily abandoned his classical models and had dramatized an event which had taken place in the lifetime of many of the spectators. It had been recounted to him, he said, by a gentleman at Court, the Chevalier de Nantouillet, who in his turn had had it from the French Ambassador at Constantinople.

The Sultan Amurat, forced to be absent from Constantinople in order to lead his armies in the field, has left his Sultaness, Roxane, in charge of affairs at home. In her custody he has left his younger brother Bajazet, whom he intends to have put to death at a convenient time because he is a potential rival for the throne. The order for Bajazet's execution presently reaches Roxane, but in the meantime she has fallen passionately in love with him and is hatching a plot to marry him and reign with him in Amurat's place. The Grand Vizir, Acomat, abets her in her plans. Bajazet's life depends on their success, yet he is an unwilling pawn since his real love is not for Roxane but for the young princess Atalide, who lies equally helpless in Roxane's power. The play turns on the hesitations of Bajazet— unable, although life is at stake, to feign a convincing response to Roxane's passion. Gradually Roxane realizes the truth and has Bajazet strangled. She herself is killed by Amurat's messenger, who immediately after is slain by her partisans. Atalide commits suicide and at the final curtain only the Grand Vizir Acomat is left, determined to perish in battle against the supporters of the Sultan.

This orgy of blood and passion was an instant success. During its first month at the Hôtel it was given the honour of a command performance at the marriage of Monsieur to his second wife, the square little Princess Palatine. Liselotte must have been bewildered by it. To her, newly arrived from her German backwoods, Turks and Frenchmen, Versailles and Constantinople, were equally incomprehensible, equally exotic. Did she look behind the curtains for the mute with the bowstring before going to bed at Saint-Germain? Was she further confused by being told that, according to a popular 'key' to the play, Roxane represented Queen Christina of Sweden who, while visiting France a few years earlier, had caused her lover Monaldeschi to be murdered at Fontainebleau? Did anyone whisper that Roxane was not unlike the Montespan and that Atalide had something in common with La Vallière? We can never be sure whether Racine intended the veiled allusions to contemporary scandals which were attributed to him. But whether by luck or design, they increased the appeal of his tragedies.

That useful barometer of society's taste, Madame de Sévigné, had heard marvels of *Bajazet* even before she went to see it. At last she finds an opportunity of visiting the Hôtel. She writes to Madame de Grignan:

"Racine's play seemed quite good to me. My 'daughter-in-law' struck me as the most marvellous actress I have ever seen; she surpasses the Des Oeillets by a thousand miles. I thought I was pretty good at acting myself, but I am not worthy to light the candles when she appears. She is ugly at close view and I am not surprised that my son was suffocated by her presence, but when she speaks verse she is adorable. *Bajazet* is a fine play. I thought it a little confused at the end, but it is full of passion—a passion less wild [sic] than in *Bérénice*. However, in my humble opinion it does not surpass *Andromaque*, and as for the noble plays of Corneille, they are incomparably above it . . ."

Nevertheless she thoroughly enjoyed her afternoon at the theatre.

"I wish you had been with me after dinner," she chats on. "You would certainly not have been bored. You might perhaps have shed one little tear, since I shed more than twenty; you would have admired your sister-in-law; you would have seen *the angels* in front of you [the de Grancy sisters] and the Bourdeaux woman, wearing such a *girlish* frock. Monsieur le Duc sat behind, Pomenars up aloft in the gallery with his nose hidden in his cloak because the Comte de Créance swears he will have him hanged, struggle he never so hard.[1] All the best people were on the stage. The Marquis de Villeroi was in a ball costume, the Comte de Guiche slim and trim like his wit, all the others dressed as bandits . . ."

It is easy to see why the silent gesture and the subtle effect were unknown on the seventeenth-century stage. A playwright had not only to please his audience, but to compete with it. Such fashionable concourses, however, greatly increased the prospects of a play. They made of a performance a social occasion which might have little to do with the

[1] The Marquis de Pomenars had eloped with the Comte de Créance's daughter. "Fourteen years later," asserts an eighteenth-century memoir-writer, "she perceived that she was living with him, returned to her father, and brought an action for rape".

intrinsic merits of the piece. Hence Madame de Sévigné's enthusiasm despite her loyalty to Corneille.

But once the glamour of the spectacle had worn off, she returned to her old admiration. She read the play and found it far inferior to *Andromaque*. Its Turkish atmosphere was not true to life: *Ils ne font pas tant de façons pour se marier.* The character of Prince Bajazet was *glacé*. Away from the Champmeslé's acting the tragedy seemed flat. "Long live our old friend Corneille!" she exclaims. "His best passages are master-strokes which no one can imitate." Then comes the sentence which Louis Racine refused to believe when his indignant eyes fell upon it. "Despréaux says so even more strongly than I do. In short, this is true taste—hold to it."

It would seem that word had gone out from the Corneille camp to find *Bajazet* deficient in local psychology. It may have been Corneille himself who started it. "Mark this well," he is reported to have said in conversation with Segrais. "There is not a single character in the *Bajazet* who has the feelings which he should have, and which they have in Constantinople. All of them, under their Turkish clothes, have the feelings which people have in the heart of France."

Yes, the characters were too French. They were not Turkish as Corneille's Romans had been Roman. De Visé, who had just launched his new paper, *Le Mercure Galant*, presented this criticism with a new twist. Perfidiously affecting to defend Racine, he remarked:

"I cannot agree with those who say that this play is not sufficiently Turkish. There are Turks who are *galant*. And then if the play is popular, it does not matter why. When one has to invent, it costs no more to invent courteous gentlemen and tender and *galant* women than to fabricate barbarians who are not in the taste of the ladies of to-day—and the first rule, of course, is to please *them*."

All these were mere grumblings of jealous writers and were without effect on the success of *Bajazet* which ran for two months, or about twenty-five performances.[1] Racine's Preface, printed while the play was still being acted, can, as usual, be taken as an indication of the author's immediate reactions. It is very easily the shortest he ever wrote, as though to show that for this play at least he felt no need of a detailed justification. He affirms, without ill-humour, he has taken the greatest care to render accurately the customs of the Turks and then leaves his tragedy to speak for itself.

Bajazet appeared without a dedication. From now on, Racine dispenses with these verbal bribes for patronage. The patrons he possesses are sufficient.

2

In Bajazet, Racine returned to the character-plan which had first become apparent in Britannicus. Four main characters appear on the stage: Roxane, the queen; Bajazet and Atalide, the prince and princess—both entirely virtuous and entirely helpless; and Acomat, the counsellor, whose part is here expanded until he becomes an essential factor in the development of the plot. Off-stage is Amurat, the king, whose threats and orders constitute a necessary dramatic force. But his person, incarnated by an actor, could only be an embarrassment.

Although the tragedy is entitled Bajazet, it is Roxane who steals the thunder. Racine has given her the ferocity of a tigress, bent on the satisfaction of an elemental desire. She considers Bajazet more as her prey than as her prospective lover. Holding his life in the hollow of her hand, she derives a voluptuous pleasure from the thought that she can either deliver him up to the bowstring of the executioner or place him on the throne as her own mate. Even at the beginning, before she has any doubt of his love for her, she complacently shows her claws, then re-sheathes them with a smile of provisional reassurance.

[1] The première was on 5th January. The next play at the Hôtel (Thomas Corneille's Ariane) was first produced on 4th March.

Et moi, vous le savez, je tiens sous ma puissance
Cette foule de chefs, d'esclaves, de muets,
Peuple que dans ses murs renferme ce palais,
Et dont à ma faveur les âmes asservies
M'ont vendu dès longtemps leur silence et leurs vies.
Commencez maintenant : c'est à vous de courir
Dans le champ glorieux que j'ai su vous ouvrir.

But when she smells treachery, with what instinctive cruelty she acts. How she lingers over the prospect of Atalide contemplating the corpse of her murdered lover.

Ah! si pour son amant facile à s'attendrir,
La peur de son trépas la fit presque mourir,
Quel surcroît de vengeance et de douceur nouvelle
De le montrer bientôt pâle et mort devant elle,
De voir sur cet objet ses regards arrêtés
Me payer les plaisirs que je leur ai prêtés!

This is a development of Néron's

Je me fais de sa peine une image charmante,

and it shows also the strength which lies stored in Racine's restrained vocabulary. *Cet objet* in this speech is more blood-chilling than any realistic description of a strangled corpse.

If Roxane's language is silky, her actions are ruthless. Determined to give Bajazet a final chance of reprieve, she invites him to come with her and see Atalide put to death, then, "freed of this love fatal to your honour", to pledge himself to her.

Ma rivale est ici : suis-moi sans différer;
Dans les mains des muets viens la voir expirer;
Et, libre d'un amour à ta gloire funeste,
Viens m'engager ta foi; le temps fera le reste.
Ta grâce est à ce prix, si tu veux l'obtenir.

If this were the whole of Roxane's character, she would be too unsympathetic and too crude to hold the spectator's interest, but Racine—without endowing her with any

[175]

great subtlety—gives her a more vulnerable side and makes it possible to pity her. Her excesses are the result of her passion, or, more precisely, they spring from a possessive and uncompromising nature tormented by passion. As much as Hermione and Phèdre, she is in the grip of implacable Venus. It brings her suffering, within the limits of her nature, but not much self-questioning. Having perceived, with a shock of indignation, that Bajazet prefers Atalide to herself, she does not stop to ask why. She instantly conceives the problem in terms of a duel, with Bajazet as the prize. She is ready to fight with all the weapons at her disposal, and they are formidable. But it is a duel to the death; should she lose Bajazet, she has no wish to survive.

> *Je saurai le surprendre avec son Atalide,*
> *Et, d'un même poignard les unissant tous deux,*
> *Les percer l'un et l'autre, et moi-même après eux.*

This vulnerable aspect of Racine's queen makes the character capable of development not, indeed, in this play, but in a future play, following his system of variations on a basic theme. In *Bajazet* for the first time he gives the queen ruthlessness in love, hatred for her rival and a blind, disastrous attachment to the prince.

Of the character of Bajazet there is little to be said. From one point of view he is a weak and vacillating prince, too immature to deceive, too unconfident to attempt to command. From another—and the majority of audiences at any period must love him for this—he is handsome, courteously passionate, physically brave, and as sincere as he is stupid. It is difficult to decide whether Racine intended him as a satire or a model of mankind, or whether, without bias in any direction, he simply considered such a character essential to any well-made play. He had been Britannicus and would be Xipharès.

If Bajazet lacks enterprise—this was no doubt what Madame de Sévigné meant when she described him as *glacé*—his feminine partner on the same moral plane is a much more lively creation. She is as unselfish in her love as he is, but more intelligently so. Let him feign to adore Roxane and she will choke down her tears. Since there's no help for it, she forces her will to conquer her inclination, but without any Cornelian conviction that she is serving a moral purpose or that virtue lies elsewhere than in the natural happiness which she might have enjoyed with Bajazet. She is lucid and practical in her actions. Atalide is, one feels, out of place in this tragedy of daggers and bowstrings, and especially out of place in a seraglio. She is strikingly modern in a situation which can only be described as Biblical: a seventeenth-century girl—almost a twentieth-century girl—in a dilemma which might have come out of the Old Testament. This is what makes her so attractive, and not least, it would seem, to her creator. Her reactions and the language she uses to express them, are those of any young woman brought up according to the highest standards of West European society. (Except religious standards. Until after *Phèdre* there are no 'religious' characters in Racine; none remotely resembling the dedicated virgins of Port-Royal.)

At the first moment which she has alone with her confidant, she calls herself by her own name:

> *Zaïre, c'en est fait, Atalide est perdue!*

In rather childish words, but with perfect mental clarity, she goes on to expound the situation.

> *Si tu venais d'entendre*
> *Quel funeste dessein Roxane vient de prendre,*
> *Quelles conditions elle veut imposer!*
> *Bajazet doit périr, dit-elle, ou l'épouser.*
> *S'il se rend, que deviens-je en ce malheur extrême?*
> *Et, s'il ne se rend pas, que devient-il lui-même?*

The brush with the tigress has flustered her, but she does not waste time in pouting helplessly. She seeks out the adored but resourceless Bajazet and urges him to make a false declaration of love to Roxane. Having screwed up his resolution as high as she can, she sends him into the dangerous presence as though he were a small boy.

ATALIDE: *Allez, seigneur, sauvez votre vie et la mienne.*
BAJAZET: *Hé bien . . . Mais quels discours faut-il que je lui tienne?*
ATALIDE: *Ah! daignez sur ce choix ne me point consulter.*
           L'occasion, le ciel pourra vous les dicter.
           Allez: entre elle et vous je ne dois point paraître;
           Votre trouble ou le mien nous ferait reconnaître.
           Allez: encore un coup, je n'ose m'y trouver.
           Dites . . . tout ce qu'il faut, seigneur, pour vous sauver.

Her own resolution breaks down for a moment when she believes that, after all, Bajazet has preferred her rival. But later, when Bajazet has reassured her and Roxane's suspicions of the two have become a certainty, Atalide rises to her greatest heights. She seeks out Roxane, argues that if Bajazet loves her it is only because she persuaded him to do so, and offers to kill herself in order to clear the way. But Roxane has already sent Bajazet to his death. She replies coldly:

> *Je ne mérite pas un si grand sacrifice:*
> *Je me connais, madame, et je me fais justice.*
> *Loin de vous séparer, je prétends aujourd'hui*
> *Par des nœuds éternels vous unir avec lui:*
> *Vous jouirez bientot de son aimable vue.*
> *Levez-vous.*

According to all modern readings, this is predominantly Roxane's play, to a degree probably going beyond Racine's intentions. He put into the part of Atalide all the charm, spirit, and pathos that it would hold and hung it high in his gallery of young princesses which, it is evident, he painted with loving care. If his *jeunes premières* are overshadowed by some of his more experienced characters, this is in the first place a law of nature rather than of art; for not even the highest art can make of an immature character the centre

of a mature work. The Atalides, Junies, Ophelias, Corde-
lias, and even the Desdemonas of dramatic literature can
only be exquisite and heart-rending side-issues. The Roxanes,
Gonerils, and Gertrudes triumph by reason of their greater
ripeness and depravity. But sometimes the margin is narrow
and it appears that in the estimation of the seventeenth
century Atalide outshone Roxane.

It is probable that the part of Atalide was created by the
Champmeslé. Such is the conclusion of her biographer,
M. Emile Mas, and, although there is no certain testimony
going back to 1672, she was celebrated in later years for
her interpretation of the part. "The manoeuvres of the
Champmeslé", wrote Madame de Sévigné in 1689, "to
retain all her lovers, without prejudice to the parts of
Atalide, Bérénice, and Phèdre, cover five leagues of
country very easily." Two years after this, Boursault gave
his advice in print 'To a Young Lady of Quality who was to
play the Role of Atalide in the Tragedy of *Bajazet* by M.
Racine', thus showing that the part was prized by society
amateurs.

Racine may have meant to hold the balance even between
his two creations, and to this end he wrote parts for them
of roughly equal length (Roxane has some twenty more lines
to speak than Atalide). An uncertain authority—which
belongs to the mid-eighteenth century and is chiefly
interesting because it shows what a historian of the theatre
could accept at that date—has it that he first cast the Champmeslé as Atalide, then switched her to Roxane, and finally
changed her back to Atalide.[1].

If that was so, Roxane was created by the Dennebaut.
The Sieur de Champmeslé was certainly Bajazet. La Fleur,
who had played Burrhus in *Britannicus*, was the Vizir Acomat.
Hauteroche, who had created Narcisse, had the confidant's
part of Osmin. The veteran Floridor was no longer with
them. He had died almost in harness the previous year,
after playing his last Racinian part as Titus in *Bérénice*.

[1] This is from the Brothers Parfaict, who began publishing the fifteen
volumes of their *Histoire du théâtre françois* in 1745.

3

Although *Bajazet* cannot be ranked among Racine's greatest tragedies, it is one of his most interesting experiments. In the development of his theatre as a whole, it might be considered as only a sketch for *Phèdre* and—judged by the standards of pure classical tragedy—it is much inferior to *Phèdre*, and, indeed, to *Andromaque* and *Britannicus*. But a truer judgment can be formed by considering *Bajazet* as a play written in holiday mood after the victory of *Bérénice*, as a reaction after the genteel restraint of that production and as a conscious approach to melodrama—the nearest that Racine ever made. It even suggests to an English reader that Racine might have competed on equal terms with the Jacobean 'horror' dramatists if his lot had happened to set him down among them. As it was, he respected the stage conventions of his time, but within those limits packed every permissible device with which to thrill the audience. It is significant that *Bajazet* contains the most important piece of 'business' used in a Racinian tragedy, and one of the very few he employed. Timid enough when judged by Jacobean standards, the business of the letter surprised on the swooning Atalide is sufficiently outstanding to taint the play for the classical purist. Unlike Bérénice's letter which foreshadows it, or the cup of poison dashed from Monime's hand in *Mithridate*, or the sword snatched from Hippolyte in *Phèdre*—for all of which some verbal invention could have been substituted without much loss—Bajazet's letter is essential to the plot. Remove it, and considerable circumlocution would be necessary, with a consequent weakening of the dramatic impact.

The same is true of Roxane's final dismissal of Bajazet. This, by reason of the circumstances which surround it, is also a kind of 'business', although physically it consists only of a word and a gesture. When Bajazet stands before the Sultaness, stumbling through his clumsy defence of Atalide, she cuts short his protestations with the one word:

Sortez! The audience know, though he does not, that beyond the door through which he has been sent the mutes stand ready to garrot him. The flick of Roxane's hand is thus the order for his instant execution.

But most of the surprises in *Bajazet* result, as in *Andromaque* and *Phèdre*, from the closely-woven texture of the play. The characters tread on each other's heels with telling effect. No sooner has Bajazet reassured Atalide of his love for her than Roxane is upon them. When Roxane hesitates, uncertain whether to believe in Bajazet's love or not, news comes of the arrival of the Sultan's messenger, bearing no doubt a second demand for Bajazet's execution. She must make up her mind in the instant on a matter of life and death. The scenes of this drama—even the 'tender' scenes—give the spectator no breathing-space. The tension is heightened by the constant menace of the Sultan's intervention or return, the unknown quantity which at any moment may upset the calculations of the characters on the stage and which forces the pace of their actions as though they were racing against an unseen clock. Reinforcing the pressure of time is the pressure of place: the brooding, sultry atmosphere of the harem, with its mute guards lurking in intricate corridors and its walls washed by the sea on which Acomat's ships wait ready for flight. In this forbidden place the characters meet, not just in fear and suspicion of each other, but in fear of the law which they are breaking by meeting there at all. Herein, as M. François Mauriac has pointed out, lies the true local colour of the tragedy. Atalide and Bajazet—though less Roxane and Acomat—may be oriental only in costume and name, but the atmosphere of the harem which Racine contrives to suggest was not the atmosphere of Versailles or of any Western court. It differs also from the atmosphere of his Greek and Roman plays where the exits lead from the 'cage of passions' towards the open air and where the characters, even when they are going to their deaths, seem to be escaping into the sunlight.

The illusion that this blood-soaked tragedy really occurs

in the seraglio of Byzantium and not in a palace on the Tiber or in Epirus can be reinforced by décor and lighting, particularly in a modern production. But, independently of anything that can be achieved by such means, the feverish, oppressive climate of *Bajazet* is already established by Racine's text. The sense of hurrying time and of brooding disaster are apparent even at a reading of the play and are created by the dialogue, in which it is hard to find a line which does not have a direct bearing on the march of external events. Here there is little introspection and certainly no ornament. In *Bajazet*, unlike *Bérénice*, there are no passages which could be "chanted", except Atalide's final incantation, whose purpose, like the last speech of Oreste, is to bring down the curtain on a high note of sorrow.

Since everything is stated, or indicated, in the lines of the actors, it might appear that they—and the producer—can do no more than amplify for a mass audience the effect which already exists, powerful and complete, on the printed page. In writing *Bajazet*, Racine made the film; the acting of the play is merely its projection on the screen.

This consideration, which applies more or less to all Racine's tragedies, is most evident in *Bajazet*. It once led a modern producer, Gaston Baty, to maintain that it is not worth while acting Racine. Since the author has included everything, he reasons, the actor's task is limited to reproducing, one after another, all the indications provided him. "If he is mediocre, he will distort the model. The whole triumph of his talent can only be to present a faithful copy, a second 'print', of the clear, complete figure which emerges from the reading. Roxane's '*Sortez!*' is much admired; but on the stage, the actress's gesture accompanies the line and the effect is weakened because it is expressed twice. A silent gesture would have much greater force."[1]

[1] G. Baty. *Le Masque et l'encensoir*. (Paris, 1926.)
Quoted by permission of MM. Bloud & Gay et Cie, Paris.

Perhaps this is nothing more than a family quarrel between author and producer, the producer grumbling because the author's text does not allow him sufficient latitude. And it is true that, while considerable liberties can be taken with the texts of Shakespeare and Molière, and the result still holds the stage, Racine's plays are so delicately balanced that it is dangerous to tamper with them. The smallest alteration may disturb the whole intricate mechanism. It must be remembered that Racine, unlike Molière and Shakespeare, was neither an actor nor the leader of a company. Although by the date of *Bajazet* his influence at the Hôtel was no doubt sufficiently strong for his advice to be sought and, if he wished it, imposed, yet he was not in a position to modify his plays at rehearsals. The innumerable touches which the producer or the actor-manager find by experiment had, by him, to be thought out beforehand and encrusted in the script as the safest way of ensuring their preservation. If challenged by an actor, he only had to point out the necessary implication of his lines in order to have his way, provided that the actor was intelligent and reasonable. But he dare not rely on the inspiration of the moment. Before his plays went into rehearsal, he had foreseen the effects he wanted and, by writing a text in which the stage-directions were implicit, had done all that was humanly possible to ensure that his wishes were carried out.

The existence of the modern producer makes such precautions less necessary and a truly inventive producer may well complain, like M. Gaston Baty, that Racine's situations are too clear-cut and his characters 'without mystery'. But it is more difficult to accept his final conclusion that Racine was not a 'man of the theatre'. All that we can readily admit is the self-evident fact that Racine was not of the theatrical profession. But that his plays were not carefully devised for the stage, with a full knowledge of what was possible and effective upon it, is belied by the experience of generations of actors and audiences.

The intensive study which Racine's great interpreters have always thought it necessary to give to their parts suggests that he is an exacting dramatist, for the actor, but also, when the effort to understand his intentions has been made, a rewarding one. If his plays were merely literature, yielding up their full content to the solitary reader, such study would, on the contrary, prove barren.

CHAPTER XIV

THE FRUITS OF SUCCESS

MITHRIDATE, IPHIGÉNIE

OLLOWING his now settled rhythm of one play
a year, Racine produced *Mithridate* in January 1673,
probably on the thirteenth of the month. It seems
to have run without a break until Easter and may
well have been taken up again in the summer. Louis XIV
saw it for the first time on February 11th at Saint-Germain;
his approval was such that he came to regard it as his favourite Racinian tragedy. In May, Monsieur commanded a performance in his château at Saint-Cloud for the entertainment
of the Duke of Monmouth and the British Ambassador and
his wife. They saw it in a room "decorated with a marvellous
profusion of flowers arranged in silver bowls and vases".

Like some other immediately successful plays, *Mithridate*
has hardly any history. After the *turquerie* of *Bajazet*,
Racine had returned to the Roman chroniclers and out of
the lamentable story of Mithridates Eupator, King of
Pontus, had evolved a play in which virtue and youth
triumphed over villainy and age. There was one considerable female role for the Champmeslé: that of Monime, a
sweet and touching princess; two princely roles to divide
between the Sieur de Champmeslé and Brécourt, though
it is not known which of them played the virtuous Xipharès
and which the treacherous Pharnace; the title role for La
Fleur who, as Mithridate, represented one of the noblest
of the Racinian kings. He sees in time through the villainy
of Pharnace, and with his dying words unites the innocent

lovers, Xipharès and Monime. More fortunate than
Bajazet and Atalide, this pair survive while the obstacles to
their happiness disappear. The tragedy ends on a solemn
yet hopeful note. The audience comes away neither thrilled
nor stunned by a last-act massacre, but agreeably moved
and satisfied that ultimately justice has been done.

Once again, it would seem, Racine had delighted his
public. The almost complete absence of, controversy
around *Mithridate* (only de Visé alluded, once again, to the
lack of local character) was a sign, not of disinterest, but
of acceptance. Robinet, though no critic, proved a
weather-cock of public opinion in the banal verses with
which he praised the play:

> *Mais en un mot, l'Auteur adroit*
> *Que l'on nomme Monsieur Racine,*
> *Lequel à l'Hôtel prend racine,*
> *A ce sujet fort bien traité;*
> *Et l'on y peut, en vérité,*
> *Quantité de grands vers entendre,*
> *Et quantité d'un style tendre.*

It might be thought that in so perfectly crossing the t's
of his own reputation, Racine had been too complacent.
For, if *Mithridate* has sometimes been held up as his most
technically perfect play, it contains little that is new. All
the elements which his admirers had most appreciated in
his previous work are present in it: the 'political' background, sufficiently solid to give an air of gravity to the love-
story; the warrior-king, not barbarous but sufficiently stern
to kill comparisons with the frivolous pastoral novels;
the chivalrous prince, to revive carefully restrained ideas
of romance; the appealing heroine through whom, now
that so many safeguards have been established, the current
of emotion can be allowed to flow.

All this, though blended in different proportions, had
been used and tested before. Without, in the common
meaning of the term, 'repeating himself', Racine seems
to have paused to exploit the professional experience which

he had gathered in his previous plays. It was his right to do so. Through disappointment and experiment he had found the formula which best suited his talent and which appealed most strongly to the contemporary public. Thanks to this formula, and without resorting to shoddy craftsmanship or to sensational devices, he had written the equivalent of a best-seller. Who should blame him? Where is the pure artist who would not do as much if it could be achieved without the sacrifice of quality but only, it might be argued, by slightly restraining the creative urge? From one point of view this can be called a ripening of talent, and the fact that *Mithridate* contains little that is embryonic or experimental can legitimately be quoted in its praise. It is a mature work. Only if Racine had continued to write a number of similar plays, as carefully compounded as this one to please both the academic critics and the audiences of his time, could he be accused of complacency. As it is, *Mithridate* stands as a model of what the Racinian tragedy is supposed to be, but, significantly, it stands alone.

If, when placed beside some of the more adventurous tragedies, *Mithridate* appears a little colourless, that would be a false indication of the author's mind, The 'noble abstractions' of classicism which, as a young man, he had believed to be the essence of poetry, did not so greatly impress him now. Writing for his cultured public, he must, in moderation, use the literary idiom of the age—but without supposing that it held a monopoly of virtue. He was as sensitive as any Romantic to the individual flavour of a style, a character, or a period. With what relish, having devised his disciplined tragedy, his modern heroine and his sober happy ending, did he go back to the source which had first inspired him: Plutarch in Amyot's translation. Conserving in part the original spelling—although, beyond heightening the archaic flavour, it serves no purpose—he quotes lovingly to his polished contemporaries what he describes as the words of Amyot, "for they have a grace in the old style of this translator which I am sure I cannot equal in our modern language".

[187]

"And she had much renown among the Greeks for that, though hotly entreated by the King who lusted after her, she never would hearken to all his pursuings until there was promise of marriage made between them, and he had sent her the diadem or royal headband and had called her Queen. The poor lady, since the King had wed her, had lived in great displeasure, doing continually no other thing but lament the unhappy beauty of her body which instead of a husband had got her a master and instead of conjugal society such as befits an honourable lady, had given her a guard and a garrison of barbarous men who held her captive far from the fair land of Greece, in a place where she had only a shadow and a dream of the sweets she had hoped for; and on the contrary had really lost those true sweets which she had enjoyed in the land of her birth. And when the eunuch was come in unto her, and had signified to her in the King's name that she was to die, then did she tear from off her temples her royal headband and, knotting it round her neck, did hang herself therewith. But the headband was not stout enough and broke incontinently. And then she cried out: 'O accursed and ill-starred Stuff, wilt thou not serve me even for this sad usage?' So saying, she cast it upon the ground, spitting upon it, and stretched out her throat to the eunuch."[1]

So Racine—not, as he claims, quoting the exact words of Amyot, but rearranging them to suit his purposes in the final Preface to his play as he published it in 1676.

Some critics, noting the 'Roman' subject of *Mithridate*, have seen it as the *coup de grâce* administered to the already defeated Corneille. There is, however, no reason to believe that Racine, having triumphed in *Bérénice* and having felt free after that to make the bold excursion of *Bajazet*, was again glancing at his old rival's reputation. His own reputation was now solidly established; his manner was recognized and admired. Nothing that Corneille had written lately could have disturbed him. If he had returned

[1] The barbaric tone of this passage from Plutarch recalls the Old Testament sources of the strongest passages in *Esther* and *Athalie*.

to the old enmity in *Mithridate*, it would have been a retro-grade step without significance at that date. Moreover, *Mithridate* has little that is 'Roman' except its source. It is, as we have seen, a synthesis of Racinian elements. Its existence seems sufficiently explained by Racine's desire to write another impressive and successful play.

2

As *Mithridate* began its run, Racine found himself in possession of a signal honour. On 12th January 1673—and so probably on the eve of the première—he was installed in the chair in the Academy left vacant by the death of La Motte le Vayer. With Fléchier and the obscure Abbé Gallois, he shared the distinction of being the first new member elected since the Academy's status had been raised by the bestowal of the King's official patronage.

At thirty-three, he became the youngest member of a company which included his patrons Colbert and Saint-Aignan, as well as that essential friend Chapelain. He took his seat beside high dignitaries of the Church—François de Harlay, Archbishop of Paris, Bossuet, Bishop of Condom—learned judges like Bazin de Bezons, anti-Jansenists like Desmarets de Saint-Sorlin, quizzical aristocrats like Bussy-Rabutin. The presence of some of these men may have disturbed him when he first joined their company. But a greater ordeal was to appear before his fellow-writers and dramatists—the Abbé Boyer, Philippe Quinault, nearly as young and quite as brilliant as himself, Michel Le Clerc, who dabbled in the theatre but was more at home in the salon and the law-court, Corneille, Segrais, Pellisson, Charles Perrault—none of whom bore him any great love.

Before this reconstitution of the Awful Seat, it is not surprising that he was overcome and almost broke down. His speech of thanks, says his son Louis, was uttered in so low a voice as to be nearly inaudible, and he did not after-wards publish it or even preserve it among his papers. It is also possible that the thought of his tragedy, to be produced on the morrow, heightened the tension for him. Fléchier and Gallois, on the other hand, acquitted themselves like experienced orators and were warmly applauded.

But confidence quickly returned, and within a few months "the illustrious M. Racine" was exchanging ripostes at a meeting of the Academy with "the celebrated M. Corneille". The subject of their interchange was Boursault's latest play, of which Corneille pugnaciously remarked that had it only been signed 'Racine' the sheep-like public would have considered it perfect. Racine made some equally biting reply.

For his reassurance to be complete, he had only to look at the men of talent who were still absent from the Immortals. He had been honoured before La Fontaine, his old friend and senior by eighteen years; before Boileau-Despréaux, his new friend and would-be counsellor; before the younger Corneille, fashionable playwright though he was; before Benserade the veteran lyric-writer; before Molière, whose election it would soon be too late to consider.

Within two years, the new Academician received another mark of the appreciation of Colbert and the King. In October 1674 he was appointed *Trésorier de France en la généralité de Moulins*—a town in central France which he never visited. This financial office carried with it the technical right to be called *chevalier*, which he ignored, and also, as a friend reminded him some years later, "the honourable satisfaction of being buried with golden spurs on". Racine wore the honour modestly enough, but derived an income of 2,400 *livres* from the sinecure.

Such offices could be bought, and were usually considered as favourable investments open to men with the right connexions. Racine, however, acquired Moulins as a free gift from his patrons.[1]

---

[1] The Letters Patent, granted on 20th September 1674, speak of the beneficiary in terms somewhat warmer than was usual even in such documents: "Louis by the grace of God King of France and of Navarre,

3

The death of Molière on 17th February 1673 altered the whole balance of power in the Parisian theatre. No sooner was Molière buried than his company began to break up. Four of its members joined the Hôtel de Bourgogne—among them Baron, whose arrival brought Racine a new and brilliant *jeune premier*. The King, not uninfluenced by Lully, then stepped in to order the amalgamation of the rump of Molière's troupe with the company of the Marais and their removal across the river to a hall in the Faubourg Saint-Germain. Of the two theatres thus vacated, the old Marais was closed for good, and the fine hall of the Palais-Royal, whose stage had been enlarged and modernized by Molière during his twelve-year tenure, was given to the Florentine for the exclusive performance of operas.

Henceforth the Hôtel de Bourgogne had only one immed-iate competitor to face instead of two: the merged com-pany in the Faubourg Saint-Germain, which became known as the Théâtre Guénégaud (or sometimes as the Théâtre Mazarine; it lay in the angle of the two streets). It is doubtful, however, whether the elimination of the Marais, which of recent years had been little disposed to challenge the Hôtel on its own ground of straight tragedy, brought much comfort to the Burgundians. They would, in fact, have more to fear from the combined talents of the new association than from two weak companies, one languishing and the other leaderless. But the real threats to their future did not lie here. They were of a more far-reaching nature.

---

to all who shall see these present Letters, salutations. Be it known that We, having every confidence in the person of our dear and well-beloved Maître Jean Racine, and in his judgment, ability, uprightness, integrity, experience and capacity in the matter of Our Finances, and in his loyalty and attachment to Our service, and out of Our regard for his excellent qualities and his merit, have given and granted him and do give and grant by these presents the office of Our Counsellor-Treasurer of France and General of Our Finances in the Generality of Moulins.''

First, the strong personalities of the theatre were disappearing. Molière, the greatest, was dead. Corneille was finished, and so much out of favour in influential quarters that after 1673 his yearly pension ceased to be paid. Racine's official influence was not of the kind and scope that were necessary. Of the remaining authors and actors none was of sufficient calibre to stand up to the encroachments of officialdom. There were always bureaucrats eager to step in and regulate the theatre in the interests of tidiness and economy, aristocrats who looked on it as a toy with which it would be amusing to play. Beyond these were the forces of the Church and the magistrature who disapproved of the comedy in the name of morality and good order. As long as the theatre had possessed determined and influential men who could invoke the King's support while retaining some independence, all these hostile influences could be warded off. But a weak theatre was at the mercy of the regulators and the arbitrary merger of 1673 set a dangerous precedent for interference.

As for the one strong man who remained, the comedians would have felt safer if he had not been there. Lully, who had already benefited most by the new dispositions, was a constant danger to them. Having supplanted the original founders of opera in Paris, the Marquis de Sourdéac and his partner Champeron—it was their abandoned theatre in the Jeu de Paume de la Bouteille which became the Théâtre Guénégaud—he obtained control of every public performance of music in France and went on to exploit the new vogue to its utmost. All Paris and Versailles flocked to the opera. By mid-afternoon the Rue Saint-Honoré was blocked with coaches, and their occupants had the choice of missing the spectacle or getting out and walking through the unnameable mud. The Lully-Quinault-Vigarani combination hit the taste of the time as unerringly as Racine had hit it a few years before in *Bérénice*.

This was the most imminent threat to the Hôtel de Bourgogne: not that a rival company of players should share their audiences, but that tragedy, even 'tender' tragedy, should go out of favour altogether. To move the public, to provoke tears—and how insistent were all the non-profession-al commentators on this aspect of theatre-going—the love-liest verse spoken by the most melting voice was inferior to music and song, especially when these were combined with the spectacular appeal of costumes, décors and *machines*. The ladies went to the opera to be moved. The men—if *Le Mercure Galant* is to be believed—went because the ladies were moved.

> *L'Opéra fort souvent peut hâter une affaire*
> *Que cent mille soupirs n'auraient jamais pu faire.*
> *Quand le chant dans le cœur a fait impression,*
> *Ce cœur n'est pas longtemps sans quelque émotion.*
> *C'est l'heure du berger, ô trop heureux Silvandre,*
> *L'objet que vous servez est tout près de se rendre.*

In face of the glamorous productions at the Palais-Royal, there was a danger that the most sweetly-modulated spoken tragedy would seem too austere and it says much for the professional skill of Racine and the Champmeslé that they, at least, were able to hold their own. That Racine was fully aware of the challenge is shown by the Preface to his next play, *Iphigénie*. The significance of this highly skilful piece of special pleading on behalf of his con-ception of tragedy must have been clear enough to con-temporaries.

Racine had found it repugnant, he says, to let his heroine be sacrificed at the end of the play, as she is in the legend recounted by Aeschylus and Sophocles. Casting about for a means to save her, he had found in other ancient authors a second character, a false Iphigenia, whom he could present in an unsympathetic light and sacrifice at the dénouement in place of his "amiable and virtuous" princess. How much preferable is this natural solution to presenting on the stage a miraculous intervention—"a goddess and a *machine* and a metamorphosis, which might find some cred-ence in the time of Euripides, but which would be too absurd and incredible for us".

By thus glancing at the Greeks, he condemns the modern rage for showy but improbable spectacles, and asserts his essential principle that the human element is the mainspring of drama. (He is typically French in rejecting the myth.) This done, he is able to use the example of the Greeks to attack from another angle the Italian inspirers of opera and of the *pièce à machines*. He has been obliged to discard, he writes, certain non-essentials in Euripides' version of the legend, "but where the passions are concerned, I have been careful to follow him more closely . . . I have observed with pleasure, having seen the effect produced on our stage by everything that I have imitated from Homer and Euripides, that good sense and reason are the same in every age. The taste of Paris has proved to be concordant with that of Athens; my audiences have been moved by the same things that in other times drew tears from the most sophisticated people in Greece."

The rest of this Preface appears to be a slightly pedantic justification of certain passages in Euripides. At first sight the modern reader might question its relevance. But when he notices that the play defended is the *Alcestis* and realizes that the *Alcestis* had just been compared disadvantageously (by Pierre Perrault) with Quinault-Lully's new and immensely popular opera *Alceste, ou Le Triomphe d'Alcide*, Racine's motive becomes clear. In defending 'his' author, he is defending by implication, and on the highest possible level, himself. He no longer refutes criticism directly: he has found a subtler and more dignified method. But his shafts are just as deadly. He quietly points out to the disparagers of Euripides, not that they are wrong in principle, not that their general approach to the question of Ancients *versus* Moderns is mistaken . . . but that they have allowed themselves to be misled by a printer's error into ascribing four lines to the wrong character. When these lines are restored to their real speaker, the conclusions drawn by the critics collapse.[1]

---

[1] More unkindly still, Racine lets it be known that the misprint occurs only in one 'wretched edition' *in Latin*. He himself read Euripides in the original Greek.

This is literary fencing at its most formidable, for such arguments cannot be answered. One may dispute for twenty years on the respective merits of the Classic and the Baroque and be little the worse at the end of it. But a precise thrust on a point of fact, delivered after the adversary has built it into his system of defence, is mortal. Racine handles his weapon with an easy nonchalance. He is courteous, lightly condescending, almost regretful. "The *Alcestis* is not really the point at issue here," he writes, "but I am under too great an obligation to Euripides not to be somewhat jealous for his memory and not to take this opportunity of reconciling him with these gentlemen. I am sure that he only stands so low in their opinion because they have not properly read the play on which they condemn him."

He makes his demonstration and concludes, not in his own words, but still modestly by quoting Quintilian.

"One must be extremely circumspect when pronouncing judgment on the works of these great men, lest it happen to us—as it has to several—to condemn what we do not understand."

This is Racine in his most confident vein writing for publication a few weeks after the success of his latest play had reassured him of the Parisian public's support for his simple-looking tragedies.

4

Iphigénie was first produced at Versailles at the summer fêtes of 1674, which had a special brilliance that year to celebrate the return of Louis from the conquest of the Franche-Comté. Ten years older than when he had caracoled as the Paladin Roger in the *Pleasures of the Enchanted Island*, the King drove out sedately in a calèche, seated between the Queen and the Montespan, to the spot in the park where the play was to be acted. The setting had a semi-natural splendour surpassing anything that Lully could contrive on an indoor stage. Against the heavy August green of the yew-hedges gleamed the new white marble of

the fountains with their tritons of gilded bronze. White
tents with baldaquin tops marked the back of the stage and
represented the encampment of the Greek armies bound for
the attack on Troy. Through a central opening between
the tents, the eye ran on down the Allée de l'Orangerie to
a little temple with pilasters of lapis lazuli and a door of
beaten gold, which closed the vista. It was already dusk,
but the orange and pomegranate trees on either side were lit
by an immense number of crystal candelabra whose flames
swayed lightly in the evening air. The place was sweet with
the perfume of cut flowers in porcelain vases. Violins
played softly. In such surroundings "the company of the
King's Players performed the tragedy of *Iphigénie*, the
latest work of the Sieur Racine, which was received by the
whole Court with the esteem which the plays of this author
have always enjoyed".

No doubt that is how *Iphigénie* should always be produced.
It is the only one of Racine's tragedies which gives the
illusion of happening in the open air, under a clear sky on
the shore of a windless sea. The lightness and grace of its
atmosphere rise almost palpably from the poetry even as it
stands on the printed page. How much more when properly spoken by voices which cannot be prevented here from
floating into a slight 'chant'.

The mood is established by the opening scene in Agamemnon's tent just before dawn.

> *A peine un faible jour vous éclaire et me guide,*
> *Vos yeux seuls et les miens sont ouverts dans l'Aulide.*
> *Avez-vous dans les airs entendu quelque bruit?*
> *Les vents nous auraient-ils exaucés cette nuit?*
> *Mais tout dort, et l'armée, et les vents, et Neptune.*

By the end of the first act full daylight has come, and the
crafty Ulysses has painted his vigorous picture of the waves
whitening round the ships of the triumphant Greeks.

> *Voyez tout l'Hellespont blanchissant sous nos rames,*
> *Et la perfide Troie abandonnée aux flammes,*

Ses peuples dans vos fers, Priam à vos genoux,
Hélène par vos mains rendue à son époux;
Voyez de vos vaisseaux les poupes couronnées
Dans cette même Aulide avec vous retournées . . .

Achilles has arrived, sea-borne from Lesbos, clamouring for his bride and then for the new adventure of Troy. Clytemnestra is approaching with her daughter, whose arrival Agamemnon dreads above all else, since he must sacrifice her to appease the oracle. She would be here already, declares a messenger, but

Elle s'est quelque temps égarée
Dans ces bois qui du camp semblent cacher l'entrée.
A peine nous avons, dans leur obscurité,
Retrouvé le chemin que nous avons quitté.

Thus half in the Greek country of the legend and half among the hornbeams of Versailles, the story was unfolded in Racine's verses, musical yet never merely ornamental for, as he himself pointed out, "the loveliest scenes are in danger of being found tedious the moment they can be separated from the action". For the right use of poetry on the stage—particularly that stage—it would be hard to improve on Clytemnestra's vision of herself returning alone after her daughter's sacrifice. Four lines suffice to reveal the full pathos of a situation and a character.

Et moi, qui l'amenai triomphante, adorée,
Je m'en retournerai seule et désespérée;
Je verrai les chemins encore tout parfumés
Des fleurs dont sous ses pieds on les avait semés.

It says much for the cynical Court of Versailles that they were responsive to this mood and this poetry. An age which has seemed to other ages hard-bitten because it was normally unsentimental over the relations of husbands to wives and parents to children, turned from wild nature with a fastidious shudder, and ignored the nostalgia of the native place, nevertheless had its Achilles' heel. The spectacle of innocent beauty in distress moved it deeply. And when the lovely voice of the Champmeslé had died away and the candles still blazed on their azure-and-gold stands, Racine stepped forward to receive what must have been the most satisfying homage of his professional career. While half the Court, their eyes on Louis, applauded the author loudly, many others, swept away by his art, wept unrestrainedly. He had touched their most sensitive chord and for a few moments they were his.

Even the reporter Robinet, proud to be present at such a fête, caught—however prosaically—the emotion of that instant.

> La très touchante Iphigénie,
> Ce chef-d'oeuvre du beau génie
> De Racine, ravit la Cour . . .
> Et pour lors, la Cour toute pleine
> De pleureurs, fit une autre scène,
> Ou l'on vit maint des plus beaux yeux,
> Voire des plus impérieux,
> Pleurer sans aucun artifice
> Sur ce fabuleux sacrifice.
> L'auteur fut beaucoup applaudi . . .
> Et même notre auguste Sire
> L'en louangea fort, c'est tout dire.

When Paris saw *Iphigénie*, probably in January 1675,[1] it endorsed the opinion of Versailles. The play ran at the Hôtel for three months, or some forty performances. By what can only have been an accident, it cruelly underlined the eclipse of Corneille, for the old dramatist's *Suréna*,

[1] The exact date of the Paris première is unknown. It must have been after 15th December 1674, when Minutoli (*Lettres*, quoted Mélèse: *Le Théâtre et le public sous Louis XIV*) wrote that Corneille's new play at the Hôtel de Bourgogne was not proving a success. It must have been before 28th January 1675 when Racine was granted the *privilège* authorizing the publication of *Iphigénie*. Allowing a short interval for Corneille's play to expire, late December or early January seems the correct date for *Iphigénie*, and this accords with other, less precise, contemporary allusions.

produced by the Hôtel immediately before *Iphigénie*, had proved an instant failure. Admitting tardily that the odds against him were too heavy, Corneille wrote no more for the theatre.

5

In *Iphigénie*, for the first time since *Andromaque*, Racine had turned back to the Greeks for his inspiration. What he took from them now were, not the Eumenides-driven Oreste and Hermione, but the calm, noble figures of Agamemnon and his daughter. He had found in Euripides that version of the legend in which Iphigénie, after being led to the sacrificial altar, was suddenly saved by the intervention of a god. That—or so Racine maintained in his Preface—was inacceptable in his time. Equally repugnant would have been the death of Iphigénie. It was only the "very fortunate" discovery of the personage of Eriphile that enabled him to write his tragedy at all. Having intrigued against Iphigénie, Eriphile "deserves in some sort to be punished" and can be sacrificed without violation of natural laws or of the sympathies of the audience. Iphigénie lives on to wed Achille, whom Racine presents as her fiery and devoted lover.

This solution, though it made the play possible on the seventeenth-century tragic stage, is not really defensible. In eliminating the supernatural machinery which Euripides had used to save the heroine, Racine did not go far enough, for other mythical postulates remained. Agamemnon and the other Grecian chiefs accept the oracle's demand for a sacrifice and assume that it will be efficacious. It is so. When it is made—the desired victim proving to be Eriphile—the heavens thunder and the winds rise. All this, however muted down by Racine, still belongs to the ancient world and makes the psychology of his play inconsistent.[1] The character of Agamemnon, poised as he is

---

[1] Racine's awareness of the dilemma is shown in his handling of Ulysses' description of the sacrifice (Act V, Sc. vi). Ulysse—the trustworthy eyewitness—has himself seen only phenomena (thunder, lightning, the

between the two worlds, suffers particularly. If closely examined, he is as incredible as was Créon in *La Thébaïde* when he proclaimed himself indifferent to the death of his son provided his own ambitions were furthered thereby. Only Racine's greatly increased skill now persuades the spectator to accept a situation which in the earlier tragedy he rejects out of hand. The chief remaining characters are modern. Clytemnestre has no belief in, or awe of, the oracle. When her husband's design can no longer be hidden from her she reacts, like any normal mother, by finding it outrageous. The reaction of Achille is the same; he attempts to rescue his mistress by force from the hands of the priests. Iphigénie herself is no more prompted by a sense of religious dedication than Bérénice or Atalide had been. She consents to be sacrificed for the honour of her father—an entirely human motive.

Such flaws—for so they must surely be called—prevent an otherwise fine tragedy, possessed of a perfume and lightness all its own, from being placed among Racine's greatest. He had, in reality, only two extreme choices. Either he must leave Euripides intact, in which case the ritual and religious element would predominate, or he must entirely modernize his characters and setting and require of Iphigénie some different sacrifice which her father could demand more plausibly. The middle course of an adaptation to the seventeenth-century idiom was impracticable.

When he came to *Phèdre*, in which the same kind of problems arose, he achieved a more perfect synthesis. That was, in part, because the subject was more amenable. The supernatural element was no longer an essential of the plot, but could be used, it might be said, as an intangible part of the décor. Wisely, he preserved it and did not, as in *Iphigénie*, avoid the intervention of a god to bring about his

---

roaring sea) which a modern can call natural although Ulysse attributes them to the gods. He merely *reports* the vision of Diana descending in a cloud as having been seen by the superstitious soldiery. The distinction is ingenious, but Racine no doubt knew that he had not solved the larger problem.

dénouement. This time it did not matter. The actions of the characters throughout the length of the play had not been focused upon it. It simply gave added solemnity to the death of one of them who was doomed in any case.

But, in spite of its inconsistencies, *Iphigénie* can still give considerable pleasure. It is, as many critics have pointed out, a 'serene' play—serene in the character of its heroine, in its poetry and its philosophy. Not only are the guilty punished but the innocent are rewarded. Almost alone of Racine's princesses, Iphigénie is spared and restored to her lover. She takes her place beside the Monime of *Mithridate*, who was also innocent and was also spared, and it is natural that the light should shine more brightly on these two in contrast with the darkness which engulfs their fellow-creations. What does the relative optimism of these two consecutive plays portend? Does it reflect a new-found serenity in Racine's own life, based either on his personal relationships or on his sense of material achievement, or on both combined? Had something prompted him, after *Bajazet*, to begin weaving a moral purpose into tragedy and to exalt the innocent at all costs, as later in *Esther* and *Athalie*? Or was he only obeying a sentimental consideration which drew him towards the 'happy ending'—and how far is it possible to distinguish between his personal convictions and his sense of what the public desired?

Such questions will always be asked, but the material to base an answer on is lacking. In its absence we can do no more than point out that *Iphigénie* is the most 'moral' of Racine's great secular plays, in that it is the only one which fully satisfies the popular conception of poetic justice. Compared to *Iphigénie*, *Phèdre* will be an 'immoral' play.

6

The contemporary success of *Iphigénie*, while increasing Racine's reputation, made him more vulnerable to attack. His genius, it seemed, had crystallized and would give no more surprises but only repeat the pattern. Its beauties would continue to please the public until the next change of fashion, but at the cost of its weaknesses becoming familiar to the expert eye. All highly successful authors incur this danger, though rarely at the age of thirty-five. Then the very magnitude of his triumph made him a more tempting target for the envious to shoot at. He was as outstanding and as irksome to others as Corneille had seemed to him a few years earlier. In that venomous age it was unlikely that he would be allowed to enjoy his rewards in peace.

After *Iphigénie* had exhausted its first run at the Hôtel, the rival company of the Théâtre Guénégaud performed another *Iphigénie*, by Le Clerc and Coras, which ran for five performances only in May-June 1675. This tragedy, produced too late to have any effect on Racine's play, and a failure in any case, might merely have been one more example of the *rencontres* so familiar to the theatre of the seventeenth century. A subject which was 'in the air' or had already proved successful in one version, was treated by a second author not necessarily actuated by malice against the first. Such was the explanation given by Le Clerc, in the Introduction which he wrote for the new play.

"I must say in all good faith," he protests, "that when I undertook to treat the subject of *Iphigénie en Aulide*, I believed that M. Racine had chosen that of *Iphigénie en Tauride*, which is no less fine than the other. Thus chance alone was the cause of our encounter, as it happened to M. Corneille and him in the two *Bérénices*."

This disingenuous statement can hardly be reconciled with the rest of Le Clerc's Preface, in which he goes on to praise his own piece at the expense of Racine's. Moreover, had the confusion been genuine, Le Clerc and Coras had had plenty of time in which to correct it. Their tragedy was not acted until some four months after the Paris première of Racine's *Iphigénie* and nine months after the triumphant production at Versailles.

There can be little doubt that circles hostile to Racine outside the theatre had encouraged this obscure pair of authors to produce a rival play. The jealousy which prompted the attack was more conspicuous than the effectiveness of its timing. In order to make way for the new *Iphigénie*, the Théâtre Guénégaud interrupted the highly successful run of *Circé*, a *pièce à machines* by de Visé and Thomas Corneille, which had been playing to packed houses for two months. When, after five performances, *Iphigénie* was withdrawn, *Circé* resumed its triumphal progress well into the autumn and was long remembered as one of the great successes of the spectacular stage. "If Molière's company had been allowed to perform with music and dances, and the instruments which they would have liked," wrote a contemporary, "*Circé* would easily have eclipsed all the operas we have so far seen." But, hampered by Lully's monopoly, the Théâtre Guénégaud was restricted to an orchestra of six violins and six other instruments.

In following this uncommercial procedure, the Théâtre Guénégaud, it might be said, had merely cut off its nose to spite its face. It had incurred a loss both in receipts and prestige in the hope that a wild blow at Racine might slightly detract from his reputation. The affair bears the marks of a *cabale* motivated by spite rather than by strictly professional considerations. Racine avenged himself in the following epigram on the two unfortunate authors:

> *Entre Le Clerc et son ami Coras,*
> *Tous deux auteurs rimant de compagnie,*
> *N'a pas longtemps sourdirent grands débats*
> *Sur le propos de son* Iphigénie.
> *Coras lui dit: " La pièce est de mon cru."*
> *Le Clerc répond: "Elle est mienne et non vôtre."*
> *Mais aussitôt que l'ouvrage a paru,*
> *Plus n'ont voulu l'avoir fait l'un ni l'autre.*

He paid no heed to another, still clumsier, attack launched in the following year by his old enemy Barbier d'Aucour. The man who had come to the defence of Port-Royal ten years earlier had not forgotten his rancour. In a satirical poem, entitled *Apollon vendeur de Mithridate*, he related, with a wealth of hackneyed puns, how the tender 'racine' planted by Port-Royal had grown thorns to wound its gardeners. With this personal history he mingled criticisms of Racine's work as a dramatist, accusing him of plagiarism, particularly among the Ancients. Each of his points had already been made by previous critics. Barbier d'Aucour's doubtful merit was to have strung them together with the heavy facetiousness peculiar to the ecclesiastical polemists which had so infuriated Racine when he found it in Nicole and in the Abbé de Villars, critic of *Bérénice*.

These attacks were straws in the wind, but Racine does not seem to have been much disturbed by them. In 1676 appeared the first collected edition of his plays and he took the opportunity to re-write some of the Prefaces in a more objective style. He discarded some of his more biting remarks and from the new Preface to *Britannicus* omitted all reference to the 'evil-intentioned old poet'. The echoes of this and other dated polemics die down and there remain chiefly calm and scholarly discussions of the sources from which these now established tragedies had been drawn. Only for *Bajazet* does he feel the need of justifying at much greater length his excursion into near-contemporary history. He alleges the principle—familiar enough to-day, but novel then—that a removal in space is equivalent to a removal in time.

"Turkish characters, however modern they may be, have a dignity on our stage. They come very early to be considered as Ancients. . . . We have so few dealings with the princes and other persons who live in the seraglio that we consider them, so to speak, as people living in another age than ours."

In the new Preface to *Andromaque* he remarks—with his eye perhaps not on this tragedy only—that "one should not quibble with poets about a few changes which they may make in the original legend; one should rather consider the excellent use which they have made of these changes and the ingenious manner in which they have contrived to adapt the legend to their subject".

CHAPTER XV

THE QUARREL OF *PHÈDRE*

HE slowing rhythm of Racine's production after *Mithridate* became still more accentuated after *Iphigénie*. Between the production of that play at Versailles and the first performance of his next tragedy more than twenty-eight months elapsed.

Part of the long interval may have been filled with experiments which he did not bring to a conclusion. Perhaps it was then that he made the plan of the first act of an *Iphigénie en Tauride* which was found among his papers. It would be a natural sequel to the *Iphigénie en Aulide* which he had successfully completed. Le Clerc's statement on this point cannot be trusted far, but it lends colour to the supposition that at one time Racine was hesitating between the two subjects. According to Le Clerc's version, Racine would have approached the *Iphigénie en Tauride* first, then discarded it in favour of the other *Iphigénie*. But this would not bar him from returning to it afterwards. He is also said to have begun an *Alceste*, but there may be some confusion here between the study (and perhaps translation) which he was making of the *Alcestis* of Euripides at the time when he wrote the Preface to *Iphigénie*, and the composition of an original play.[1]

In any case, these projects and experiments are not unlikely to have been part of his search for a new subject which finally led him to *Phèdre*. They have some significance if they belong to the years 1674-6, when his mind was full of Euripides, but little if—as his son Jean-Baptiste believed

[1] For La Grange-Chancel's remarks on the *Alceste see* p. 286.

—they occupied him after *Phèdre* and his open renunciation of the theatre.

Once found, the subject of *Phèdre* required long meditation. It was not, after all, to be a clever variation of his old successes, written to keep his name before his patrons and the public. It was to be a new creation, riper and more splendid than any that had gone before, though recognizably of the same family.

To perfect it, in the midst of his growing social obligations, a year would seem short and two years hardly too long. This gestation was necessary in order to bring to birth the brown-skinned young hunter Hippolyte; the pure Aricie, tender but also courageous, most flawless of her line of virgin princesses; the complex figure of Phèdre, sum-total of several experiments; the simple, pernicious Oenone; the half-fabulous pirate Thésée.

To set these characters, inevitable when born, yet any one of which might have miscarried, against the noblest, most significant background that Racine knew, since it belonged to his boyhood, to fit them for the contemporary stage without falsifying their Greek origins, to clothe them with an aura of poetry and myth yet make them acceptable to a realistic, 'reasonable' seventeenth-century audience— this was the task which Racine set himself to perform. *Phèdre*, he hoped, would be the peak of his achievement, but not only in the vulgar sense of his most brilliant or successful play. Its composition corresponded to an over-riding necessity. He was, as the event proved, so far from being written-out that his greatest tragedy was still within him. As an artist, he must translate into formal reality— for him, a play acted on a stage—the still formless elements which chaotically moved his mind. Until that was done, he could find no rest, and even when it was done he would wonder anxiously, with the humility of a true artist before what he feels to be the supreme subject, whether he had done it well enough. "I dare not yet affirm that this is indeed the best of my tragedies", he will write when, for better or worse, it has been launched.

In such circumstances, having lived with his work so intimately that he could no longer see it in perspective, the judgment of others assumed great importance. Temporarily dazed and exhausted, it was the only guide to show him whether he had produced a masterpiece or a monster.

2

That Racine was actively working on a new play had been public knowledge for some time before its production. His subject was no secret and it is probable that his text, or portions of it, had circulated through some of the salons.[1] This practice, while it brought an author useful opinions and stimulated interest in his forthcoming work, had the disadvantage of opening the door to an unscrupulous plagiarist.

Such was Pradon, the undistinguished author of two sentimental tragedies which the Hôtel de Bourgogne had produced without much success. Appropriating Racine's title and characters, but bowdlerizing the plot so as to avoid giving offence to the most prudish tastes, he set out to write a play which should surpass Racine's.

Pradon's self-conceit needed little bolstering. He possessed, however, a powerful backing which made his challenge more serious than the bid of a small author to ride to notoriety on the back of a great one. Supporting him was the circle of the Duchess of Bouillon, the youngest of the five stormy nieces of Cardinal Mazarin.

She had made of her house in Paris a little court to which some of the greatest names in France were proud to belong and in which men of letters, chosen for the most part with discriminating taste, were encouraged and protected.

[1] The first precise mention of the play is found in a letter written by Bayle to Minutoli on 4th October 1676: "M. de Racine travaille à la tragédie d'Hippolyte, dont on attend un grand succès."
To judge by one of Racine's own letters, he probably submitted Phèdre for criticism to the grammarian Bouhours at some unspecified time in the same year.

Among them were the delicate poets of the older generation—Ménage, Benserade, Segrais, La Fontaine—poets of
the theatre such as Boyer and sometimes old Corneille, one
poetess: Madame Deshoulières. The Duchess herself
dabbled in literature, and because of her amateur practice
of letters was all the more dogmatic in her judgment of
professionals. Her closest ally was her brother, Philippe
Mancini, Duke of Nevers—also a poet and patron of the
arts.

These two, brother and sister, formed one of those
little islands of resistance which held out in French society
against the encroachments of Versailles. Very powerful
in their family connections, feeling themselves superior
to the law and the common rules of conduct, they had no
scruples to prevent them from satisfying their dangerous
caprices. The fact that they were highly cultivated people,
capable of setting an esoteric fashion in opposition to the
broader fashion set by royalty, made them still more a
tribunal to be reckoned with.

For reasons which have never been fully clarified, the
Duchess of Bouillon determined that the new tragedy which
Racine was preparing should fail. Perhaps she had motive
enough if she listened to the jealous insinuations of her
protégés, but it would be a mistake to describe her salon
as a last stronghold of the Cornelians. Some of its clients
were admirers of Corneille, but others, just as certainly,
were not. Contemporaries did not see in the *cabale de
Phèdre* a last engagement in the Corneille-Racine struggle;
that was already considered as closed. It is more probable
that the Duchess was prompted by some different animosity
—in his rise to fame and his defence of his position, Racine
had given offence to many people—and that she was above
all curious to test her power. She was a woman who would
be irresistibly interested by the prospect of destroying the
accepted idol of the Court and the public. She was
probably fascinated by the intrigue, just as Henriette
d'Angleterre may have been when she suggested the two
Bérénices to Racine and Corneille. The effect of her

manoeuvre upon Racine himself would hardly enter into her calculations.

With this powerful machine behind him, Pradon sat down to compose his *Phèdre et Hippolyte*. He had, according to his own account, no more than three months in which to complete the task. Racine's tragedy was to be produced at the Hôtel at the beginning of the New Year; Pradon hoped to be ready at the Théâtre Guénégaud by the same date.

At one time it looked as though his effort of hurried composition would be wasted and the play produced too late to serve its main purpose. For Racine, having got wind of the plot against him, was calling on the influences which he possessed to defend his position. The two best actresses at the Théâtre Guénégaud declined the leading part in Pradon's play. Not without difficulty, a third actress was persuaded to take it. Racine then sought an injunction banning the rival production altogether. Such a proceeding was no novelty. If Pradon is to be believed, he had attempted a similar step against the *Iphigénie* of Le Clerc and Coras in 1675. Other, more certain, instances are on record. In an age when there was no general protection of copyright, Racine was justified in seeking legal protection in advance for his latest work if—as he had every reason to do—he suspected plagiarism. Pradon, indeed, maintained that he went further by seeking a ban, not only on the production but on the publication of the rival play.[1]

---

[1] Most of this information derives from Pradon himself, whose partiality is obvious. But in the matter of the injunction at least, it seems that his word must be accepted. As Paul Mesnard pointed out, he would hardly have lied to contemporaries on a matter on which they would have independent knowledge, nor would he have dared to claim falsely that his play had been saved by "the kindness and justice of the King", whose decision, he implied, had overridden Racine's objections.

As for the actresses, the fact that they declined to appear is confirmed independently by the *Gazette d'Amsterdam*. In a paragraph dated "Paris, 8th January 1677" and published on the 14th, the paper reported that the Théâtre Guénégaud had despaired of being able to give Pradon's

But Racine's counter-measures were without effect. The Bouillon faction wielded too much influence for his manoeuvres to win him more than the shortest advance. His tragedy was produced at the Hôtel on 1st January, 1677. Two days later, Pradon's play followed at the Théâtre Guénégaud.

What then happened was not—as was so long believed on the word of Louis Racine—that the Duchess of Bouillon bought up the *premières loges* at the two theatres and packed them with her own satellites. That colourful story must be discarded and the less palatable fact be recorded that for several performances public opinion, misled by the Duchess of Bouillon's coterie, hesitated between Pradon's play and Racine's.[1] The Théâtre Guénégaud was almost as

---

play, "because two of their best actresses had refused the chief part, *through intrigue or caprice*". Pressure by the Racinian camp remains suspected but unproved—as the gossip-writer no doubt intended. An alternative suggestion from the Racinian side is that the actresses—probably the de Brie and Molière's widow—withdrew of their own accord to avoid unfavourable comparisons with the Champmeslé appearing in a stronger play.

[1] A good review of the factual evidence is given, with additional discoveries of his own, by Professor H. C. Lancaster in his *History of French Dramatic Literature in the Seventeenth Century*, Vol. IV, Part I.

The most conclusive testimony is provided by the books of the Théâtre Guénégaud, which reveal no mass bookings by the Duchess of Bouillon or by anyone else. Varying numbers of boxes were reserved at different performances by individuals, some of whom could by no stretch of reasoning be connected with the *cabale*.

As for the mass bookings at the Hôtel de Bourgogne, they were equally mythical. Madame Deshoulières' daughter, interviewed by Brossette in 1711, declared that when her mother sent to book a *première loge* at the Hôtel de Bourgogne for the first performance of *Phèdre*, Champmeslé informed the messenger that there was none available—"as he always did when Madame Deshoulières attempted to book at this theatre". She was obliged to disguise herself and sit incognito in a *seconde loge*, for which a friend bought the tickets. For the second performance, Professor Lancaster has discovered that two *premières loges* were reserved by Condé, a supporter of Racine. Neither of these events could have occurred if the Duchess of Bouillon had already obtained control of the seats.

In view of Mlle. Deshoulières' statement, several critics, beginning

full as the Hôtel de Bourgogne. The audiences, primed though they may have been, appeared as enthusiastic on the Left Bank as on the Right. This explains the bitterness of Racine's first reaction. Far worse than a check arbitrarily brought about by the power of money was the failure of this play into which he had put so much to establish its immediate superiority over an insipid imitation. For a moment Racine doubted his public, which was unable to distinguish between his own ripest work and that of a second-rate hack. For a moment he may even have doubted his own genius. It was of this period and for this reason that his friend Valincour wrote: "I saw M. Racine in despair".

Before Racine could recover, he had a new dispute on his hands. He became involved in an exchange of libellous sonnets whose scandalous echoes drowned all reasonable voices and for a short period aroused as much interest as the plays themselves. Seen from a distance, they introduce a note of gross comedy into the affair. At the time, the participants were too angry to distinguish between trivial and serious issues.

The first sonnet was the work of Madame Deshoulières, the poetess who advised and befriended Pradon, and who may have first brought him to the notice of the Duchess of Bouillon. Having witnessed the première of Racine's tragedy, she returned home to sup with Pradon and a few

---

with Sainte-Beuve, assumed that the Duchess bought up the *loges*, not for the first six performances (as Louis Racine declared), but at a later date, after the Affair of the Sonnets. Apart from the uncertainty of where this date should be placed, and the uselessness of such a gesture once Racine's play had established itself, this hypothesis is also destroyed by Professor Lancaster's examination of the accounts of the Théâtre Guénégaud, which show no such bookings at any period of Pradon's run.

It may be added that the figure of 15,000 *livres* given by Louis Racine as the price paid by the Duchess for buying up the *premières loges* at both theatres for the first six performances would have been excessively high. According to La Grange's *Registre*, the first six performances of Pradon's play grossed 4,647 *livres for all the seats in the theatre*.

other friends and it was over this meal that she composed
her rudimentary description of *Phèdre*:

> Dans un fauteuil doré, Phèdre tremblante et blême
> Dit des vers où d'abord personne n'entend rien.
> La nourrice lui fait un sermon fort chrétien
> Contre l'affreux dessein d'attenter à soi-même.
> Hippolyte la hait presque autant qu'elle l'aime.
> Rien ne change son air ni son chaste maintien.
> La nourrice l'accuse—elle s'en punit bien.
> Thésée a pour son fils une rigueur extrême.
>
> Une grosse Aricie au cuir noir, aux crins blonds,
> N'est là que pour montrer deux énormes tétons
> Que malgré sa froideur Hippolyte idolâtre.
> Il meurt enfin, traîné par des coursiers ingrats,
> Et Phèdre, après avoir pris de la mort aux rats,
> Vient en se confessant mourir sur le théâtre.

The sonnet was at once copied and circulated. Racine
and his friends did not suspect the gentle Madame Deshoulières of being its authoress. For them, she was the
writer of idyllic verses in which she hymned her pet lambs
and other domestic animals. They thought they recognized
the hand of the Duke of Nevers, whom they knew to be
concerned in the *cabale*. They therefore flung back at him
a sonnet constructed on the same rhymes, but more slander-
ous in content:

> Dans un palais doré, Damon jaloux et blême,
> Fait des vers où jamais personne n'entend rien.
> Il n'est ni courtisan, ni guerrier ni chrétien,
> Et souvent pour rimer se dérobe à lui-même.
> La Muse par malheur le hait autant qu'il l'aime.
> Il a d'un franc poète et l'air et le maintien;
> Il veut juger de tout et n'en juge pas bien.
> Il a pour le phébus une tendresse extrême.
>
> Une sœur vagabonde aux crins plus noirs que blonds
> Va par tout l'univers étaler deux tétons
> Dont malgré son pays Damon est idolâtre.

[212]

PORTRAIT OF A YOUNG MAN.
Musée de Langres, attributed to François de Troy.

BOILEAU'S APOTHEOSIS: THE ASCENT TO PARNASSUS.

Frontispiece to Brossette's edition of his works, 1718.

Il se tue à rimer pour des lecteurs ingrats;
L'Enéide est pour lui pis que la mort aux rats,
Et selon lui, Pradon est le roi du théâtre.

This sonnet, with its libellous reference, not to the
Duchess of Bouillon, but to her sister the Duchess of Mazarin
who, after an adventurous career, was then at the Court of
St. James vying with the Duchess of Portsmouth for the
favour of Charles II, infuriated her brother Nevers. He
replied with dignity, but also with a threat which he was
fully capable of putting into effect:

Racine et Despréaux, l'œil triste et le teint blême,
Viennent demander grâce et ne confessent rien.
Il faut leur pardonner parce qu'on est chrétien,
Mais on sait ce qu'on doit au public, à soi-même.
Damon, qui pour l'honneur de cette sœur qu'il aime
Doit de ces insolents abattre le maintien,
Deviendrait le mépris de tous les gens de bien
S'il ne punissait pas leur insolence extrême.
Ce fut une Furie aux crins plus noirs que blonds
Qui leur coula du pus de ses affreux tétons
Ce sonnet qu'en secret leur cabale idolâtre.
On vous verra punir, satiriques ingrats,
Non pas en trahison d'un bol de mort aux rats,
Mais de coups de bâton donnés sur le théâtre.

Racine did not have to suffer this indignity, although an
anonymous enemy, in yet another sonnet on the same
rhymes, tried to spread the rumour that Boileau had been
waylaid and beaten in the street. Both were in fact saved
by the intervention of a protector more powerful than
Nevers. Old Condé, watching the affair with amusement,
decided that things had gone far enough and commanded
his son to write to the two friends:

"If you did not write the sonnet, come to the Hôtel de
Condé, where Monsieur le Prince will see to it that you
are protected from these threats, since you are innocent.
And if you did write it, come none the less to the Hôtel de

Condé, where Monsieur le Prince will still take you under his protection, because the sonnet is most diverting and full of wit."

Were they responsible for the second sonnet? Racine's pen, at least, was usually more subtle, though in the heat of the moment he was capable of writing in a coarser vein. The explanation given twenty-five years later by Boileau's biographer, Brossette, was that some courtier friends of Racine's—d'Effiat, Manicamp, Fiesque, and Nantouillet—wrote the first two quatrains collectively while dining. As to the sextet containing the attack on the Duchess of Mazarin, it was written by "other persons, whose names M. Despréaux said he did not know".

However innocent the two poets may have been, the sonnet was currently believed to be theirs, and the shocked reactions of some of the nobility, less broad-minded than Condé, must have shown Racine with startling clarity the weakness of his position. Who was he, a mere poet, to attack the character of the Duke of Nevers? Bussy-Rabutin, not without malice towards several, summed up the attitude of many of his class.

"Never," he wrote at the end of January, "never was there anything so insolent as this sonnet. Two scribblers allege that an officer of the Crown is neither a courtier, nor a soldier, nor a Christian; that his sister, the Duchess of Mazarin, is a trollop, and that he is in love with her, although he is an Italian. And even if these insults were true, they ought to warrant a thousand cuts with the stirrup-leather on people of that sort."

The affair of the sonnets blew over and Racine's *Phèdre* survived the *cabale*. Its superiority was soon admitted by the temporarily bewildered public, while, once the wonder of the *cabale* had diminished, Pradon's play began to languish. After sixteen consecutive performances, it was taken off. But on Racine the experience had already had its effect. He had realized the vulnerability of his position: his professional reputation was exposed to the whims of coteries and his person was not safe from the

attacks of a fantastical nobleman. This time a great protector had stepped in before it was too late, but not before
he had caught a frightening glimpse of the vindictiveness of
his foes and of his own social insignificance. The sight had
made him sober.

3

These events befell him at a transitional stage of life when
the impulsion of youth falters and many men who have led
full and successful lives hesitate before entering on a more
settled period of maturity. As he reached his late thirties,
it is probable that Racine halted to question himself. His
self-examination would be made more bitter by the sordid
ending of his liaison with the Champmeslé. Their relationship had been deteriorating for some time and now she
had openly replaced him by the Comte de Clermont-
Tonnerre. She was about to pass permanently out of his
life, though during the rest of a long career she remained
the foremost interpreter of the parts which he had written.
In these circumstances and at this age Racine would look
back nostalgically towards his adolescence, then forward
in an attempt to assess how much might still be saved or
altered. There would arise in him a strong desire for greater
security, spiritual as well as material. Perhaps in the first
shock of the *cabale* and the ribald mud-slinging of the
sonnets, his old misgivings were re-born. "I seem to bring
disaster to every affair in which I am interested," he had
cried at Uzès. Did he carry within him a malignant demon
which prevented him from ever entirely attaining his
objective, or, if for a moment he attained it, from possessing
it tranquilly?

When, therefore, he received an intimation that the
King was disposed to offer him, jointly with Boileau, the
post of Historiographer Royal in succession to Pellisson, he
readily accepted. The office promised everything of which
he stood most in need: a recognized position, official as
much as literary, the opportunity of being in close touch

with the highest influences—his duties would be to accompany the King and chronicle his exploits from personal knowledge—and material security in the form of an annual pension of 6,000 *livres*. He would be expected to cease writing for the theatre in order to devote his whole attention to his new task. A similar condition was imposed on Boileau.[1]

Racine's acceptance of such a condition has outraged some of his admirers. Whether any masterpieces comparable to *Phèdre* were lost by it must always be a subject of conjecture. We leave consideration of the point to the following chapter. Meanwhile, it is clear that, in the circumstances in which he found himself in 1677, Racine had no hesitation in acquiescing.

The offer almost certainly came to him, through the Montespan and Colbert, in the spring of 1677, when the battle of *Phèdre* was scarcely over. Official confirmation, in the form of an order for 6,000 *livres* on the Royal Chest, came in the following September. Before this, Racine had married. His bride was Catherine de Romanet, a girl of twenty-five, twelve years his junior. She came of a prosperous legal family. Her father had been mayor of Montdidier, a small town in Picardy, and her mother the daughter of a rich notary established in Paris. At the time of her marriage Catherine's parents were both dead and she was living in Paris with an uncle, Louis Le Mazier, a successful member of the bar. She was thus related to Marguerite Le Mazier, Nicolas Vitart's wife, whose family background was similar to hers. No doubt the Vitarts were responsible for arranging the match. They displayed no little wisdom and practical affection in uniting their hypersensitive cousin to the unspoilt and equable Catherine de Romanet, who was also a small heiress. The wives of

[1] Boileau wrote very little during the thirty-four remaining years of his life. In the Preface to the 1683 edition of his Collected Works, which contained five new *Epîtres*, he excused himself by saying that these were composed "long before I became engaged in the noble employment which extricated me from the profession of poetry".

famous men have rarely been approved by their husbands' admirers and Racine's wife has been no exception. Affectionate, temperately pious, a good housekeeper and a sensible mother, she was quite ignorant of dramatic poetry and was surprised to learn one day that rhymes could be either masculine or feminine. She brought to the marriage an income of about 5,000 *livres* and "a chest of German ebony with nine dozen towels and eight pairs of sheets".

The marriage took place in the church of Saint-Séverin on 1st June 1677. Numerous members of the Le Mazier family were present on Catherine's side. Racine's sponsors were Boileau and Nicolas Vitart. Among those who signed the register were his old friends Antoine Poignant and François Le Vasseur, Prior of Oulchy. La Fontaine was not present and, on the evidence of the register, there was not a single representative of the theatre or—except Boileau and Besset de la Chapelle—of the world of letters. On the other hand, this was no bourgeois family wedding. The Great Condé and his son the Duke Henri-Jules, the Duke of Chevreuse, Colbert, his wife and his son de Seignelay, the judge Guillaume Lamoignon, First President of the Parlement de Paris (the same judge who had taken it upon himself to ban *Tartuffe* during one of the absences of the King), and his son the Advocate General—all these came to show their friendship for the repentant poet.   *

4

The Preface to *Phèdre*, published on 15th March 1677, contains a famous reference to the moral lessons which can be learnt from that tragedy in particular and to the moral utility of tragedy in general. The ancient theatre, argued Racine, was a school for the teaching of virtue. If modern writers would keep in view the same sound principle, "it would perhaps be a means of reconciling tragedy with a number of persons celebrated for their piety and their doctrine, who in recent times have condemned it".

It is not necessary to assume that these pious persons were all Jansenists. In throwing out a feeler to those who had condemned the theatre recently ('*dans ces derniers temps*') Racine could have thought of many instances later than his dispute with Nicole eleven years before. During his successful years, the theatre had been subjected to attacks of increasing violence by ecclesiastics directly opposed to Port-Royal on other points. Preachers and divines—the same who sometimes thundered against the corruption of the Court and boldly urged Louis to put away the Montespan—deplored the alluring mask which Vice wore on the stage. Whatever the worldly abbés might hold, the parish priests still considered the actor as an outcast from the Christian flock. Racine, who had publicly consorted with actors, was only too well aware of the disrepute in which the profession was held by many decent people. More than that, leanings towards a new seriousness were beginning to appear in the Court itself. Although the Montespan still reigned, her supremacy was no longer unchallenged. The years of careless glory were drawing to a close. The King was by starts devout and promiscuously carnal, a sure sign of the approaching climacteric. By and by the tone of the Court would change and sobriety under the name of piety would prevail. The perspicacious might already see the pure star of Madame de Maintenon appearing on the horizon. There lay the future.

The piety which Racine began to manifest immediately after his retirement from the theatre was therefore completely consistent with his other actions. He had renounced a disreputable way of life. He was about to serve the King in a position of honour in a society whose esteem he valued. The one thing lacking was a basis of moral solidity and this he could acquire by a reconciliation with the Church. He effected this reconciliation through the priest of his parish then, a little later, approached the great figures of Port-Royal and made his individual peace with them.

Even Louis Racine—whose account of this passage of his father's life is too tendentious to be trusted on any point not confirmed elsewhere—gives the events in this same order: first, the approach to the parish priest (whom Racine saw at an early date when, in the bitterness of his reaction against the theatre, he thought of becoming a Carthusian monk), then marriage, then the reconciliation with Port-Royal. Nicole was visited and readily forgave his errant pupil. Then the Great Arnauld, persuaded, says Louis Racine, by Boileau and by the blameless morality of Phèdre, also forgave him. These meetings with the Jansenist divines perhaps occurred in the summer or autumn of 1677, at about the time when Racine's appointment as Historiographer Royal was officially announced.

Thus the circle was complete. Everything necessary had been done to bury the past and to fit him for the new and honourable life which the King's offer opened up.

If we stress these events and the order in which they happened, it is because—as any reader unfamiliar with the subject must be warned—the most divergent explanations have been given of Racine's retirement from the theatre. The extreme left has maintained that he renounced it in a fit of pique and for the sake of the material rewards which his new post promised. The extreme right has held that he experienced something approaching a religious conversion. Between these extremes and their over-simple alternatives of a materialistic Racine and a spiritual Racine are a number of more subtle gradations. We think that the answer which satisfies all that is known of the facts, of Racine's character and the mentality of his age, lies to the left-centre. While he did not embrace piety through calculation, but because it was consistent with his respect for the Monarch and his search for social respectability, he certainly did not experience a true 'conversion'. For a long time to come he remained fully in the world, seeking the advantages which it offered to any gifted and honest citizen. Had he been a true Jansenist, or had his crisis been of the intensity of Pascal's, he would hardly have let himself be dissuaded from entering a religious order. But while continuing a worldly career, he performed the disinterested act of making his peace with Port-Royal and from that moment he stood loyally by his old masters even though they were dangerously out of favour. This was not the act of a courtier, but of a man whose conscience demanded that he should be faithful to the friends and ideals of his boyhood.

Phèdre is sometimes quoted as evidence that the reconciliation with Port-Royal was long premeditated by Racine. But if, at some time in 1675 or 1676, he had been resolved to hold out an olive branch, he could have done so best by ceasing to write at once. Another tragedy, however exemplary, would be a weaker pledge of his intentions.

The nature of *Phèdre*, when it is examined, increases the improbability that it was deliberately written as a gesture towards either the Jansenists or the Church in general. Only after it had been composed and produced, and at a time when his mind was beginning to contemplate reform, was Racine able to look at his latest tragedy and to point to its moral value in the Preface from which we have quoted. It was thus used, but not planned, as an instrument of conciliation.

CHAPTER XVI

PHÈDRE

"THE criticisms have vanished," Racine had once written. "The play remains." What had been true of *Britannicus* was truer still of *Phèdre*. The prestige which his last secular tragedy rapidly acquired in the French theatre has been maintained almost uninterrupted until this day. Amid revolutionary changes of taste, it has, with only minor fluctuations, preserved its fascination for the critic and the scholar, its power of moving an audience and its attraction for great actresses who have looked to it for the crowning role of their careers.

The character of Phèdre, as we have already suggested, was the product of a long secretion of feeling and of experience in writing for the theatre. She is a woman "in the August of her life", married to a roving and absent husband, the mother of a child old enough to be considered as the next King of Athens. It is impossible to assign an exact age to her. It varies according to the ideas of the period, the producer, the actress. The Champmeslé was about thirty-five when she created the part, but this means little since she continued to play it for twenty years. In the next century, Adrienne Lecouvreur played it triumphantly as a young actress of twenty-five. Mlle Clairon, still more daring, made her début in it at eighteen. Rachel, in the nineteenth century, essayed it at the age of twenty-three, though the Phèdre of her middle years was considered better. At the other end of the scale, many contemporary playgoers will have mixed memories of Sarah Bernhardt

presenting scenes from *Phèdre* at the age of seventy. All
that can be deduced from the text is that Phèdre is a mature
woman, full of experience and disillusion, but also capable
of an irresistible infatuation which torments and wastes her.

This aspect of Phèdre, as she writhes helpless in the grip
of "implacable Venus", imparts a crescendo movement to
the character and the action; it is so powerful that it might
seem at first to be the whole character and the whole play.
Like Roxane, she is impelled by a sensual urge which over-
whelms prudence and every other interest; like Roxane,
she is made ruthless by jealousy and frustration; like Roxane
—and, in this, also like Hermione—she goes on to destroy
the object of her desire and is then destroyed herself. But
even in her blindest moments she is more than Roxane,
who was carried so high by the unreasoning optimism of the
blood that she could not see the obstacles which lay in her
path. Phèdre has suffered too much to expect an easy
satisfaction of her desires, even after the false news of
Thésée's death appears to have set her free and to have
removed the first barrier between herself and Hippolyte.
Her passion, overshadowed by experience, is a sad passion.
In her mistrust of life she approaches Agrippine, although
the situations in which the two queens are placed are
totally dissimilar. But it is not without significance that in
the year in which Racine was composing *Phèdre*, he re-
wrote the Preface to *Britannicus* in terms which showed
that he had given new thought to the character of Agrippine,
whom he had not considered worthy of mention when the
play had first been published six years earlier. He spoke
now of her pride and ferocity and of the evil influence
exerted upon her by Pallas, and added: "I will say no more
of Agrippine, for there would be too much to be said. It
is she above all whom I have endeavoured to depict ad-
equately, and my tragedy consists as much in the fall of
Agrippine as in the death of Britannicus." Strained though
such an interpretation seems to be of the Roman play, it
reflects the processes of Racine's mind at a date when he
was transforming the Greek tragedy of Hippolytus—in

which the young Prince was the central character—into the tragedy of Phèdre.

Seen, then, from one angle, Agrippine and Phèdre have certain resemblances and we may suppose that, in reflecting on his new and supreme character, Racine recognized her kinship with an earlier creation. Both are accustomed to the wielding of influence, aware of the pitfalls of life, and in the grip of a dominating but joyless passion—with Agrippine, the lust for power; with Phèdre, lust.

But the factor which makes of Phèdre a tragic character *par excellence* is entirely lacking in Agrippine. This is the sense of fatality. Not only does she feel that she is being swept towards her doom, but she can name the particular force that is driving her on—heredity, personified in the enmity of the gods:

> PHÈDRE: *O haine de Vénus! O fatale colère!*
> *Dans quels égarements l'amour jeta ma mère!*
> OENONE: *Oublions-les, madame; et qu'à tout l'avenir*
> *Un silence éternel cache ce souvenir.*
> PHÈDRE: *Ariane, ma soeur, de quel amour blessée*
> *Vous mourûtes aux bords où vous fûtes laissée!*
> OENONE: *Que faites-vous, madame? et quel mortel ennui*
> *Contre tout votre sang vous anime aujourd'hui?*
> PHÈDRE: *Puisque Vénus le veut, de ce sang déplorable*
> *Je péris la dernière et la plus misérable.*

She recalls her vain efforts to cheat her destiny:

> *Je reconnus Vénus et ses feux redoutables,*
> *D'un sang qu'elle poursuit tourments inévitables.*
> *Par des vœux assidus je crus les détourner:*
> *Je lui bâtis un temple et pris soin de l'orner;*
> *De victimes moi-même à toute heure entourée,*
> *Je cherchais dans leurs flancs ma raison égarée;*
> *D'un incurable amour remèdes impuissants!*

By her constant awareness of her danger, Phèdre differs from some of Racine's other characters, but by no means from all. Oreste at least half suspected his in the opening scene of *Andromaque*, though it was not until the end, when he stood on the brink of madness, that he allowed himself to see the truth with complete lucidity:

> *Grâce aux dieux, mon malheur passe mon espérance!*
> *Oui, je te loue, ô ciel, de ta persévérance!*
> *Appliqué sans relâche au soin de me punir,*
> *Au comble des douleurs tu m'as fait parvenir;*
> *Ta haine a pris plaisir à former ma misère;*
> *J'étais né pour servir d'exemple à ta colère,*
> *Pour être du malheur un modèle accompli.*
> *Hé bien! je meurs content, et mon sort est rempli.*

And, linking the first of Racine's secular tragedies with his last, the mistily-drawn figure of Jocaste in *La Thébaïde* had lamented to the sun the necessary doom which awaited her incestuous race:

> *O toi, soleil, ô toi qui rends le jour au monde,*
> *Que ne l'as-tu laissé dans une nuit profonde?*
> *A de si noirs forfaits prêtes-tu tes rayons?*
> *Et peux-tu, sans horreur, voir ce que nous voyons?*
> *Mais ces monstres, hélas, ne t'épouvantent guères:*
> *La race de Laïus les a rendus vulgaires;*
> *Tu peux voir sans frayeur les crimes de mes fils,*
> *Après ceux que le père et la mère ont commis.*
> *Tu ne t'étonnes pas si mes fils sont perfides,*
> *S'ils sont tous deux méchants, et s'ils sont parricides;*
> *Tu sais qu'ils sont sortis d'un sang incestueux,*
> *Et tu t'étonnerais s'ils étaient vertueux.*

A character helpless but still conscious in the hand of supernatural forces was therefore not an innovation confined to Racine's last tragedy. There would be no question that he took the conception from the Greeks, were it not that—as a pupil of Port-Royal—he might also be supposed to be imbued with the Jansenist doctrine of predestination. Following this theory, Phèdre is "a Christian to whom grace has been denied". Because she is not one of the elect, she sins inevitably and cannot escape damnation.

It is obvious, however, that all the accessories with which Racine surrounded the character are Greek and that an actress steeped in the mythology and imagery of Euripides could give a rendering which would be wholly satisfactory, whereas an actress conceiving the part in a 'modern' or Christian light would have to treat very many of her lines as allegory and would thus distort the part as written. However aptly the character might be used afterwards to illustrate the Christian teaching of the drama, there is nothing in it that could not have developed normally from Racine's earlier tragedies, or that a seventeenth-century mind free of religious preoccupations could not have adapted from the ancient writers. That Phèdre was predestined according to the tradition of the Greeks when she might equally have been foredamned by the Jansenists is surely nothing more than a coincidence. And when her fate overtakes her, the punishment is not for her 'sins'—a word essential to the Christian concept, which Racine never uses—but for her *crimes*, her *forfaits*, her *fureur* (excess), and her impurity. For the Greeks, who had had no Fall, human nature in itself was not sinful. It could be led or driven into offending by excess, and the conduct of the individual then became punishable as a monstrous departure from the norm. But the original essence of the personality was not involved, as it is in the Christian doctrine. The difference is fundamental.

Phèdre is at least half innocent and it is this, combined with the inevitability of her wrong-doing, which lifts the part so high among tragic roles and presents almost inexhaustible subtleties of interpretation to the great actress. As Racine himself pointed out, "she is involved, by her destiny and by the anger of the gods, in an unlawful passion by which she is the first to be horrified. She makes every effort to overcome it. She prefers to pine and die rather than to declare it to anyone; and when she is forced to reveal it, she speaks of it with a confusion which shows plainly that her crime is rather a punishment of the gods than an effect of her own will.''

But Phèdre has to accomplish one act which goes beyond blind passion. In denouncing the innocent Hippolyte to his father Thésée, she acts with a certain premeditation. The malice of her accusation is attenuated by the desperate state of her mind when she makes it; after it has been made she repents and intends to withdraw it, but is silenced by the shock of learning that Hippolyte loves Aricie. He has spurned her not because of his youthful chastity, but because he prefers her "rival". Yet these attenuations are not enough. In spite of them, Phèdre might still appear odious to an audience which is not, while in the theatre, in a position to weigh with care the psychological circumstances surrounding the act, but sees chiefly the act and its consequences. Racine therefore seeks to remove the most obvious blame from Phèdre by laying it on the nurse, Oenone. It is Oenone who suggests the accusation to her mistress, Oenone who makes it to Thésée with her mistress's passive consent:

> Fais ce que tu voudras, je m'abandonne à toi.
> Dans le trouble où je suis, je ne puis rien pour moi.

Finally, it is Oenone who lurks anxiously in the background when she fears that Phèdre may have withdrawn the calumny and confessed the truth to Thésée.

Oenone is far removed from the conventional confidante, who is merely an echoing wall. When she gives back Phèdre's thoughts, she gives them back darkly distorted, she draws the extreme practical conclusions from her mistress's inner promptings and desires. She is an example of the "low and servile" mind (the words are Racine's) whose grossness prevents it from moving easily in the domain of emotion and which instinctively seeks to transpose into external action the subtle movements of the mind and heart. These, in the convention of the classical theatre, were the preserve of the princes and princesses who were characters of refined and complex sensibilities, whereas the plebeian characters stood for insensibility and stupidity. The hierarchy is of course psychological and not social. As a "low and servile" character (i.e. a woman of action) Oenone simplifies what she cannot abide and, by cutting through the intricate knot of another's emotions, unleashes huge forces which neither she nor anyone else can afterwards control.

From psychological stupidity springs misplaced external activity and from such activity springs disaster: such is the lesson of Oenone. This gross, well-intentioned, bustling character does not rate as an evil genius, since she cannot compose but only mistranslate. She is not a second Narcisse, who was pernicious with intent. She is, however, the willing servant of the evil which lies *in posse* in Phèdre's emotions, waiting for some interpreter bold enough and fool enough to define it as a policy.

> *La nourrice l'accuse, elle s'en punit bien*

wrote Madame Deshoulières, whose satirical summary of the play shows, on some points, a certain rough penetration. Oenone too, on her own level, can be justified. She is actuated throughout by loyalty to her mistress and when at length Phèdre turns upon her and curses her for meddling, she employs the heroic logic of the simple-hearted and goes out to kill herself. In other theatres at other periods she might well be the heroine of a play, but not in seventeenth-century tragedy.

The character of Phèdre complemented by Oenone is so tremendous that it dwarfs the other personages of the drama. But these too are necessary and fully drawn. If they could exist in a play with a less impressive central character, they would be seen to be of respectable stature. Racine's tragedy, like Pradon's, was first produced and published under the title of *Phèdre et Hippolyte*. Racine adopted the shorter title in the 1687 edition of his works. In the subject as he found it in Euripides and Seneca, the character of Hippolytus was of primary importance. To the Greeks he was a chaste young charioteer, absorbed in manly sports, plain-spoken and uncourtly. Hunting he loved but love he laughed to scorn. His defence against Phaedra was his inability to understand her passion, which seemed to him womanly and ridiculous. This figure of the splendid young athlete, untamed by society and unbroken to love, was native to the Greeks and could be idealized by them, as, in most of its essentials, it can be appreciated by northern peoples. Racine also understood it—he was too familiar with the Greek world not to have done—but he realized the practical impossibility of presenting such a figure unmodified on the stage of his own country and time. There, he knew that the noble profile of the free adolescent, redolent of the forest and of the sea, would seem too immature to be accepted as a serious character. A minority of the audience would credit him with unnatural vices, since they could see no other reason for shunning women. Even a modern Frenchman of great artistic insight, M. Jean-Louis Barrault, sees mainly in Hippolyte the perfect animal:

"Hippolyte is the most handsome youth in Greece. His costume is his muscles. They must be strong and harmonious. It is essential that Hippolyte should give out a young and vigorous *virility*. Hippolyte is the finest horse in Troezen. His mane is blond, a warm blond. . . ."

Between the Greek conception and the French realization something has disappeared, but this was hardly Racine's fault. He preserved as much as he dared of the original character and saved it from being laughed off the stage— and thus ruining his most tremendous play—by providing Hippolyte with a shy and delicate passion for a princess of
* equal freshness and innocence.

The unworldly Arnauld, looking for nothing in the play beyond the moral lesson of Phèdre's expiation, was one of the first to ask: "Why did he make Hippolyte fall in love?" The answer we have already given, but in his Preface Racine gave yet another reason to justify his invention. It was that, in order that Hippolyte's death should not seem

[228]

entirely unmerited, he had had to make him "a little
guilty" towards his father Thésée. He had therefore
represented him as being in love with Aricie, whose family
had been the mortal enemies of Thésée.

This ' political ' argument, however unconvincing,
must be respected as Racine's official explanation.

Aricie, though by her existence she saves Hippolyte from
the mockery of the *petits maîtres*, draws on herself the laughter
of some of the female members of the audience. Blonde—
she must be blonde—she stands on the stage exposed
to the ribaldry of the disillusioned. Her timidity and her
bourgeois insistence on marriage before she will run away
with Hippolyte have been scoffed at by later critics than
Madame Deshoulières. And at the best, it might be objected
that she is only another princess of the line of Junie,
Atalide, and Monime. But at least she is a worthy representative of that line and when, emboldened by the
certainty that Hippolyte loves her, she can emerge a little
from her virginal reticence (so accurately observed, so
delicately drawn), she is both touching and energetic in
the defence of his interests and hers.

This pair of lovers are not insipid, though their carefully
modulated flute-notes may sound thin beside the brasses of
Phèdre's passion. One of their functions is to throw this
passion more sharply into relief. Their hesitating purity
accompanies (always by implication) the stampeding
impurity of Phèdre's desire, which gains in force when it
can be seen against such a background. Thus Aricie is at
once a device to heighten the psychological interest of
Phèdre—and incidentally, to increase her torments by
adding that of jealousy—and she is also, like Oenone, a
living character which an actress can incarnate on a fully
human plane.

Of the other characters, Thésée, the King, is primarily a
device to influence the plot at three decisive points: when
his death is falsely reported, when he returns unexpectedly,
when he decides on his son's death. He can, however, be
clothed with a kind of mythical life, all the more acceptable

because he does not appear until near the end of the third act, when a background of legend has already been built up for him, and when, both for the other characters and the audience, he seems to have escaped almost miraculously from the country of the dead. An actor who can contrive to keep a little of this superhuman haze about him will maintain the tragedy at its intended height and will be able to invoke the intervention of a god without violating dramatic truth. The actor who interprets Thésée merely as a husband who returns from a journey to find his wife unfaithful will introduce a note of realism where it is least in place.

Théramène, the *gouverneur* of Hippolyte is, like Burrhus in *Britannicus*, as plainly real as he is virtuous. But under the shock of profound emotion he rises to the rhetorical heights of the much-discussed *récit* of the final act. That he uses over ninety lines of verse to describe the manner in which Hippolyte met his death and the subsequent grief of Aricie, and this at a moment when the tragedy might be expected to be moving rapidly towards its close, has very often been construed as a defect in dramatic construction. As early as 1677 Subligny protested against the *invraisemblance* of Théramène's detailed oration. Fénelon followed him by remarking that Théramène should have panted out his tidings in two brief lines of agitated verse and then stopped, overcome by grief and horror. Of a realistic drama this would undoubtedly be true and the fact that Racine is following the Greek convention of the 'messenger' speech and that he had used this convention uncriticized several times before—in *Britannicus*, *Mithridate*, and *Iphigénie*—at much the same point in the dénouement, would hardly excuse him. But *Phèdre* is not a work of realism. It presents psychological truth on a different plane—the plane first reached, though more unevenly, in *Andromaque*. In this poetic projection of reality, it is fitting that the death of Hippolyte—the concrete disaster towards which so much of the previous action has tended—should be hymned in a solemn recitative. It is not so much news which Théramène brings, as a confirmation of the doom which during the whole play has been gathering over the head of an innocent character. The bow has been drawn; the fascination now is to watch the long, certain flight of the arrow.

A more valid criticism would bear, not on the length and nature of the recitative, but on the choice of speaker. Théramène appears too familiar a character, whose human limits are too well known, to be entrusted with a speech which is almost a piece of ritual. In *Iphigénie*, the corresponding recitative is spoken by Ulysse who, although he is a character in the tragedy and fulfils a definite dramatic function, has been absent from the stage since the first act and reappears before the audience with something of the novelty and prestige of a herald. There is no equivalent character in *Phèdre*; the dignified and disinterested Théramène is therefore the only possible choice. But the want of a Messenger or a Chorus, excluded by the dramatic convention which he was following, was undoubtedly felt by Racine. When, in *Esther* and *Athalie*, he was able to use freer forms, he gladly did so, thus realizing "a project which has often passed through my mind, which was to link chorus and song with the action, as in the ancient Greek tragedy".

2

With its six principal personages the character-pattern of *Phèdre* is complete and does not differ in outline from the pattern of the earlier tragedies. The psychological exploration has been carried farther and in some respects is more subtle, yet the advance since *Andromaque* is not so great as might have been expected. That is not a disparagement of *Phèdre* but a tribute to the relative maturity of Racine's first great tragedy, produced nine years before. The only character which Racine could surely not have encompassed in 1667 was the character of the queen and it is in one sense true to say that the finest result of his years of experience and experiment was this study of Phèdre which had slowly flowered from his mind with a kind of organic growth and which, if looked at in isolation, has the inevitability of a finished work of art. The detail of the study is impeccable. Everything is there, yet not a line is wasted. So perfect is the portrait that one is tempted to think that she could be moved bodily into some other medium or period, and still remain as great and as true.

But this is an illusion. No great character is transposable —or if it is, the transposition would cost as much original talent as the creation and therefore the attempt is hardly ever made.

Phèdre is bound to the other characters of the tragedy by so many fibres, psychological and dramatic, that if she were torn away from them she would no longer live. Nothing that they say or do is without effect on her and vice versa. To transplant her successfully into, for example, a modern novel or play, would entail the almost impossible feat of transplanting the other characters also, without severing the delicately-spun relationships which bind them all together. No one who has considered the tight construction of Racine's play would presume to take it to pieces and rebuild it in any different setting. If a demonstration is needed, the experiment can be made of displacing any scene, any entrance or exit, of re-timing any event or statement and comparing the new effect with the old. It becomes immediately apparent that you touch this wonderfully-made machine at your peril. The sequence and linking of the scenes, the march of emotional development, recall. by their masterly workmanship *Andromaque* and *Bajazet*. The only difference is that the author has become more expert; he handles his dramatic effects with a surer and quieter touch. There is nothing in *Phèdre* as brilliant or as startling as the: *Qui te l'a dit?* of Hermione, or the: *Sortez!* of Roxane. Such fireworks are no longer necessary. The movement of the action and the interest of the characterization are sufficient in themselves to enthral the audience without the interjection of sudden surprises. It is pointless to crack a whip in an express train.

The poetry of *Phèdre* is an inseparable part of the composition. It flows naturally from the characters, from the situations, from the atmosphere, half human, half fabulous, through which the action moves. *Phèdre* is a poetic drama, with the emphasis laid equally on the two halves of the term. Since the verse is meant to be spoken by an actor or actress in its dramatic context, there perhaps it should be left. Nevertheless, so memorable are many of the lines that they would still deserve attention as poetry wherever they were found. No notes are necessary to explain the beauty of

> *Cet heureux temps n'est plus. Tout a changé de face*
> *Depuis que sur ces bords les dieux ont envoyé*
> *La fille de Minos et de Pasiphaé,*

or of

> *On ne voit point deux fois le rivage des morts,*
> *Seigneur: puisque Thésée a vu les sombres bords,*
> *En vain vous espérez qu'un dieu vous le renvoie,*
> *Et l'avare Achéron ne lâche point sa proie.*

It is unnecessary to watch an actress flinging off the veils which stifle her in order to hear the querulous sigh in

> *Que ces vains ornements, que ces voiles me pèsent!*
> *Quelle importune main, en formant tous ces nœuds,*
> *A pris soin sur mon front d'assembler mes cheveux?*
> *Tout m'afflige et me nuit et conspire à me nuire.*

And those simple, mainly monosyllabic, lines which Hippolyte secretes have an existence independent of the play and the character—or perhaps it would be truer to say that Hippolyte was worth creating if only to give a voice to

> *Dans le fond des forêts votre image me suit*

or to

> *Le jour n'est pas plus pur que le fond de mon cœur.*

Such words merge intimately into the character, but, after fulfilling their dramatic functions, they float on into more indefinite associations. They suggest a little more than they state, have more resonance and more mystery than a less generous dramatist, confining himself to the ideal minimum, would have judged it necessary to offer. This poetic haze, hanging over the whole of *Phèdre* more consistently than over any other of his tragedies, lends remoteness and nobility to a story which, treated in a different idiom, might only be a sordid tale for a police-court. Racine draws his musical and evocative effects from the simplest material. His vocabulary is economical to the point of poverty, his images are taken from the conventional classical mythology over which so many other writers have ranged. Yet with these unpromising instruments he contrives to be a great poet. Dropped entirely is the adolescent exuberance of his Port-Royal odes to nature; dropped almost equally is the mechanical pseudo-classicism of his early official odes. But the spirit which animated both is still alive and in *Phèdre* at last the two tendencies are harmoniously reconciled to produce a work which was his fulfilment as a poet as well as a dramatist.

3

Between *Phèdre* and the earlier tragedies there is no solution of continuity, only a magnificent progression. Every element in his last secular play—including its poetic qualities, which were foreshadowed in *Iphigénie*—can be found in embryo in his previous writings. This seems finally to dispose of the theory that *Phèdre* was Jansenist-inspired, which could only be maintained if the tragedy showed a marked deviation from his earlier work. Whatever is relatively new in *Phèdre* can be traced to the influence of Euripides, and even this, as we have seen, is not entirely new.

More debatable is the question whether, in accepting the conditions attached to his official appointment, Racine submitted to frustration as an artist. What of the plays which the Historiographer Royal could no longer write? Could he have gone higher in the particular idiom that he was using? Were the twelve years which passed before he found a new inspiration and a new approach all wasted years from the point of view of the drama? In order to suggest an answer we have to imagine Racine, reassured by the ultimate success of *Phèdre*, and still a private citizen, casting about for the subject of his next play. Would he have treated the other great themes which seemed worthy of his pen, have written a *Medea* or an *Oedipus Rex*? It is unlikely, for, always sensitive to public opinion, he would scarcely have chosen subjects which would be judged barbaric. *Phèdre* had already been blamed by some for excessive coarseness. The *motif*, and especially the word, of incest had given offence "even to the least delicate of the ladies", as Subligny remarked. While it is repugnant to think of a Racine subservient to the *premières loges*, it is all too probable that, after the lesson of the *cabale de Phèdre*, he would have sought support wherever he could have found it and have been especially careful to shock no one. Perhaps he would have worked again on the subjects which seem to have interested him, the Alcestis or the Iphigenia in Tauris. What then? Would the over-strong *Phèdre* have been followed by a mellifluous second *Iphigénie*, as the virile *Britannicus* had been followed by *Bérénice*? And if so, are we to deplore this hypothetical loss?

All this is speculative, but not more so than the assumption that Racine, continuing to write for the theatre with no break after *Phèdre*, would have gone on to produce as great, or greater plays. It is only on this assumption that his long retirement from the theatre can be considered a disaster. On the other hand, material circumstances allied to his own good sense may have saved him from the pathetic fate of old Corneille. His public were to witness no decline in power, or even in originality. He left them when he was at the peak of his achievement, tolerably certain that posterity would say of him that his only weak plays had been his first.

It is difficult to believe that, among the several considerations which prompted Racine's retirement, this did not figure too. The author of *Phèdre* was too sound a judge to be much mistaken in the worth of his latest tragedy. He knew what he had tried to do in it and, after the first weeks of bitterness and uncertainty, he no doubt felt that he had succeeded. He was content to go out on that high note. And we may assume that, in making that decision, he had no plans of comparable magnitude in mind. Had he had any, the artist in him was sufficiently vigorous to override both the susceptible personality and the sober opportunist and to insist that the work of creation must go on. Whatever the alternatives, no writer of Racine's stature would allow his growth to be stunted if he still felt himself to be in the prime of invention.

An interesting parallel, which in some ways is curiously close, is furnished by another of France's great poets, Victor Hugo. In his late thirties, the great Romantic seemed to have come to the end of his creative vein. A dozen years of intense activity had seen the composition of all the lyric poems, the plays, and the novel on which the reputation of *Victor Hugo*, *première manière*, is based. With the apparent exhaustion of his lyric inspiration and the failure of his last play, *Les Burgraves*, Hugo turned to a political career in which he was encouraged by Louis-Philippe. An emotional crisis centring on the death of his daughter Léopoldine, which occurred while he was absent in the Pyrenees with his mistress, furnished a subsidiary guilt-motive for silence roughly equivalent to the shock of snapping the Racine-Champmeslé liaison. For ten years he published nothing and it was only the change of régime, leading to his removal from professional politics and his exile, which opened up his second existence as a creative writer. At almost the precise age when Racine, at the command of Madame de Maintenon, was writing *Esther*, Hugo, burning with indignation against Louis Napoleon, was composing *Les Châtiments*. Though the two men are poles apart in taste and temperament, they experienced the same pause toward their fortieth year and the same revival of creative vigour in the early fifties, kindled apparently by an accidental spark,

No rule is intended to be proved, nor indeed is one sought, but if the careers of other great writers are scrutinized it will be found that Racine's silence after the age of thirty-seven was by no means abnormal. It has received exceptional attention because of the clearly-marked circumstances which surrounded it and because he seems to have stopped in the plenitude of his powers. But we do not know how painful and exhausting was the effort of creating *Phèdre*. The long interval which separated it from *Iphigénie* may have reflected an immense labour of composition which—in the absence of very precise encouragement— he hesitated to undertake again.

PART III

The Promised Land

CHAPTER XVII

TOWARDS SECURITY

I N accepting the post of Historiographer Royal, Racine had committed himself to a delicate task. Some of the difficulties he had no doubt foreseen. Others became apparent when he began to fulfil his duties.

As if by instinct, he made his first approach to the work as a man of letters. The habit of mind implanted during his years of playwriting caused him to conceive the King's history as a new literary genre whose rules it was necessary to study before he began to compose. But his own century offered him little guidance. He could not accept as 'history' the collections of anecdotes and biographical apologies which passed under that name among his contemporaries. Rejecting such easy solutions, he went back to the ancient historians with whose works he had become familiar when constructing his tragedies. In an attempt to assimilate their approach, he made for his own use an analysis of Lucian's treatise *On the Writing of History*. Guided by such models, he probably hoped to produce a general history of the reign, with the Sun-King as the central figure, but with some perspective in the treatment of military, political, and even economic developments.

But such a plan was hardly practicable at that date. The field was too vast and he was too near it—and then his dependence on the royal approval was a formidable barrier to objectivity. In the end he contented himself with gathering factual material from the sources open to him—

informants at Versailles, the official archives, near-contemporary memoirs—and presenting this material in the
form of isolated *relations*. These *relations*, recording the
more striking events of the reign, and particularly the
military campaigns, would be the documents which he
and Boileau occasionally read aloud to the King. Their
fragmentary nature can be guessed from the fact that neither
of the historiographers saw fit to publish them. On
Racine's death, they were entrusted to his friend and successor Valincour. They disappeared for ever when Valincour's house was burnt down in 1726.

Ironically enough, the only surviving work which
illustrates Racine's talent as a historian is his *Abrégé de
l'histoire de Port-Royal*. It is at once factual, persuasive and
highly readable—the work of a polemist who has taken
great pains to be accurate. It shows Racine as a chronicler
of considerable ability, but hardly as a historian in the
modern sense, or even as the word may be applied to
Voltaire. Had this clandestine composition been discovered, Racine would, of course, have been disqualified on
ideological grounds from serving as the Historiographer
Royal.

Racine's scholarly approach to his official duties was not
appreciated by many of his contemporaries. It was felt at
Court that the first requirement of the man who was to
record the King's actions was that he should himself be
familiar by birth and upbringing with the society in which
the King moved. Madame de Sévigné—doubly biased
because her cousin Bussy-Rabutin had been disappointed
in his candidature for the same post—expressed her doubts
whether the history of Louis could ever be worthily
written by "those two bourgeois". Subligny, who, as a
fellow-writer, might have been expected to be more
tolerant, had already singled out examples of social ignorance in *Phèdre*. He had found it surprising that Hippolyte,
a prince, should be described as feeding his horses with his
own hand; shocking that Oenone, a servant, should signify
to Hippolyte, a King's son, that Phèdre wished to be alone

[241]

and that he should retire. "C'est manquer de civilité; c'est choquer les règles de la bienséance; *c'est ignorer l'usage de la cour.*" A full two years after Racine had renounced the theatre, this supposed taint still clung about him. An Italian visitor to Versailles, Primi Visconti, making thumbnail sketches of the Court for his Memoirs, noted in 1679:

"Racine was the author of several comedies—a better poet than Pellisson—but as he had made Alexander express plebeian sentiments in his verses, the Maréchal d'Estrades told me that he feared he would do the same in his history of Louis, since he was a man of the people. I said that it was excusable for him not to understand the sentiments of the King."

Years later, when Racine was an experienced and—by many—an esteemed courtier, a German envoy, the Baron von Spanheim, marked the progress which he had evidently made, yet still insisted on his plebeian origins:

"M. de Racine has passed from the theatre to the Court, where he has become a clever courtier, devout also. The merit of his dramatic works does not equal his success in adapting himself to these new surroundings, where he plays all kinds of parts. . . . For a man risen from nothing, he has easily picked up the manners of the Court. The comedians had given him a spurious manner; he has corrected it and he is acceptable everywhere—even at the King's bedside, where he sometimes has the honour to read aloud, which he does better than most."

These foreign observers were surely echoing an opinion which they found ready-made at Versailles, based on the contempt of the aristocrat and the amateur for the parvenu and the professional. Racine's first steps as an official cannot have been easy, and many were the social rebuffs which he must have suffered. To the moral ordeal was added physical discomfort when his duties required him to accompany Louis to the wars.

Racine and Boileau had been too late to take part in the spring campaign of 1677 and—according to the anecdote—had paid for their absence cheaply by telling Louis that he had defeated his enemies too rapidly for their tailor. Before their campaigning clothes were ready, every town had fallen before the invincible monarch. But such excuses could not be used twice. In 1678 they rode with the King to the sieges of Gand and Ypres. It was a totally new experience for both of them. Neither had ever heard a shot fired with intent to kill. It is improbable that Racine had ridden a full day's journey on horseback for fifteen years. Boileau's lack of practice in equitation was even greater. Besides the fatigue and the element of danger, they were quite unfamiliar with the routine of campaigning, yet it was their duty to be at the King's side at every moment which might prove memorable, and to obtain a coherent picture of the campaign which, when written, would not provoke the laughter of the experts. The opportunities for leg-pulling at their expense were un-limited. Even the soldier-courtiers who were their friends could not resist taking advantage of them.

As for their enemies, they seized their pens to profit by this unexpected chance. Madame de Sévigné and her circle exchanged ironically pitying comments on the two poets at war. Pradon related or invented the story that, having inquired of a general where they should stable their horses, they were met by the freezing reply: "Give them to me, gentlemen, I will hold them myself."

Such hostility was gradually overcome. It is true that Boileau rode out only once again, in 1683; after that, ill-health retained him in Paris. But Racine persevered and had to his credit two tours of inspection and four campaigns in all—the last being the unsuccessful campaign of the Netherlands in 1693, when Louis made his final appearance in the field. Racine's perseverance says much for his moral and physical courage. As he grew more familiar with war conditions, he became, as his informal letters to Boileau and others show, a highly conscientious and intelligent reporter. He reconnoitred the enemy positions at a certain risk, took pains to ascertain the names of all the units engaged and their strength, questioned experts like Vauban on technical points. By interrogating serving soldiers he tried to piece together accurate accounts of earlier engagements in which they had fought. The war correspondent, no less than the historian, will hail him as a brother when he comes upon these lines in one of his letters to Boileau:

"Seriously, this M. d'Espagne is a very sound man, and I could feel that he was speaking the truth in all that he told me of the battle of Saint-Gothard. But, my dear sir, what he said is not borne out either by M. de Montecuculli or by M. de Bissy, or by the Maréchal de la Feuillade, and I can see that the truth, which we are always being asked for, is more difficult to find than to write."

He had moreover an eye for the picturesque detail and did not observe only the King and the great captains. His sympathy with the enemy and the common soldier breaks out on occasion. He sees the horrors of war as well as its glory.

"I also saw eight prisoners being brought in. They were a horrible sight. One had a bayonet wound in his side, another a musket wound in the mouth. The other six had their faces and hands all burnt by the ignition of the gunpowder which had been in their pouches."

That was written during the siege of Namur in 1692, by which time Racine was accustomed to the sights of battle. Who can doubt that in his first campaign the carnage sickened him and, joined to his own rawness and relative discomfort, made the experience an unhappy one? But he came through it without seriously disgracing himself and without forfeiting the approval of the King. So long as he had that, he could afford to ignore the gibes of soldiers and courtiers and go steadily on his way, confident that the minor humiliations which he had to endure would gradually cease.

2

Racine was becoming settled in his new life and was looking forward confidently to a continuation of the royal

AN ARTIST'S CONCEPTION OF THE CLIMAX OF *ATHALIE*.

From the edition of 1691.

François d'Aubigné Marquise de Maintenon
Institutrice des Demoiselles de la Maison Royale de St Cir.

MADAME DE MAINTENON, FOUNDER OF SAINT-CYR AND INSPIRER OF RACINE.

Racine
Dessiné par
Son fils aîné.

RACINE IN HIS FIFTIES.
Sketch by Jean-Baptiste on the fly-leaf of a Horace.

favour when a danger took shape which threatened to destroy his whole position.

Two years after the Quarrel of *Phèdre* a chance word spoken at a dinner table set the police on the trail of a fraternity of sorcerers and poisoners who had been operating undetected for years in the background of French society. One arrest quickly led to others, and by 10th April 1679, enough suspects had fallen into the net for the work of justice to begin. A special court, the Chambre Ardente, was set up in the Palais de l'Arsenal. It was presided over by an examining magistrate of exceptional integrity and ability, Gabriel Nicolas de la Reynie, who was assisted by Bazin de Bezons, another shrewd and cultured man of law. These two had to sift a mass of testimony provided, sometimes willingly, sometimes after the routine torture, by men and women whose guilt varied widely in kind and degree. Some were alchemists, some adventurers ready to commit any crime provided it was profitable, some were abortionists or baby-farmers, others foolish women who did little more than tell fortunes and provide their credulous clients with charms. Their misdeeds ranged from treason, murder, and black magic to petty fraud. However, it was early apparent that the most interesting of the accused was the woman Catherine Monvoisin, known as La Voisin, and her activities became the crux of the investigations.

She was a woman of low condition, now middle-aged, who had taken to soothsaying in order to support her family in greater comfort. From petty fortune-telling, she rose to the standing of a fashionable oracle who was invited to great houses as a professional singer might be. There she appeared clad in her famous robe of crimson velvet embroidered with golden two-headed eagles. Prophesying was the most innocent of her activities. She provided her clients with charms and love-philtres, but also with poisons to rid them of tiresome husbands or of relatives from whom they hoped to inherit. Her connexions ran from the highest to the lowest. She could pay professional visits to the boudoir of the great lady and also be on familiar terms with her kitchen-maid. Among her lovers were a count, a viscount, an architect, and the headsman of Paris whose function it was to burn women convicted of crimes such as hers.

Among her friends, though not her accomplices, were the family of the actress Du Parc, whom she claimed at her interrogation to have known for fourteen years. If exact, this places the beginning of the friendship in 1665, the year of *Alexandre*, when the Du Parc was still with Molière's troupe. The acquaintance was no doubt made through the Du Parc's stepmother, Benoîte Lamarre, who—as the second wife of the charlatan-quack de Gorla—was of the same world as La Voisin. After the actress's death, her two young daughters were taken into the household of the Countess of Soissons, who was in relations with La Voisin for dark purposes of her own. A sister of the Duchess of Bouillon and of the Duke of Nevers, the Countess of Soissons belonged to the clan which had attempted the destruction of Racine at the time of the Quarrel of *Phèdre*.

Thus a youthful liaison, almost forgotten by Racine, but not by the relatives of his dead mistress, became linked in sinister fashion with the more recent vendetta. Two currents of jealousy and hatred came together and promised the most dangerous consequences.

In the eighth month of the trials, La Voisin made a statement which is reproduced here as it was recorded by the clerks of the Chambre Ardente.

Bench: How had she made the acquaintance of the Du Parc, play-actress?

Accused: She came to know her fourteen years ago, they were very good friends together, and she knew all her affairs during that time. She had intended to declare to us, some time ago, that the Du Parc must have been poisoned and that Jean Racine was suspected of it and that there was a considerable amount of talk about it; she, the respondent, has all the more reason to suppose it true because this Racine always prevented her, who was the good friend of the Du Parc, from seeing her during the whole course of the illness from which she died, although the Du Parc was always asking for her; but although she went to the Du Parc's to see her, they would never let her go in, and this on the orders of the said Racine, as she learnt from the stepmother of the Du Parc, called the Demoiselle de Gorle, and from the daughters of the Du Parc, who are at the Hôtel de Soissons, and who have told her that this Racine was the cause of their misfortunes.

—— Was any proposition ever made to her to get rid of the Du Parc by poison?

—— She would have given a rough welcome to anyone asking that.

—— Does she not know that the Demoiselle de la Grange[1] was approached for that purpose?

—— She has no knowledge of that.

—— Does she know a lame player?

—— Yes, and it is the man Béjart,[2] whom she has only seen twice.

—— Did not this Béjart bear some grudge against the Du Parc?

—— No, and what she learnt concerning the said Racine was firstly through the Demoiselle de Gorle.

—— Will she state to us exactly what the De Gorle told her?

—— The De Gorle told her that this Racine, having secretly married the Du Parc, was jealous of everyone and particularly of her, the respondent, of whom he had a great mistrust, and that he had got rid of her by poison and because of his extreme jealousy, and that during the illness of the Du Parc, Racine never left the Du Parc's bedside, and that he drew from her finger a valuable diamond and also misappropriated the jewels and principal effects of the Du Parc, which were worth a considerable sum of money; and that she had not even been allowed to speak to Nanon,

[1] The wife of the actor in Molière's troupe.

[2] Louis Béjart, one of Molière's troupe. He had died in the previous year, 1678.

[247]

her chamber-maid, who is a midwife,[1] although she asked for Nanon and had a letter written asking her to come to Paris to see her, as well as herself, the respondent.

—— Did the De Gorle ever tell her in what way the poisoning had been done and who had been used to do it?

—— No.

The cross-examination then diverged to other suspected cases of poisoning having no connexion with Racine or the Du Parc. But enough had been said to cast deep suspicion on the Historiographer Royal.

The judges moved slowly. They could not do otherwise in face of the great mass of incriminations which were slowly emerging from the inquiry and which implicated persons of the highest rank. The accusation against Racine, made on the twenty-first of November, was methodically communicated to the Minister of Justice at Versailles. On the eleventh of January 1680, Louvois wrote back to the Commissaire Instructeur, Bazin de Bezons: "The royal warrant necessary for the arrest of the Sieur Racine will be sent to you as soon as you ask for it."

Keeping this authority by them to use if they thought fit, the magistrates went after bigger game. With great boldness, they had demanded and obtained that the Duchess of Bouillon should appear before them to answer charges of having conspired to poison her husband and so be free to marry her lover. The Duchess obeyed this summons in a typical way, behaving on the same occasion as a *grande dame* and a spoilt schoolgirl. Followed by twenty coachloads of the aristocracy, she arrived triumphantly at the court and entered holding her husband by one hand and her alleged lover, the Duke of Richelieu, by the other. La Reynie

[1] The meaning is evidently that the Du Parc had not been allowed to speak to La Voisin's chambermaid Nanon, although she (the Du Parc) asked for her.

The French transcription of the whole of this important extract from the archives of the Palais de l'Arsenal is given in an appendix to this book (p. 339).

questioned her gravely on the séances which had been held
at her house.

"Did you ever see the Devil, Madam?" he asked in a
tone of resigned irony which was lost on the Duchess.

"No," she answered, with a pert stare at the magistrate,
"but I see one now. An ugly old devil he is too."

Her delighted friends laughed and applauded as she left
the court. They felt more amused than indignant that the
drab men of the law should venture to question the high
nobility on their comings and goings. With typical
frivolity, Madame de Sévigné informed her daughter that
"the Duchess of Bouillon went to La Voisin to ask for a
pinch of poison to put away an old husband she had who
was slaying her with boredom, and to obtain some means
of marrying a young man who had influence over her, unknown to everyone".

But even the Duchess of Bouillon was not wholly above
the law. Soon afterwards she received a royal order
exiling her to her country estates. As for her sister, the
Countess of Soissons, she fled from France without facing
the court, and remained abroad for the rest of her life.

If even the greatest were disturbed by the investigations,
what must have been the state of mind of Racine who could
not override the court and whose fate was of so little social
consequence? What desperate appeals and expedients did
he resort to in those months during which the prophetess's
accusations and the authority for his arrest hung over his
head? The King he dared not invoke, but he could cautious-
ly approach Colbert, the Minister of the Interior, could
canvass his legal connections—from his wife's family up to
the Advocate General Lamoignon[1] and could redouble his
efforts to please his protectress nearest the King.

---

[1] It will be recalled that the Lamoignons had been among the guests
at Racine's wedding. The elder, Guillaume Lamoignon, *premier président
du parlement de Paris*, had presided in 1676 at an earlier poisoning trial,
that of the Marquise de Brinvilliers. He died in 1677, and his son,
Chrétien-François, the Advocate General, now suspected that he had
been poisoned by one of his own servants, possibly at the instance of the

On the suggestion of Madame de Montespan, he and Boileau began working on the libretto of an opera on the fall of Phaëton, an undertaking of a more frivolous kind than any tragedy, and which ran entirely contrary to his sober resolution to quit the theatre. The project was dropped on the representations of Quinault, anxiously defending his position as premier librettist. Racine also patiently re-wrote a long extract from Plato's *Banquet* which had been translated by Madame de Montespan's sister, the Abbess of Fontevrault.

* These services, although they cannot be dated exactly, were probably rendered during the first session of the Chambre Ardente, which lasted from 10th April 1679 until 1st October 1680. By the second date, evidence of so dangerous a character had been brought to light that the sittings were abruptly suspended by direct order from the King. Madame de Montespan, whom Louis had associated so openly with his glory, who had borne him seven children whom he honoured next only to the legitimate princes of the blood, was herself implicated. She had 'conjured' and attended Black Masses to obtain his favours. She had had love-philtres secretly poured in his wine, by which his health was probably affected. She had finally, when she felt her influence over him slipping, plotted to poison him and the beautiful eighteen-year-old Mademoiselle de Fontanges. This, the latest charge against her—the facts to which it related had occurred on the eve of La Voisin's arrest—was also the most serious. Louis could not allow any more to be revealed without compromising the throne itself. The Montespan was not publicly charged or repudiated, but from then on she was in eclipse, and this protectress on whom Racine had set such hopes could no longer be of great use to him.

But by that date (October 1680), the cloud was moving away. La Voisin's accusation against him was not followed

---

Countess of Soissons. Chrétien-François Lamoignon remained on terms of friendship with both Racine and Boileau. He was invited to a performance of *Esther* in 1689.

up and, like the majority of the several hundred persons who were implicated by name in the inquiry, Racine suffered no worse punishment than intense anxiety. When the court resumed its sittings in the following year, the judges were more circumspect. They did their best to limit investigations and revelations of guilt to the profess-ional criminals whom they already held under arrest. The final sentences nearly all fell upon these and their immediate tools. More than thirty of them were condemned to death, including La Voisin, who was burnt alive. Others were sent to the galleys. Others again—some of the least guilty—were shut away for the rest of their lives in prisons or convents because of the dangerous knowledge they held. Open scandal was avoided and the fabric of society was re-knit, to outward appearances, on the old pattern.

3

That Racine had poisoned, or contemplated poisoning, the Du Parc is a charge which will not stand an instant's scrutiny. If La Voisin's declaration were accepted as literally true, we should be faced with a crime such as only a sadist could commit. We should have to imagine Racine, having administered the poison because of his "extreme jealousy"—this is the only motive imputed to him—shutting himself up with his mistress to watch her die. The Racine who reveals himself in his personal correspond-ence was incapable of this. On the other hand, the facts as La Voisin relates them would not be inconsistent with a death in childbirth or as the result of an abortion for which Racine might have had some share of responsibility. In that eventuality—but also in the eventuality of a natural death—the anxious presence of Racine at his mistress's side would be fully understandable, as would be his insist-ence that neither La Voisin nor the midwife Nanon, who may have been an equally sinister figure, should be admitted to the sickroom. The ring which he drew from her finger may have been his ring, and the "jewels and effects" which he took away, his gifts which he could not bear to leave to the sordid creatures who surrounded her. No action is attributed to him which would not be excusable in an innocent and anguished lover.

But there is the further consideration that La Voisin's evidence was circumstantial. She was not present during the Du Parc's last illness. It was not she who supplied the poison. "I should have given a rough welcome to anyone asking that!" she had exclaimed indignantly. Her whole account was hearsay taken from the Du Parc's daughters and stepmother, who over the years may well have fostered a growing sense of grievance against the poet who had dropped them as soon as his mistress was dead. This would explain Benoîte Lamarre's declaration—if indeed she made it—that Racine had "secretly married" Marquise. If marriage had made him her son-in-law, she would have had a certain moral claim on his bounty, and the Du Parc's daughters would have been his step-children. If there was no marriage, his obligations towards them were reduced to vanishing point.

Had a marriage in fact taken place, there was no apparent reason for keeping it secret, given the circumstances in which the two principals found themselves at that date.

The whole of La Voisin's testimony is so weak and inconclusive that in itself it could hardly have justified Louvois's written offer to authorize Racine's arrest. On purely legal grounds, neither the magistrates nor the Minister should have given it serious consideration. The fact that they did so is a strong argument for believing that extra-legal forces were at work to destroy the Historiographer Royal and that they seized on La Voisin's charge as a pretext. In the event, the influences which Racine was able to invoke, reinforced by the vagueness of the charge when closely examined, reinforced perhaps also by the sudden realization on the part of the Soissons-Bouillon faction that they themselves were vulnerable, brought the charge to nothing.

But for a moment Racine had seen the pit at his feet. The sins of his youth—as by then he must have regarded them—were about to be visited on him a hundredfold. All that he had striven for and all that he prized most—position, moral standing, the esteem of his friends and patrons, his access to the King—could be swept away in a night. And then it passed like a bad dream. There is good reason to believe that his undated *Ode tirée du Psaume XVII* was written as an act of thanksgiving for his deliverance. Like David he could say:

> *Déjà dans mon âme éperdue*
> *La nuit répandant ses terreurs,*
> *Présentait partout à ma vue*
> *Et ses tourments et ses horreurs;*
> *Ma perte était inévitable;*
> *J'invoquai ton nom redoutable,*
> *Et tu fus sensible à mes cris;*
> *Tu vis leur trame sacrilège,*
> *Et ta pitié rompit le piège*
> *Où leurs complots m'avaient surpris.*[1]

This ode was never published by Racine among his other translations and imitations of sacred songs. Louis Racine, finding the manuscript written in his father's hand, also left it unpublished. Was it because he guessed that it referred to a secret ordeal of which it was better not to speak?

After a survey of the facts, it seems almost superfluous to add that the poisoning trials could have had no connexion with Racine's retirement from the theatre. La Voisin was not arrested until two years after his decision to retire had been taken, and her accusation of him came nearly three

---

[1] The suggestion that the Ode was linked with the poisoning trials is M. François Mauriac's (see his *Vie de Racine*. Paris, 1928).

The Psalm is No. XVIII in the English Revised Version. Cp. vv. 4, 6, 17.

"The sorrows of death compassed me, and the floods of ungodly men made me afraid . . . In my distress I called upon the Lord . . . and my cry came before him . . . He delivered me from my strong enemy, and from them which hated me."

years after *Phèdre*. Nor is the theory sometimes put forward, that remorse for the death of the Du Parc was a factor in his decision, any more plausible. If he felt remorse, we should have to suppose that some act of his had contributed to her death, and the only suggestion of this lies in La Voisin's declaration, whose value we have already seen. We should further have to suppose that remorse did not begin to operate until some eight years after the death had occurred. Even if Racine had been in some measure guilty, it is inconceivable that at that distance of time the man who had gone on to new successes, new activities and the favours of the Champmeslé, should suddenly have looked back to the past with an anguish deep enough to prompt so radical a change in his way of life. Among the various motives underlying Racine's abandonment of the theatre, the Du Parc's death can hardly be included.

CHAPTER XVIII

THE DRAMATIST RE-BORN

ESTHER and *ATHALIE*

AFTER the storm had passed, Racine steadily strengthened his position at Court. Never presuming to step above his rank, he made many friends by his modesty and affability, and in time acquired the protection of the woman who, together with Louis's confessor, wielded the strongest influence over the King's later years. The Queen died in 1683. The Montespan, though still at Versailles, was only held in regard as the mother of the King's children. Madame de Maintenon was his true helpmate and probably soon became his morganatic wife. If Racine cultivated her friendship he was not necessarily obeying an ulterior motive. Her character and his were sufficiently compatible to draw them together.

In the summer of 1687 he writes to Boileau, who is taking the waters at Bourbon:

"I have had the honour of seeing Madame de Maintenon, with whom I spent the best part of an afternoon, and she made it clear that the time had not seemed too long to her. She is still the same as when you saw her, full of intelligence, of sense, of piety, and of much kindness towards us. She asked for news of our work [as historians]. I told her that your indisposition and mine, my journey to Luxembourg and yours to Bourbon, had put us a little behindhand, but that nevertheless we were not wasting our time."

Boileau replies sententiously:

"You are quite right to cultivate Madame de Maintenon. Never was anyone so worthy as she is of the position which she occupies, and hers is the only virtue in which I have not yet observed a flaw. Her esteem for you is a mark of her good taste."

In the previous year Madame de Maintenon, always interested in problems of education, had founded at Saint-Cyr a school for daughters of the impoverished nobility. The school, for which she carefully fostered the King's interest and patronage, became one of the chief interests of her life. She herself chose the mistresses, drew up the curriculum, and often escaped from Versailles to spend tranquil days at Saint-Cyr.

One of the school activities which she encouraged was the production of plays. But the choice was difficult. The Mother Superior, Madame de Brinon, composed several herself. Though morally suitable, they were otherwise—in the words of one of her pupils—"detestable". They then tried some of the great contemporary tragedies—Corneille's *Cinna*, Racine's *Iphigénie* and *Andromaque*. This last work proved to be too ardent. "Our little girls have acted it so well," Madame de Maintenon told the author, "that they will never act it again as long as they live—nor any of your other plays."

But she was perspicacious enough to distinguish between the worldly dramatist of twelve years ago and the sober, God-fearing courtier of to-day, and her estimate of his present character caused her to put forward a bold suggestion. It can hardly be described better than in the words of her shrewd young niece, Madame de Caylus:

"She asked him in this same letter [in which she had deplored the effects of *Andromaque*] to write for her, in his leisure moments, some kind of moral or historical poem, from which love would be entirely excluded, and in which he must not think that his reputation would be involved, because the play would remain buried at Saint-Cyr. She added that it mattered little to her if it was not written according to the rules provided that it contributed to her plans for entertaining the young ladies of Saint-Cyr while also educating them.

"This letter threw Racine into great agitation. He wished to please Madame de Maintenon. Refusal was impossible for a courtier, yet it was a delicate commission for a man like him who had a great reputation to maintain and who, although he had given up writing for the theatre, certainly did not wish to destroy the high opinion which his works had earned for him. Despréaux, whom he consulted, decided bluntly against the plan. But that was not Racine's view. Finally, after a little reflection, he found in the subject of *Esther* everything that was necessary to please the Court. Despréaux himself was delighted with it and urged him on to work with as much enthusiasm as he had displayed in advising him against it."

So *Esther* began to take shape. It became a dramatic poem in three acts, interspersed with choruses, part recited and part sung. There were half a dozen good speaking parts for the girls who were capable of acting, and room for a considerable number of others in the chorus of Jewish maidens or as the guards of King Ahasuerus. The *convenances* were scrupulously observed. As Racine primly remarked in his Preface:

"I think that it is wise to point out here that, although there are masculine roles in *Esther*, these roles were acted by girls with all the propriety befitting their sex. The thing was made all the easier for them because in ancient times the costumes of the Persians and the Jews consisted of long robes reaching to the ground."

Racine spent many hours at Saint-Cyr coaching the young actresses who were to interpret his first dramatic work since *Phèdre*. In spite of Madame de Maintenon's assurances, he was fully aware that it could affect his reputation, and he had composed it as a serious work of art. Nothing in this sacred production for amateurs should have recalled the wings of the Hôtel de Bourgogne. Yet the old professional habit was still strong, and he chose and drilled his school-girl cast with something of the anxious care that had gone

[257]

to the preparation of his great secular tragedies for the Parisian public. When little Mademoiselle de Maisonfort forgot her part at one of the performances and fled blushing into the wings, Racine became for a moment the overstrung author-producer storming at one of his experienced professional actresses. "Ah, Mademoiselle," he cried, in his most withering tones, "you have ruined my play." The girl burst into tears. Suddenly remembering where he was, Racine pulled out his handkerchief to dry them, and then, overcome with remorse and sympathy, wept unfeignedly himself.

Racine was justified in his pains, for *Esther* was acted before the most distinguished audiences he had ever had, if they were not the most critical. The first performance, on 26th January 1689, was witnessed by the King, the Dauphin, four dukes—Chevreuse, Beauvilliers, Noailles, and La Rochefoucauld—all of them patrons or friends of the author—three bishops (among them Bossuet), and the Minister Louvois. Entry was by invitation. The King was so charmed by the spectacle that he ordered another performance three days later. This time the Duc d'Orléans, the Dauphine and the princes of the Royal blood were present. Some "pious persons" were also given seats, among them eight Jesuits.

The play was repeated four times in February,[1] each time before a select audience who prized their invitations as the highest badge of social merit. Its success became a *succès de snobisme*. On the fifth of the month the guests of honour were James II of England and his Queen, who had lately arrived in France after the loss of their throne. Madame de Sévigné received an invitation for 19th February. She was placed "in the second row behind the duchesses", and next to the Maréchal de Bellefonds, who had gallantly requested the honour of sitting beside her. "The Marshal and I listened to the tragedy with an absorption which *was noticed* and at the right places we murmured appreciative remarks which perhaps were a little above the heads of some of the ladies there."

[1] February 3rd, 5th, 15th, and 19th.

On such an occasion, Madame de Sévigné can be forgiven for describing her own triumph in greater detail than the play. On his way out, the King stopped to speak to her. " 'Madame, I am certain that you were pleased with it.' Keeping my head, I replied: 'Sire, I was delighted. I cannot tell you how much I enjoyed it.' The King said: 'Racine is a very clever man.' I said: 'He is, Your Majesty, but these young people are clever too. They entered into the spirit of it as though they had been doing it all their lives.' 'Ah,' he replied, 'Yes, that is quite true.' And His Majesty went away, leaving me an object of general envy.''

There were no more performances of *Esther* for that year. The ostensible reason for discontinuing them was the death of the Queen of Spain, which caused the French Court to go into official mourning. But in reality, Madame de Maintenon had grown concerned at the effect of these frequent entertainments upon her young protégées. The distraction was too great and the atmosphere too worldly. In spite of the decency of their costumes, the girls were seen to too much advantage on the stage. Intrigues occurred with young gentlemen of the Court. One, between Mademoiselle de Marcilly—who played Zarès— and the Marquis de Villette, led to a marriage.[1] Others did not. The profane atmosphere was recklessly heightened by importing singers from the Paris Opera to strengthen the choir of "timid doves". This innovation was made, ironically enough, at the performance in honour of the dour James II. At the same performance young Madame de Caylus, who originally had only spoken the prologue, played the part of Esther with conspicuous success. She was of an irreproachable character and *milieu*,

[1] By her second marriage in 1720 to Henry St. John, Mlle. de Marcilly became Viscountess Bolingbroke and played a prominent part in social and literary circles, both in England and France. She died and was buried at Battersea, where her memorial, with the charming epitaph written by her husband, is still to be seen in the riverside parish church.

but she was no longer an ordinary pupil of the school.
Although still only seventeen, she had been married in law
for three years. She acquitted herself, as Dangeau and others
tactlessly remarked, "better than the Champmeslé".
Such comparisons were hardly calculated to please Madame
de Maintenon; still less the pious persons to whose opinion
in spiritual matters she attached such importance. The
ascetic Bishop of Chartres, in whose diocese Saint-Cyr lay,
was particularly concerned. He wielded a quiet but strong
influence over Madame de Maintenon, who had procured
the bishopric for him. The *curé* of Versailles, more vocal,
protested with a vehemence in which religious zeal was
linked with a personal hatred of Racine—inspired perhaps
by his known relations with Port-Royal. "M. Racine",
he wrote in his *Mémoires*, "delighted to have an opportunity
of winning consideration at the Court and of making his
fortune, did not hesitate for a moment to return to his old
profession of poet. He saw that now it would prove incomparably more lucrative than it had been in Paris, where
he had worked for a long time without becoming very rich."

This was slander. Racine's conscience was clear enough.
He did not make a penny out of *Esther*. The orders of
Madame de Maintenon, the nature of the subject and the
innocence of the actresses removed any other scruples that
he might have had. Moreover, the men whom he looked
upon in secret as his ultimate moral tribunal approved the
play. The Great Arnauld received a copy in exile and
found it perfectly edifying. The Jansenist Father Quesnel
was also edified by it, but wished that it had only been
printed, not acted. He feared the dangers of any appearance,
however decorous, upon a stage. On this point the Jansenists and the Jesuits were at one. Although *Esther* was
performed some six or seven times at Carnival time in the
following year (1690), its second impact on contemporaries
was much slighter, and it may be supposed that the invitations were more restricted and the production less ambitious. The lavish costumes of the original production—they
had cost over 14,000 *livres*, and some were sewn with

jewels from the King's own ballsuits—were probably not used.

When, in 1691, Racine executed his second commission for Madame de Maintenon by writing a masterpiece which stands on equal terms with the greatest of his secular tragedies, the performances were given almost furtively. *Athalie* was staged very simply in a schoolroom by girls wearing their ordinary school costume. Since this play demands a grandiose setting, striking costumes, and spectacular crowd-movements, it is not surprising that it fell flat.

The failure of *Athalie* has even been compared to Racine's disappointment at the time of *Phèdre*. If this is an obvious exaggeration it is nevertheless understandable that he should be disappointed in its production and reception. The fact that not he but the Abbé Boyer was asked to write the next play for Saint-Cyr suggests that an intrigue was mounted against him. If so, it was probably inspired by an ecclesiastical faction.

Although both his sacred plays were frequently performed in private by the school, he was never to see an adequate production of them. They did not reach the professional stage, and hence the general public, until the next reign. *Athalie* was first produced at the Comédie Française in 1716 and *Esther* in 1721. The great qualities of the first gradually became apparent. They were increasingly appreciated, by Voltaire and others, during the course of the eighteenth century.

2

Although *Esther* appears slight compared with Racine's great tragedies, it shows no decline in his literary skill. Besides fulfilling perfectly, in its form and tone, the requirements of Saint-Cyr, it allowed Racine to make an experiment which had long tempted him. He had already looked enviously at the device of the chorus by means of which the Greek dramatists mingled comment and exposition with dialogue. He had seen something similar in contemporary opera and perhaps, in beginning *Phaëton* a few years earlier, he had been prompted by artistic curiosity as much as by compulsion in this attempted invasion of Quinault's domain. He may also have looked back to the lyrical monologues found in French tragedy of an earlier generation, one of which he himself had included, strictly pruned, in his first play. Now at last, twenty-five years after *La Thébaïde*, he was able to use stanzas not unlike the Stanza on Ambition which he had once quoted to Le Vasseur, then discarded with the reflexion that "it may come in elsewhere".[1]

The choruses, impossible in a regular tragedy on the professional stage, found a natural place in *Esther* and satisfied both author and performers. Written with a harmonious simplicity which occasionally admits picturesque turns of language echoing Racine's reading of the Bible, and which were equally inadmissible in the professional theatre, they form an accompaniment to the tragedy proper.

Its theme, however, is complete without them. It follows the broad lines of the Old Testament story, omitting of necessity all reference to the King's concubines and to Esther's equivocal position in the royal household. Racine softens a few other details too crude for his purpose and introduces secondary characters of his own invention. For dramatic purposes, he heightens the ferocity and insolence of Haman and thus points the contrast with the Israelite people who, since they are represented on the stage only by a chorus of maidens, are given a helplessness and innocence going well beyond the Old Testament characterization. Their peril is made more acute by the fact that the order for their massacre is to take effect in ten days; any dramatist would realise that the Biblical interval of eleven months was far too long. The counter-massacre by which the Old Testament Jews avenged themselves after the triumph of Esther is of course omitted. But Racine seems not entirely consistent here. His Aman

[1] *See* p. 63.

is torn to pieces by the "peuple en fureur" whereas the Biblical Haman was only hanged. The main reason for this was that, in the interests of a swift dénouement, he wished Aman's death off-stage to occur as rapidly as possible: the mob might be supposed to be more expeditious than the hangman. Secondly, in the society for which he was writing, he did not wish to stress the reference to hanging. Good taste forbade a reference to the gallows and demanded a paraphrase:

> Que tardez-vous? Allez, et faites promptement
> Elever de sa mort le honteux instrument.

Instead of the Biblical directness of: "Hang him thereon", his Assuérus cries:

> Qu'à ce monstre à l'instant l'âme soit arrachée;
> Et que devant sa porte, au lieu de Mardochée,
> Apaisant par sa mort et la terre et les cieux,
> De mes peuples vengés il repaisse les yeux.

So the word *potence*, with its association with the public executioner, was avoided and what in fact was a far more barbaric conception substituted.

These various changes of emphasis do not seriously distort the Biblical story and are perfectly permissible to a writer adapting it to a new medium and a new public. They only spring into relief when confronted with Racine's surprising statement in his Preface that: "It seemed to me that, without altering any of the smallest circumstances of the Holy Scripture (which, in my opinion, would be a kind of sacrilege), I could construct the whole of my action just from the scenes which God himself, in a manner of speaking, had prepared."

One appreciates Racine all the more on finding that, covered by this sweeping claim, he has proceeded to remodel his material with the assurance of a master-craftsman. He strikes out the non-essential, introduces new elements where necessary, retouches whatever is not dramatically effective and finally compares Holy Writ with the Gentile historians to make sure that nothing has been forgotten. "I thought nevertheless that I might borrow two or three indications from Herodotus, to complete the portrait of Ahasuerus."

The first dramatist of France is conscious of knowing his own business best. Reverence and humility may characterize his general approach, but when a play has to be constructed the execution is in his hands alone.

He is even able, in one of the most interesting passages of the play, to interject an account of the King's dream, which has obvious significance from two different points of view. The Book of Esther mentions no dream. It merely records:

"On that night could not the King sleep, and he commanded to bring the book of records of the chronicles; and they were read before the King."

Racine develops this considerably (Act II, sc. 1).

HYDASPE: "*Le roi d'un noir chagrin paraît enveloppé;*
Quelque songe effrayant cette nuit l'a frappé.
Pendant que tout gardait un silence paisible,
Sa voix s'est fait entendre avec un cri terrible:
J'ai couru. Le désordre était dans ses discours:
Il s'est plaint d'un péril qui menaçait ses jours:
Il parlait d'ennemi, de ravisseur farouche;
Même le nom d'Esther est sorti de sa bouche.
Il a dans ces horreurs passé toute la nuit."

So far, this is a dramatist's expansion of the Biblical text, lying, it is true, within the limits of his play, but difficult to read without believing that it is also an allusion to a scene witnessed in the royal bedchamber at Versailles. Racine then returns to the Bible in order to use the trait which it places so aptly in his courtier's hands:

Enfin, las d'appeler un sommeil qui le fuit,
Pour écarter de lui ces images funèbres,
Il s'est fait apporter ces annales célèbres
Où les faits de son règne, avec soin amassés,

Par de fidèles mains chaque jour sont tracés;
On y conserve écrits le service et l'offense,
Monuments éternels d'amour et de vengeance.
Le roi, qui j'ai laissé plus calme dans son lit,
D'une oreille attentive écoute ce récit.

Having woven into his dramatic poem this evocation of
the sleepless Sun-King murmuring the name of Esther,
then calling for the annals of his reign to be read to him—
no doubt by one of their two compilers[1]—Racine might
seem to have exhausted the possibilities of his interpolation.
But an invented trait is often more tenacious of life in an
author's mind than a borrowed one, and the embryonic
dream of Assuérus will grow until in his next play it
becomes an integral part of the heroine's psychology, as
well as of the machinery of the plot. What in *Esther* was a
luxury, allowed himself by the poet and courtier, in
Athalie is a necessity, and therefore incomparably more
impressive.

It is necessary to say something of the 'keys' to *Esther*.
Assuérus is descended from the secular Racinian kings and
fulfils the same materially decisive function in the drama.
Except in the specific allusion to his sleeplessness, he is
hardly Louis XIV, but rather a personification of Racine's
ideas of kingship, based on observation of Louis XIV and
elaborated with the knowledge that Louis was closely
interested in the play. The same is true of the character
of Esther. She was not Madame de Maintenon, but if
Madame de Maintenon cared to see resemblances between

[1] The nights of royal insomnia when Racine is definitely known to
have calmed the King by reading to him occurred later, in 1696. The
book he then used was not the History, but Plutarch's *Lives*. But since
Dangeau had already noted in 1686 (*Journal*, March 20th) that: "Le
Roi s'est fait lire dans ses dernières après-dinées l'histoire que font
Racine et Despréaux, et en paraît fort content," and since Louis Racine
also describes his father reading the History to the King "after dinner"
in the presence of both Madame de Maintenon and Madame de Montespan, there must have been earlier occasions to inspire the passage in
Esther.

the Biblical queen and herself, she would find them not unflattering. In this play, as in *Alexandre* and *Bérénice*, Racine created characters which great personages could identify with themselves with a certain pleasure. It was more than a fortunate chance but it was less than a courtier's deliberate calculation. The *dramatis persona* and the topical application perhaps grew up together, but the first was the elder child and was always upheld in his rights of primogeniture if the two happened to clash.

Twentieth-century criticism goes too far in tracing the descent of all these characters to Racine's subconscious mind. The seventeenth and eighteenth centuries went to the other extreme in interpreting them as objective portraits of living persons. Each age has been convinced that Racine was up to some trick: the only question is which trick? If the psycho-analytical explanation sometimes gives fantastic results, the 'key' system has also produced its absurdities. At a pinch, it is permissible to say, by a broad simplification, that Assuérus "was" Louis and that Esther "was" Madame de Maintenon. But it is unjustifiable to develop the second application as Madame de La Fayette did when she remarked that "all the difference was that Esther was a little younger and less finicky on the score of piety". She scores her point unfairly, thanks to a too literal approach. When she goes on to identify Vasthi, whom Esther has superseded before the action of the play begins, with the Montespan, she is consistent with herself, and her system is not tested to breaking point since Vasthi does not appear on the stage and is mentioned only once in a passage six lines long. But when she remarks that some people have identified Aman with Louvois—though she herself does not press the comparison—she illustrates the striking weakness of the biographical approach. For the figure of the evil counsellor which Racine found in his Biblical source and required as the necessary villain of his drama, could not have been meant for Louvois as a matter of historical fact. Racine's relations with the Minister were such that it is incredible that he should have thought of presenting him in an unfavourable light. On the contrary, he valued his patronage highly, and not long before beginning *Esther*, he was writing unambiguously to Boileau (5th September 1687):

"You and I have a very special interest in wishing him [Louvois] a long period of good health. No one could show more kindness towards us than he does."

Any attempt to read a consistent biographical intention into Racine's plays always meets at some point with an objection on the biographical plane. There may be allusions to, or borrowings from the contemporary scene, but the dramatist never binds himself to a system. He retains his freedom to transform, invent, and create. The only law which he always seeks to obey is the law of dramatic effect. This, for him, is paramount.

It therefore becomes dangerous to try to interpret his plays by any system, old or new, which is not directly related to the art of the practising dramatist. A fresh approach sometimes throws light on certain parts of his work which have been obscured or neglected. It may equally well show other parts in a totally false light. The specialists in psychology have X-rayed Racine very search-ingly in recent years. Some discoveries of considerable interest have been made, but their interest is incidental. They add very little to an understanding of the tragedies as works of art: and if they are not that, what is their signifi-cance?

It is, of course, possible to deny that aesthetic criticism has any validity to-day. But such a ruling, even if accepted, cannot be made retrospective. It can only be properly applied to those artists who work in sympathy with it and themselves conceive their works as psychological or social 'documents'. Racine's tragedies were not conceived as 'documents' and it is injudicious to praise or condemn them for elements which formed no part of the author's original design, even when they happen to be present. Like paintings, the tragedies may be looked at as carefully as desired and from any angle desired in the setting for which they were composed. Anything outside this is not criticism, but expertise irrelevant to the true meaning— and value—of the objects examined.

3

In *Athalie*, the psycho-analysing critic is no doubt right in perceiving a subconscious significance in the dream of Athalie. This powerfully rendered description of the evil queen Jezebel, painted and decked in all her finery, stooping over her daughter's bed and then, as her daughter reaches up to embrace her, disintegrating into a mass of torn flesh and bones, is too striking to be overlooked. But the discovery—or rather the recurring rediscovery—of this famous passage rarely seems to be accompanied by the realization that it expresses one of the commonplaces of human experience and of literature. There is nothing novel in the conception of a loved, admired, or desired object suddenly proving to be empty or hideous. Surely this is the secret fear of the majority of humanity, exteriorized for some in childish nightmares, for others in the brittler dreams of advancing age. As one of the universal themes of reflective literature, it appears again and again under the various symbolisms and poetic idioms used. Prettily dressed as the rose-doomed-to-wither of the Renaissance, it becomes starkly comfortless in the dry bones of T. S. Eliot's *Ash Wednesday* (the modern poet takes the conception a stage further, to the phase after dissolution has taken place, and the disintegration is of his own personality). Between the two are the metaphysical Herbert's ''But though the whole world turn to coal'', the Romantic Espronceda's ''Mud and decaying matter'', Baudelaire *passim* (most obviously in *Une Charogne*), and so on. A bare listing of examples confined to two or three literatures could probably fill this book. Do we really need the psycho-analyst to point them out or to explain their obvious psycho-physiological connotations?

And when, in the case of *Athalie*, he has insisted on doing so, what more have we learnt about Racine and his creation? We should have been informed tentatively that Racine's obsession with this particular concept may have been determined by some gruesome boyhood experience at Port-Royal, perhaps by a more recent experience on the battlefield, and possibly by a nightmare of Louis XIV's which he witnessed. That is the biographical side, after which the literary critic may step in to note the literary source of the passage in the Book of Kings and the first draft for the dream in *Esther*. *

All these factors combined account abundantly for the presence of the *songe d'Athalie* in Act II, Sc. v. Nothing has been left unanswered except two essential questions. The first, which is artistic, is in what manner Racine transformed his immediate literary source into something no less powerful and moving, but quite different.

The Hebrew chronicler had the easier task. He had already placed himself—assisted by the literary convention which he was following—in a favourable position for his effect. All that remained for him to do was to continue his direct narrative and to end his chapter on a high note by relating the facts of Jezebel's death as austerely as possible. His chief problems were those of emphasis and selection, for we do not know how much material he had to discard.

He begins with the death, in about a hundred (English) words:

> And when Jehu was come to Jezreel, Jezebel heard of it; and she painted her face and tired her head and looked out at a window.
>
> And as Jehu entered in at the gate, she said: "Had Zimri peace, who slew his master?"
>
> And he lifted up his face to the window and said: "Who is on my side, who?"
>
> And there looked out to him two or three eunuchs. And he said: "Throw her down."

[269]

So they threw her down. And some of her blood was
sprinkled on the wall, and on the horses. And he trod
her underfoot.

The Hebrew author, writing with perfect timing and
economy, would now have finished, if he were concerned
solely with narrative effect. But he still has one unused
fact which will heighten the horror of his story, provided
he can link it up without anti-climax. He is also expected
to point to the fulfilment of a prophecy, a convention no
less binding on him than was Racine's obligation to conduct
his tragedies to a morally defensible conclusion. He does
this with remarkable skill and contrives to rise to a second
climax higher than the first.

And when he was come in, he did eat and drink and
said: "Go, see now this cursed woman and bury her, for
she is a king's daughter."
And they went to bury her: but they found no more
of her than the skull, and the feet, and the palms of her
hands.
Wherefore they came again and told him. And he
said: "This is the word of the Lord, which he spoke by
his servant Elijah the Tishbite, saying: In the portion of
Jezreel shall dogs eat the flesh of Jezebel. And the
carcase of Jezebel shall be as dung upon the face of the
field in the portion of Jezreel, so that they shall not say:
This is Jezebel."

Stirred or reminded by the last part of this passage,
Racine proceeded to transpose it. The death of Jezebel
being outside his play, he must recall it by some other
method than straight narrative. The solution of a dream
serves at the same time to indicate the psychological
condition of his chief character and to advance the dramatic
action. The audience is prepared for the recounting of the
dream by the entrance of Athalie in a state of doubt and
agitation so strong that her counsellor at once remarks
it. She draws Mathan and Abner aside and begins, in

self-reassurance, to recall the achievements of her reign, seeking to prove thereby that she is neither guilty nor in danger. Gradually the tension increases. The actress, having completed her exposition of the facts, is ready to soar into her *tirade*.

> *Un songe (me devrais-je inquiéter d'un songe?)*
> *Entretient dans mon cœur un chagrin qui le ronge:*
> *Je l'évite partout, partout il me poursuit.*

With this line she is up, reabsorbed in her dream which has suddenly swung out of memory into reality:

> *C'était pendant l'horreur d'une profonde nuit;*
> *Ma mère Jézabel devant moi s'est montrée,*
> *Comme au jour de sa mort pompeusement parée;*
> *Ses malheurs n'avaient point abattu sa fierté;*
> *Même elle avait encor cet éclat emprunté*
> *Dont elle eut soin de peindre et d'orner son visage,*
> *Pour réparer des ans l'irréparable outrage.*

Racine, with his sublime preciosity, has now carried us into an element quite different from that of the Biblical writer, deliberately earth-bound with his five simple words: "And she painted her face". At this point the device of the prophecy can be introduced with complete aptness:

> *Tremble, m'a-t-elle dit, fille digne de moi;*
> *Le cruel Dieu des Juifs l'emporte aussi sur toi.*
> *Je te plains de tomber dans ses mains redoutables,*
> *Ma fille.*

The actress's voice soars for a moment longer but the sense of her words begins to falter into the nightmare tangle which leads, before the very eyes of the horrified onlookers, to the final, spectacular crash:

> *En achevant ces mots épouvantables,*
> *Son ombre vers mon lit a paru se baisser;*
> *Et moi, je lui tendais les mains pour l'embrasser;*
> *Mais je n'ai plus trouvé qu'un horrible mélange*

> D'os et de chair meurtris, et traînés dans la fange,
> Des lambeaux pleins de sang, et des membres affreux
> Que des chiens dévorants se disputaient entre eux.

ABNER: *Grand Dieu!*

The passage, though a peak one, is not isolated. After Abner's exclamation, Athalie continues with the second and perhaps more terrifying part of her dream, in which she sees the falsely reassuring figure of the child. While she is calming herself by contemplating his innocence, he steps forward and stabs her to the heart. This invention is Racine's own and it links the great *tirade* smoothly with what is to follow on the stage.

4

The second question which arises is the enigma of Athalie's character and whether it, or the play as a whole, throws any fresh light on Racine's conception of kingship.

Athalie has neither the stature nor the complexity of a Phèdre. Racine, still bound by the condition laid down for *Esther* that "love should be entirely excluded" from his play, is forced to sacrifice a whole world of human motivation and reaction. Nor has his character any other links with humanity, unless a retrospective love for her murdered mother and a perverse attraction towards her grandson and mortal enemy, the child Joas, might be faintly detected in her. But these are no more than hints in the play as it stands. What remains is a cold, lonely figure actuated by ambition and a habit of ruthlessness and troubled by forebodings which she seeks to dissipate by exterminating their physical cause. The highest precept in her moral world is to demand an eye for an eye, for it is by this means that she has succeeded in establishing peace and order in her kingdom. She justifies all the blood which is upon her hands by invoking the laws of political necessity and of vengeance. Her persecution of the followers of Jehovah is a natural measure of self-protection. If she relented towards the Levites they would destroy her—as ultimately, obeying the same moral law, they do. She is a savage with a highly developed sense of political realism, uninfluenced by either love or remorse. Since there is no flaw in her psychological armour, her downfall must be brought about by supernatural means. She is led into the trap by misgivings implanted in her mind by the dream which, Racine suggests, has been sent to her by Jehovah. She thus succumbs to an external enemy, not to a weakness in her own nature.

Yet with all her limitations there is a depth of experience in this evil, haunted queen which makes her the equal in maturity of any character in the secular plays. She is simple but not shallow—a barbarian whose single obsession is to retain power and whose single expedient is to kill. These are the lessons which experience has taught her.

In writing such a part for the entertainment of the young ladies of Saint-Cyr, Racine must have realized that he was straining them too high. How could he ever have expected a schoolgirl actress to do justice to his creation? He must have known in advance that the best of them could only give him a caricature.

It is apparent that, while still observing the outward forms which made the play suitable for the school, Racine had let himself be carried away by his subject, and had become, willy-nilly, the adult dramatist writing for adult actors and an adult audience. Recaptured by the strongest and most constant passion in his life, he found himself compelled to make his tragedy as perfect as possible in obedience to the sole laws of the drama. Considerations of his interpreters' capacities went by the board. So also did the personal applications which contemporaries might make. This time he left no courtier's margin for flattery. Whereas Assuérus had been a just king and Esther a touching and innocent favourite, his queen now is an ungodly tyrant who falls at last into the pit that has been dug for her. If she provokes a certain sympathy in the minds of a modern audience, this springs from a changed attitude towards the

implacable Jehovah of the Old Testament and from a feeling
that the scales have been weighted a little too heavily
against her. But seen from Racine's ethical position, this
pity would be a perverse pity, and it is unlikely that he
intended to arouse it. His Athalie was without doubt an
unpleasant distorting mirror if any of the great ones should
happen to glance in it.

But what of the child king, Joas, who triumphs over
her? In his Preface, Racine makes a courtier's use of this
character by observing that his natural parts are eclipsed
by the little Duc de Bourgogne, Louis's adored grandson.
That is well enough in the Preface, whose function is to
justify or conciliate, but in the play itself Racine seems to
go out of his way to strike a discordant note. He foreshadows the ultimate destiny which awaits Joas many years
after the fall of the curtain. Of three passages in the same
strain, the last (Act IV, Sc. iii) is the most striking in its
outspokenness. The High-Priest Joad is warning the
young prince with a foreboding of the future:

> Loin du trône nourri, de ce fatal honneur,
> Hélas! vous ignorez le charme empoisonneur;
> De l'absolu pouvoir vous ignorez l'ivresse,
> Et des lâches flatteurs la voix enchanteresse.
> Bientôt ils vous diront que les plus saintes lois,
> Maîtresses du vil peuple, obéissent aux rois;
> Qu'un roi n'a d'autre frein que sa volonté même;
> Qu'il doit immoler tout à sa grandeur suprême;
> Qu'aux larmes, au travail, le peuple est condamné,
> Et d'un sceptre de fer veut être gouverné;
> Que, s'il n'est opprimé, tôt ou tard il opprime;
> Ainsi de piège en piège, et d'abîme en abîme,
> Corrompant de vos mœurs l'aimable pureté,
> Ils vous feront enfin haïr la vérité,
> Vous peindront la vertu sous une affreuse image.
> Hélas! ils ont des rois égaré le plus sage.
>   Promettez sur ce livre, et devant ces témoins,
> Que Dieu fera toujours le premier de vos soins;

[274]

Que, sévère aux méchants, et des bons le refuge,
Entre le pauvre et vous, vous prendrez Dieu pour juge;
Vous souvenant, mon fils, que, caché sous ce lin,
Comme eux vous fûtes pauvre, et comme .eux orphelin.

This famous passage, with its condemnation of absolutism, and its reminder of the people's rights, acquired in time a revolutionary force and was thunderously applauded whenever an actor spoke it during the last years of the Old Régime. Are we to suppose that Racine deliberately stepped outside the limits of his story to deliver a lecture on the obligations of kingship either to Louis XIV or to his young grandson? Or had he simply, as a man of letters, allowed himself to be carried on to dangerous ground by the logical force of an idea?

First, it must be remembered that the theme of a king corrupted by servile flatterers was a recurring one in Racine's plays. The whole character of Narcisse and his relationship to Néron were built upon it. Next, Phèdre expressed her contempt for the courtly sycophant in her final dismissal of Oenone:

Détestables flatteurs, présent le plus funeste
Que puisse faire aux rois la colère celeste!

Twelve years later, the theme was picked up in *Esther* and given a precision which suggests that Racine, with a more intimate knowledge of Versailles, had grown bitterer in his opinion of the successful courtier:

Les rois craignent surtout le reproche et la plainte . . .
Quiconque ne sait pas dévorer un affront,
Ni de fausses couleurs se déguiser le front,
Loin de l'aspect des rois qu'il s'écarte, qu'il fuie.
Il est des contre-temps qu'il faut qu'un sage essuie.
Souvent avec prudence un outrage enduré
Aux honneurs les plus hauts a servi de degré.

This passage is clearly the germ of the full-length warning in *Athalie*. But there a new element is introduced. In

[275]

Athalie for the first time the People are mentioned, as though Racine, not content with protesting against sycophancy, was also presuming to advocate social justice.

That he held liberal views in political matters might perhaps be assumed on general grounds, although the assumption rests on nothing more concrete than the passages under consideration. (The existence of the memorandum on the sufferings of the common people which he is said to have written for Madame de Maintenon is problematical, and may well have been an invention of the philosophic eighteenth century.) But let us suppose, in the absence of conclusive evidence in either direction, that he felt strongly on the subject. It is still very difficult to see him, on his own initiative, affirming his opinion in a play commissioned by those nearest to Louis and in such a form that it could hardly fail to strike the ear of the King. Racine was no *lâche flatteur*, but he had enough common prudence not to give gratuitous and premeditated offence.

It is possible that he was encouraged to fly this warning kite by his friend the Duc de Beauvilliers, who was the enlightened tutor of the Duc de Bourgogne. And the support of Madame de Maintenon might also be deduced from his letter to her six years later in which he writes:

"I must confess that, when I caused there to be so much singing in *Esther* about '*Rois, chassez la calomnie*', I hardly expected that I should myself be attacked by calumny one day."[1]

If this is so, it would be a happy instance of patronage (though not Louis XIV's patronage) working in the same direction as the poet's secret convictions and leading him to develop, in memorably simple words, a point which until then had been little more than a commonplace of worldly experience.

If Joad's warning to the young king-to-be is so obtrusive that it seems to require a 'key', the other 'keys' must be used with caution, as in *Esther*. There are biographical hints, but no more, in the suggestion that the child Joas

[1] *See* below, p. 314.

was the child Racine (nurtured by his aunt Josabeth—Agnès de Sainte-Thècle); the High-Priest Joad would then be a projection of Arnauld, or some other of the great Jansenist figures, and the oppressed Israelite people would be the community of Port-Royal, in both the sacred plays. Another theory sees them as the Huguenots, then undergoing the extreme of persecution. But given Madame de Maintenon's views on the revocation of the Edict of Nantes, which seem also to have been Racine's views, this second guess can hardly be maintained. As to the first, Port-Royal may no doubt stand as a very shadowy background to the clearly executed plays, but it is so nebulous that it brings very little to an understanding of them. If * evidence is sought of Racine's attitude towards his educators, it exists in a much more concrete form which will be considered in a later chapter.

The chief significance of the two sacred tragedies for the biographer is the proof they bring that Racine's powers as an artist had not declined after twelve years of silence. They prove also that his interest in the drama was still strong, even when his stage was only a schoolroom.

CHAPTER XIX

THE ETERNAL THEATRE

EVEN had Racine wished it, he could not have made a clean break with the theatre immediately after *Phèdre*. His plays were still there, linking him to the past and steadily increasing his fame as a secular dramatist.

When the Comédie Française was established in 1680 by the arbitrary merging of the Theatres of Bourgogne and Guénégaud—an event which marked the final triumph of Louis-Quatorzien bureaucracy over the freedom of the artist—Racine's tragedies formed an important asset in the new company's repertory. *Phèdre* was chosen for their opening performance. More than this, Racine was officially called in to cast his plays among the actors whom he considered most suitable, and so was responsible for confirming the Champmeslé in her possession of the great parts which had made them both famous. There is a certain irony in this continuance of their professional association after their personal relationship had ceased, but it was inescapable. So long as both of them were powers in the theatre, their names would remain linked there.

Racine's plays were performed at least as frequently after his retirement as they had been during his most active period. From 1680 until his death one or other of them was performed, on an average, forty times a year. These numerous productions meant that, together with Corneille and Molière, he was still the principal entertainer of the theatre-going public; nothing that a younger generation of authors could write seriously shook the ascendancy of the old giants.[1]

Living as he was half at Court and half in cultivated Parisian society, it was impossible that Racine should fail to catch the echoes of these productions and to be sensitive to the reactions which they provoked.. Nor could he be indifferent to the fate of the men and women who were still his interpreters, even though he had broken with them socially as a condition of his new status.

After seven peaceful years in the Rue Guénégaud, they were forced by the theologians of the Sorbonne to vacate their theatre. More harassed than protected by their official sponsors, they had great difficulty in obtaining a new hall. Racine's attitude towards their misfortunes was one of amusement not unmixed with sympathy. Privately at least, he had not yet sided with the churchmen and magistrates who were endeavouring to make the life of the players intolerable.

"The comedians have already tried to take a new hall in five or six different places," he wrote to Boileau in August 1687, "but wherever they go it is marvellous to hear how the *curés* cry out. The *curé* of Saint-Germain-l'Auxerrois

[1] The statistics originally drawn by Eugène Despois (*Le Théâtre Français sous Louis XIV*. Paris, 1874) from the registers of the Comédie Française show that, for the period 1680-1700, performances of Racine's ten plays totalled 879, of which 756 were given to the Parisian public, 123 at the Court. Disregarding the 128 performances of *Les Plaideurs*, which would fill the second half of a double bill, the most popular revival was *Phèdre* (114 performances in Paris, 18 at Court), closely followed by *Andromaque* (111 and 14). Next, in a fairly compact group, came *Mithridate* (91 and 18), *Iphigénie* (87 and 7) and *Britannicus* (81 and 19). There was then a pronounced drop to *Bajazet* (64 and 20) and *Bérénice* (51 and 6). These relative positions were maintained for 1700-1715, although *Phèdre* slightly increased its lead over *Andromaque* while *Bajazet* and *Bérénice* dropped still further away.

During 1680-1700, Corneille was revived more frequently than Racine, with an aggregate of 1,028 performances (901 in Paris, 127 at Court). But in his case the spread was over nineteen plays, and in no single one did he equal the popularity of *Phèdre* and *Andromaque*. *Le Cid* remained the favourite Cornelian tragedy (102 and 11) and increased its popularity in the early years of the eighteenth century.

has already prevented them from taking the Hôtel de Sourdis because the organ would have been heard quite loudly in the theatre there, and in the church the violins would have been heard plainly. At present they are considering the Rue de Savoie in the Parish of Saint-André.[1] This *curé* has also been to the King to point out to him that soon there will be nothing in his parish but taverns and poulterers; if the comedians come as well his church will be empty. The Grands-Augustins have also been to the King, but there is a report that the comedians told His Majesty that these same Augustinians who do not want them as neighbours are themselves very assiduous playgoers and that they have even tried to sell to the company some houses which they own in the Rue d'Anjou in order to build a theatre there.''

Meanwhile, the players await Louvois's decision as to whether they shall be allowed to build in the Rue de Savoie. Racine comments:

''There is great alarm in the neighbourhood. All the inhabitants, who are legal folk, are horrified at the prospect of their streets being disturbed. Monsieur Billard particularly, whose house would be just opposite the pit door, complains bitterly, and when someone told him that it would be so much easier for him to go to the entertainment sometimes, he replied very tragically: 'I don't want to be entertained'.''

Finally the infant Comédie Française was allowed to settle in a tennis-hall in the Rue des Fossés-Saint-Germain-des-Prés (to-day, the Rue de l'Ancienne Comédie), some three minutes' walk from their old theatre, and ten minutes from Racine's new address in the Rue des Maçons. It would be almost as easy for him as for M. Billard to pay an occasional visit to the theatre. Although it cannot be definitely established that he did so, there is a very strong presumption that he attended plays by

[1] Until the previous November, this had been Racine's own parish. He had now moved a little further east to the Rue des Maçons, in the parish of Saint-Séverin.

other men even if he stayed away from performances of his own.[1]

Not only was Racine constantly performed: his plays were read widely. Among numerous reprintings which appeared in his life-time, the collected editions of 1687 and 1697 are particularly important. He took a sufficiently active interest in them to make corrections in the text of both. This was not the act of a man who had become indifferent to the world's opinion or who had renounced all claim to its praises.

A retired dramatist's continued concern for his reputation is natural enough, and it was to be expected that Racine would keep watch against any debasement of his work in print or on the stage. But he went further than defence. He attacked.

2

He forgave only one of his enemies, the greatest, who died in October 1684. When, three months later, the Academy received Thomas Corneille in his brother's place, it was Racine, as Director, who welcomed him to the Company. His address was an unstinted panegyric of the Great Corneille. He extolled without reservation the virtues of his old rival as the founder of regular tragedy, as a poet, and as a man. In one generous sentence he effaced the criticism which he had flung at him fifteen years before in the Preface to Britannicus.[2] He passed in silence over Corneille's weaknesses and concentrated his praises on his unquestioned qualities. His speech ranks high among the more intelligent tributes paid by one poet to another. In making these public amends, Racine seems to have followed what had become his

[1] La Grange-Chancel asserts that he attended the theatre as late as January 1694. (See below, p. 287). His epigrams and other comments on contemporary plays may have been based on his reading alone, but it is more likely that he saw these plays acted.

[2] Whereas in 1669 Racine had attacked Corneille for causing his heroes to behave and speak out-of-character, he now remarks: "Combien de rois, de princes, de héros de toutes nations nous a-t-il représentés, toujours tels qu'ils doivent l'être, toujours uniformes avec eux-mêmes!"

sincere conviction. In the privacy of his home a few years later, he was encouraging his son Jean-Baptiste to learn passages from Corneille by heart and was holding up for admiration a somewhat obvious conceit coined by the old poet.

But his tolerance was extended to none of the smaller men who were still alive. Pradon he never forgave. In his private correspondence, writing more broadly than he would have done for publication, he seized with amusement on Boileau's suggestion that the homeless troupe of the Comédie Française might ultimately come to rest in the garbage dump at Clignancourt, for "that would be a worthy theatre for the works of M. Pradon". And Racine continues: "I was about to add M. Boursault, but I am too much affected by the marks of friendship which he has so recently shown you to do so. You seem to be making furious progress along the road to perfection. What a lot of people you have forgiven!" (August 1687.)

Racine, on the contrary, continued to sharpen his arrows and to loose them when the occasion inspired him. Not all the epigrams attributed to him can be authentic, but when all those of doubtful authorship are discarded, enough remain to show that he preserved his capacity to sting almost until his last days. His epigram against Pradon's *Germanicus* cannot have been written earlier than 1694, when that tragedy first appeared:

> *Que je plains le destin du grand Germanicus!*
> *Quel fut le prix de ses rares vertus!*
> *Persécuté par le cruel Tibère,*
> *Empoisonné par le traître Pison,*
> *Il ne lui restait plus, pour dernière misère,*
> *Que d'être chanté par Pradon.*

Racine's rancour against Pradon is understandable enough on personal grounds. His contempt for the Abbé Boyer, however, must have sprung originally from the general feeling of irritation which this spectacle of plodding mediocrity aroused in him—to which, however, a more specific cause of jealousy was added shortly after *Athalie*.

Later in the same year, Boyer was called in to write for Saint-Cyr. He chose the sentimental theme of Jephtah sacrificing his daughter, and followed this up in 1695 by a second Biblical play, *Judith*, which he gave to the professional actors. The tragedy had a considerable success and became famous for the 'scene of the handkerchiefs'—so named because the female spectators, seated in serried rows on the stage, wept in unison at one particularly touching point in the story. Meanwhile—according to the anecdote—the old abbé shook his fist in the direction of the box where Racine was sitting and boomed in his Gascon accent: "Je tiengs le public, à préseng que je sais son goût. Ah! Mossieur de Racine!"

Whether Racine was in fact present at this spectacle or not, he certainly read the play, for he wrote to Boileau urging him to read it also and to give his opinion on it, "in spite of your repugnance for bad verse". He also composed an epigram as unflattering for the audiences as for the author, in which he pictured a hard-headed financier weeping bitterly over the death of Boyer's villain, so showing that the whole point of the play had escaped him.[1]

Three years after *Judith*, Boyer was dead. But Racine's implacable irony followed him beyond the grave. This is how, writing to his son Jean-Baptiste just eight months before his own death, he breaks the news of the old dramatist's disappearance:

"As academic news, I must tell you that poor Boyer died the day before yesterday, aged eighty-three or eighty-four, so they say. He is said to have written more than five

[1] *A sa Judith, Boyer, par aventure,*
Etait assis près d'un riche caissier;
Bien aise était, car le bon financier
S'attendrissait et pleurait sans mesure.
"Bon gré vous sais, lui dit le vieux rimeur,
"Le beau vous touche, et ne seriez d'humeur
"A vous saisir pour une baliverne."
Lors le richard, en larmoyant, lui dit:
" Je pleure, hélas, pour ce pauvre Holopherne,
"Si méchamment mis à mort par Judith."

[283]

hundred thousand lines of verse in his life, and I can well believe it because he did nothing else. If it was the present fashion to burn the dead, as the Romans did, he could have had the same funeral as that Cassius Parmenius who needed no other funeral pyre but his own works, which made a very fine blaze. . . . I think that the Abbé Genest will take M. Boyer's place in the Academy. He writes fewer verses, but much better ones."[1]

Another of Racine's victims was Fontenelle, who was a nephew of the Great Corneille. It is tempting to ascribe Racine's hostility towards him to his relationship to the old poet, in spite of the *amende honorable* of 1685; but no certain date can be given to the most cutting of his attacks upon him. His verses *Sur l'Aspar de M. de Fontenelle* were first published in 1692, but they could have been composed at any time after 1680, the year when *Aspar* was produced. These verses, in which Racine also lashes in passing at Pradon and Boyer, are an example of his pawky humour at its best:

> *Ces jours passés, chez un vieil histrion,*
> *Un chroniqueur émut la question*
> *Quand dans Paris commença la méthode*
> *De ces sifflets qui sont tant à la mode.*
> *"Ce fut, dit l'un, aux pièces de Boyer."*
> *Gens pour Pradon voulurent parier.*
> *"Non, dit l'acteur, je sais toute l'histoire,*
> *"Que par degrés je vais vous débrouiller.*
> *"Boyer apprit au parterre à bâiller;*
> *"Quant à Pradon, si j'ai bonne mémoire,*

---

[1] In the same letter he speaks equally laconically of the death of the Champmeslé: "'Poor M. Boyer made a very pious end—and while I am on that subject I must tell you incidentally that I owe an apology to the memory of the Champmeslé, who also died in a fairly devout state of mind, after renouncing the theatre, full of repentance for her past life, but above all very sorry to die. At least that is how M. Despréaux described it to me, having heard it from the curé of Auteuil who was present at the deathbed; for she died at Auteuil in the house of a dancing-master where she had gone for the sake of the fresh air."

"*Pommes sur lui volèrent largement;*
"*Mais quand siffllets prirent commencement,*
"*C'est (j'y jouais, j'en suis témoin fidèle)*
"*C'est à l'*Aspar *du sieur de Fontenelle.*"

In attacking Fontenelle, Racine may have been fighting Boileau's battles as well as his own; he may have been influenced by the Quarrel of the Ancients and the Moderns, which broke out in Academic circles in the late sixteen-eighties. But the fact that he made his attack, not on the critic, but on the dramatist, shows clearly enough where his own interests lay. Had the theatre not still been a living issue to him, he would have engaged the adversary on different ground—or, more probably, would not have troubled about him at all.

3

In ceasing to write for the secular stage, Racine had thus not abandoned his position as the foremost living dramatist. That much is evident and the picture of a totally repentant Racine turning his back on the theatre as soon as he became Historiographer Royal cannot be accepted even as a caricature of the facts. But is it possible to go further and to suspect that he regretted his decision never to write again professionally? Did he, in an attempt to taste the pleasures of authorship by proxy, consider training a disciple to continue his work? Such questions are inevitably raised by a curious relationship which began in the spring of 1691, a few months after *Athalie.*

It was then that he made the acquaintance of a pushing young writer named La Grange-Chancel, who was a page in the household of the Princesse de Conti. Approached by the novice, Racine consented to give an opinion on his first play, and for some time after continued to advise him on his progress. La Grange-Chancel eventually took up three of the retired dramatist's discarded projects, producing an *Oreste et Pylade ou Iphigénie en Tauride* (1697), an

Amasis (1701), and an *Alceste* (1703). For the first he made
the not unlikely claim that its plan had been approved by
Racine. The second had almost the same title as that early
lost tragedy which the young Racine had had rejected by the
Marais. As for the *Alceste*, La Grange-Chancel wrote in his
Preface: "I often heard M. Racine say that of all the
subjects of Antiquity none was more touching than this,
and that he had never produced a play since *Andromaque*
which he did not propose to follow by one on Alcestis."

After asserting that he had heard from Racine's friends
that the poet had actually carried out his intention, but that
shortly before his death he burnt the manuscript, La
Grange-Chancel added: "My reading of Euripides, combined with what I had been able to gather of the ideas
of M. Racine, kindled in me the desire to treat this
subject."

In considering what importance should be attached to
this episode, full allowance must be made for La Grange-
Chancel's character. He is the only witness to a relationship which he had every interest in exploiting to the utmost.
Racine's name in his Prefaces was an excellent advertise-
ment, and he may well have been exaggerating when he
recalled the frequency and warmth of their conversations.
He was, moreover, a Gascon, and not burdened with
modesty. His statement that Racine discerned in his first
play promise of a genius superior both to Corneille's and his
own immediately makes him suspect. The boast is too
obvious a self-puff.

But, when every reasonable discount has been made,
something remains. The whole relationship could not be
an invention. We are no doubt near the truth when we
imagine Racine, a familiar figure at the Prince de Conti's
table, agreeing to read the page's composition in order to
oblige his patrons; then, his interest aroused, beginning to
talk expansively of the old days, expounding his theory of
tragedy and discussing some of the themes over which he
himself had pondered. Only the austerest mind would
deny itself this luxury of reminiscence, while at the same

time satisfying the curiosity of an intelligent admirer. If it is unlikely that Racine ever seriously considered La Grange-Chancel as his pupil and successor, we can hardly deny that he was interested. Perhaps his interest was as much in the contemporary stage in general as in La Grange-Chancel in particular. But, however much the episode is minimized, it at least shows that, even after *Athalie*, Racine had not set his face so sternly against the secular theatre that he would refuse to advise a novice upon his work.

Later, when La Grange-Chancel had tasted success, his references to Racine became perceptibly colder. He no longer claimed that the mantle had fallen upon him but insinuated that, in his own way, he was superior. (His plays enjoyed a certain popularity in a lean period, but only the mention of Racine's name in their Prefaces would persuade the modern reader to take them up.) Finally, he stung his mentor with a remark which carries a faint echo of the master's own style. Describing the success of his tragedy *Jugurtha*, first produced in January 1694, he wrote: "Racine, whose piety no longer allowed him to attend plays since the King had ceased going to them, nevertheless came to this first performance and seemed to derive extreme pleasure from all the applause I received."

4

Other observers also noticed a deepening of Racine's piety at about this date. A number of lampoons, all belonging to the years 1693-6, echo the theme and make the easy accusation of hypocrisy. Since the pious tone of the Court became accentuated in the early sixteen-nineties and the moral standing of the theatre, harassed by its devout enemies, sank to one of its lowest points, Racine's adoption of a more puritanical attitude at that time might seem to be an example of protective colouring. Yet there can be little doubt that in his own mind he was sincere and that he saw no inconsistency between shunning (not *condemning*) public performances of plays and still nursing his old reputation. His conduct in his private life shows that he considered the two things to be separate. In his dealings with his eldest son he was certainly not wearing a mask, even though the arguments which he used to convince him were sometimes illogical.

Racine had set high hopes on Jean-Baptiste. He desired that his first-born should be an *honnête homme*, with a solid background of learning, his worthy successor in the posts which he himself held at Court. But Jean-Baptiste at the age of fifteen was more interested in his father's reputation as a dramatic poet. He read other modern poets, wrote some verses himself and trustingly sent them to his father, who was absent on a campaign. How crushing was Racine's letter in reply:

"I was pleased to have your account of the books you are reading, but I must warn you not to give all your attention to the French poets. Remember that they should only serve for your leisure moments, they should not be part of your real studies. So I could wish that you would sometimes take pleasure in speaking to me of Homer, Quintilian, and other writers of that kind. As for your epigram, I wish that you had never written it. Apart from the fact that it is not very good, I cannot advise you too strongly not to let yourself be carried away by the temptation to write French verse, for it can only serve to waste your time. *Above all, one must not write verses against anyone.*"

The remarks which Racine then makes show that he is oblivious of his own incursions into satire. He foresees that his son might quote, not his example, but that of Boileau. Boileau, he explains, is a unique case, possessing as he does an inspired gift for satire wedded to excellent powers of judgment.

Two years later Jean-Baptiste is taking his first steps at Court, anxiously watched by his father. He now shows a tendency more dangerous than the reading and writing of verse in private.

"You know what I told you about the operas and comedies which they say are to be acted at Marly," Racine writes to him in June 1695. "It is most important for you and for myself that you should not be seen at them, particularly since you are at Versailles to do your training, not to go to all these kinds of amusements. The King and the whole Court know my own scruples against going to them, and they would have a very poor opinion of you if, at your age, you showed so little consideration for me and my feelings. Above everything else, I must urge you always to think of your salvation and not to lose that love of religion which I have noticed in you."

Jean-Baptiste's reply can be guessed. Evidently he agrees not to attend the comedy, but adds some arguments which his father feels obliged to correct:

"I am very grateful for the consideration you show me in this matter of operas and comedies: but you must not mind me telling you that my satisfaction would be more complete if *le bon Dieu* entered a little into your considerations. I realize that you would not be dishonoured before men if you attended them, but do you count it as nothing to dishonour yourself before God? Do you not think yourself that men would find it strange to see you, at your age, practising maxims so different from mine? Remember that M. le duc de Bourgogne, who has a marked taste for all these things, has not yet been to a single play, and is willing to be guided on this point by the people who are responsible for his education. And where will you find people wiser and more highly esteemed than they?"

This skirmish between father and son suggests that in his fifties Racine discarded his tolerant, or at least neutral, attitude towards the theatre and adopted a view consistent with the teaching of the more rigid divines. But this was a relatively late development which did not occur until some fifteen years after *Phèdre*. If its causes were as much social as spiritual, that does not convict Racine of hypocrisy. His tendency was always to be guided by persons rather than by principles and he was betraying no one by following the lead of the public figures whose judgment he respected.

His stricter attitude towards playgoing in the last years of his life need not debar him from continuing to satirize those who still practised the drama. On the contrary, he was likely to become more severe towards them. Charity towards his enemies had never been one of his virtues and advancing age did little to develop it in him.

CHAPTER XX

THE BOURGEOIS YEARS

FAMILY AND RELIGION

RACINE in his fifties was a substantial citizen, far
removed in his outward habit of life from the
highly-strung young author of *Andromaque* and
Britannicus. Marriage had given him a pious,
practical wife and a comfortable bourgeois home established upon an income worth approximately £8,000 to-day.[1] *
He had become the father of seven children of whom the

---

[1] Reckoning the seventeenth-century *livre* at ten shillings. In the year
after his marriage Racine was receiving some 10,000 *livres* from official
sources (6,000 *livres* as Historiographer Royal, 2,400 *livres* as Treasurer
of France at Moulins, and 1,500 *livres* as a man of letters included in
Colbert's pension-list). The interest on his private capital was about
1,000 *livres*. His wife's income was about 5,000 *livres*, made up of 4,100
livres interest on Government stock (*rentes sur les gabelles*) and the
revenue from the Farm of Variville, a small estate which she owned
near her native town of Montdidier, valued at 22,000 *livres* in the
marriage contract. (*See* E. H. de Grouchy: *Documents inédits relatifs à
Jean Racine et à sa famille*. Paris, 1892.)

By 1677, Racine had ceased to derive income from ecclesiastical
livings. His earnings from the theatre also ended with the publication
of *Phèdre*. After publication, a play became public property, the author
receiving no further royalties either from the theatre for revivals or
from the publisher for new editions.

Until 1692, when his Historiographer's salary was cut to 4,000 *livres*,
Racine's income slowly increased. He seems to have received special
grants to meet the expenses of his campaigns. His post of *Gentilhomme
ordinaire du roi*, acquired in December 1690, carried a salary of 2,000
livres. At some unspecified date between 1677 and 1699, his man of
letters' pension was raised from 1,500 to 2,000 *livres*.

eldest, Jean-Baptiste, was born in 1678, and the youngest, Louis, in 1692. Between the two sons were five daughters —less important, no doubt, than the male issue, yet tenderly regarded by their parents. Mirrored in these children, products though they were of a conventional, sheltered environment, are all the features which composed the personality of Jean Racine, not excluding, to a certain degree, his talent. But it is in the two first, the early offspring of his marriage conceived before he was forty, that his image is reflected most clearly.[1]

Jean-Baptiste, as we have seen, was intended for an official career. Using the considerable influences which he possessed at Court, his father secured for him the succession of his own post of Gentlemen of the King's Bedchamber and a place in the office of the Foreign Secretary at Versailles. Here he served for some two and a half years under Colbert's nephew, de Torcy, before going as an attaché to the French Embassy at the Hague. Jean-Baptiste in adolescence bears a striking resemblance to the Jean Racine of the Collège d'Harcourt and of Uzès. He is eager, intelligent, ambitious. He has literary interests, which are carefully curbed by his father, worldly leanings which his father tries to canalize. He is impatient under admonition, and is not, as a young man, so consistent in his piety as his parents would have him, yet he surrenders with practical docility before the material argument. His materialism would even, to the idealist, appear a little startling. When, at the age of twenty, he is informed by letter that his father has been planning a marriage for him with a girl whom he has never seen, but has broken off

[1] The dates of birth of the Racine children were:

Jean-Baptiste	11th November, 1678.
Marie-Catherine	16th May, 1680.
Anne (Nanette)	29th July, 1682.
Elisabeth (Babet)	31st July, 1684.
Jeanne-Nicole-Françoise (Fanchon)	29th November, 1686.
Madeleine (Madelon)	14th March, 1688.
Louis (Lionval)	2nd November, 1692.

negotiations partly on financial grounds and partly because of the bride's volatile temperament, Jean-Baptiste seems to regret the dowry of 84,000 *livres* which has eluded him. His mother has to remark sharply that "it seems that her wealth impressed you a little too much, and that you have not reflected upon what your father wrote to you about her character. Personally," adds Madame Racine, throwing sudden light upon her own tastes, "I had another strong reason for finding her unsuitable—the young lady was red-headed."

If in broad outline Jean-Baptiste recalls his father when young, the coincidence of detail is sometimes astonishing. The son of the man who at Uzès found he could settle to nothing begins to learn German. Two months later he appears to have given it up and receives a lecture on the danger of short-lived enthusiasms. He introduces into his letters new-fangled words like *recruter* (now in the dictionary of the Academy) and is recalled to purism by the Jean Racine who had once dared to coin the word *ensaboté* (which the Academy has not yet recognized). He is exhorted to serve God because "His love is the most *solid* thing in the world; all the rest is indeed frivolous". Such is the advice of the father who had jested with Le Vasseur on M. l'Avocat's insistence on *le solide* and had put in a frivolous plea for a little *creux*. But that was three decades before the virtual enthronement at Versailles of *Votre Solidité*.

Are these examples of coincidence or of dramatic irony? Is any force at work in the background, ensuring that the pattern should repeat itself in reverse? An obvious factor is the father's lack of confidence in his own "solidity". He loves his son humanly—and therein lies the difference between his admonitions and those which he himself received in his youth—but he is anxious that he shall grow up a respected, God-fearing man. Uncertain of the value of his own example, he repeats, almost unchanged, the lessons which he himself was taught. Because he once ignored them, and has since suffered for doing so, they have acquired a greater prestige. In the respectability, the piety, which he preaches to Jean-Baptiste, there is— as we have already seen in the argument which the two had over playgoing—no consuming spiritual flame. Racine speaks to his son with the voice not of fanaticism, but of experience and, since the experience has not been profoundly assimilated, he can only express it in echoes of the warnings which were once showered upon himself.

But not all was an evocation of the past. The voice which had spoken to the author of *The Loves of Ovid* could still speak with earthly lips to the historiographer and to his son. Aunt Agnès is still at Port-Royal. Since 1689 she has been its Abbess. She watches over her nephew's family, a constant reminder of the claims of piety. She is the second factor causing the pattern to repeat itself. For Jean-Baptiste she can do no more than pray as he rides too slowly and too light-heartedly towards the Hague to take up his post under M. de Bonrepaux—stopping in Brussels, not to see the Jansenist Father Quesnel but to go to the Opera ("no doubt with the King's dispatch in your pocket!")—and her prayers can be reported approvingly in letters from Jean Racine. But over the girls of the family she can exercise a more immediate influence.

The eldest, Marie-Catherine, was born in 1680. From the age of sixteen to eighteen she traversed one of those desperate crises of adolescence which can be nearly mortal to a highly sensitive nature. Her religious vocation was clear, but because her constitution was not robust enough for the austerities of a nun's life, her parents were finally obliged to keep her in the world. The father's letters to his son are full of references to her difficulties; in his factual sentences we can follow, almost as though we had her diary, the alternations of hope and despair in her mind. First, she enters the convent of the Carmelites as a novice. In spite of some misgivings, her father sees her already as a nun. But after a few months her health breaks down and she is forced to come home. The next winter she goes to Port-Royal to be with her aunt. She is there simply as a relative, for Port-Royal, fighting the last stage of its losing battle with the Jesuits, is not allowed to receive novices. But even this life is too spartan for her. She has terrible headaches. Her father, knowing that he must soon bring her home, puts off the painful day. He finds it too difficult to insist in face of his daughter's distress. The girl of seventeen, turning desperately in her dilemma, thinks she has found a loophole. If she cannot stay at Port-Royal, perhaps she could enter the nearby Abbey of Gif, where there is no bar to receiving novices. But this is an illusion. The barrier is not the external one of the ban on Port-Royal, but the weakness of her own constitution.

"Your poor eldest sister is in tears, and in the greatest affliction she has ever known in her life. She must separate herself finally from her dear aunt and from the holy women with whom she accounted herself so happy to serve God . . . . She has written me letters which have troubled and torn me beyond description."

When, in the spring of 1698, Marie-Catherine is at last sent home, she puts on with repugnance the simple town clothes waiting for her in her old room. She makes her parents promise never to force her to wear ornaments. A young man, happening to call at the house, pays her some conventional compliment on her good looks. She answers him so sharply that, after he has gone, her father feels obliged to remonstrate with her. He watches her with pity and great gentleness, but the trap is gradually closing. Two months later he notes that she is wearing some small ornaments. "Perhaps her religious vocation will disappear. We must think of establishing her." Her irresolution, accompanied by prostrating headaches, continues all through the summer. Her parents' intention to marry her grows more definite, but a suitable husband is not to be found in a moment. The picturesque—almost the melodramatic—intrudes. Driving out to see Boileau at Auteuil, the family are caught in a thunderstorm. The horses bolt. Marie-Catherine, terrified, opens the door of the coach and flings herself into the road. The footman jumps down and picks her up, soaked and shaken, but otherwise unhurt. A neighbour of Boileau's provides her with dry clothes. Once home, she sleeps for twelve hours at a stretch, and wakes up feeling none the worse. Two months after this she is taken to Melun to see her younger sister Nanette take the veil. She returns in a state of "incredible agitation".

Life is recalcitrant material. It would have been more fitting if poor Marie-Catherine had flung herself from the coach on the return from Melun and had been killed. In fact she was married a few weeks later[1] to Colin de Moramber, a young Parisian barrister, and so became the only one of the five Racine daughters to have a husband and children. She died peacefully at the age of seventy-one, having survived the whole family except Louis.

It would be impossible to determine how much of Marie-Catherine's "agitation" was due to the natural strains of adolescence, how much to the influence of her father and mother, how much to her aunt. Whatever the true character of her religious vocation, it surely betrays at a degree of paroxysm that hypersensitiveness from which her father also suffered when young, and which he now treats with sympathy but also with practical good sense.

After Marie-Catherine, the other children presented few problems. Nanette, aged sixteen when she took her vows with the Ursulines, was of a gentle and equable temperament, and from an early age never varied in her religious vocation or in her physical stamina to follow it out. Babet, two years younger, was more mercurial and Racine would not let his lively, impulsive third daughter commit herself to convent life until her vocation had been thoroughly tested. But she was gaily determined to become a nun, and entered the convent of the Dames de Variville also at the age of sixteen.

The three others were scarcely more than infants during their father's lifetime. Under the ever-practical, ever-watchful eye of Madame Racine, they transformed the

[1] On 7th January 1699.

household into a place where her husband could relax from the cares of Court and the austerities of his hardening conscience. Occasionally there was a frightening episode, as when Fanchon, at the age of eleven, fell into a sudden fit and lay unconscious for two hours. But this forewarning of the physical or mental shadow which seems to have lain across her later life was quickly forgotten, and the little girl soon recovered her liveliness. Her sister Madelon, at the age of ten, strikes Racine as being more worldly than the others. " She reasons on every subject with an intelligence which would surprise you, and is much given to raillery, for which I often have to pull her up." But she too, without entering a convent, devoted her adult life to pious works and quiet days. The apple of Racine's eye is little Lionval or Louis, the male child born in his father's fifty-third year. "He is a very pretty child," writes Racine to Jean-Baptiste, "he learns easily and, although very quick, never gives us the least trouble." And Madame Racine writes, with devastating unsuspected powers of prophecy: "The poor little thing sends you all his love and promises that he will not go to the comedy like you do, for fear of being damned."

Never was the spirit of a childish promise more faithfully kept. How clearly it echoes through the biography which he wrote fifty-three years later, and how easy it is to understand the bias of that work. But if later biographers have been continually led to doubt Louis Racine's objectivity, that is no warrant to doubt his talent. He had a distinguished and varied career, becoming first a barrister, then for a time a priest, before devoting the remainder of his life to learning and letters. He achieved some fame as a sacred poet, but his strongest claim on the attention of English readers is the prose translation of *Paradise Lost* which he published in 1755 and accompanied by a sympathetic account of Milton's life and character. In his admiration for Milton, he ranks him only third to Homer and Virgil among the great epic poets of the world. Tasso he places very far beneath these three.

Louis became a staunch Jansenist, married and had three children, of whom only the daughters survived to prolong the line. The son, whom he had christened Jean and who was the last direct bearer of the Racine name, perished at Cadiz at the age of twenty-one in the tidal wave which followed the great earthquake of Lisbon.

Of Jean-Baptiste Racine, on whom his father had set such hopes, less can be written. Belying the worldly tendencies of his youth, he also became confirmed in his Jansenism. He left the Court soon after his father's death and spent the major part of his life among his books, studying much but producing nothing. Had his great father cast his shadow too closely over him, or had he, with the Racinian impatience, driven him too hard when what he needed was time and space in which to mature?

2

Just outside Racine's immediate family circle were his relatives at La Ferté-Milon and his wife's relatives at Montdidier. He lived on cordial terms with both these homely provincial groups, sent his children to stay with them, and was always ready to give them a helping hand.

His sister Marie was now Madame Rivière. A year before her brother's marriage she had married a doctor at La Ferté who was also an official in the salt-tax office. Now, comfortably provided for and unambitious for herself, she sends rabbits and other country produce to the Paris-dwelling Racines, prepares in a flutter of importance for the visits which they pay her in their fine coach, and acts as an agent for the small charities which her brother distributes among his poor connexions. Occasionally, his generosity is abused. "Cousin Henri has been here, dressed in rags," he writes to her. "He told my wife, in front of all our servants, that he was my cousin. You know that I do not disown my relatives and that I try to help them, but I must say that it is a little rough that a man who has put himself into that state by his debauches and his loose behaviour should come here and make us blush for his beggarly appearance. I spoke to him as he deserved, and told him that you would see that he went short of nothing if he proved worth your trouble, but that he drank everything that you had the charity to give him. Still, I did give him something to get home with. Will you please help him also, in a quiet way, but as though it came from you?"

In spite of their years of separation, brother and sister understand each other perfectly. She is more careful of his money than he is himself. And, as their correspondence shows, he treats her and her husband with an affectionate courtesy in which there is not a particle of condescension. His relations with the Romanet family at Montdidier were similar, though necessarily a little more formal. As to the Vitarts, Marguerite has been, almost inevitably, the god-mother of the Racines' first child, Jean-Baptiste. As long as she lived, it is certain that she was a constant visitor to their house. Nicolas Vitart died in 1683, at the age of fifty-seven.

While the links of the middle-class family were strong, and were accepted without question by Racine, most of his chosen friends were of a different stamp. He was on terms hardly distinguishable from personal friendship with some of the great, among them the Princes of Condé and Conti, the de Noailles family, the Dukes of Luxembourg, Chevreuse and Beauvilliers; with the high officials—men like Pontchartrain, the Comptroller-General of Finance, and de Chamlay, Marshal of the Armies; with such women as Madame de Maintenon, Madame de Caylus—who ever since *Esther* had remained his friend—and Elizabeth Hamilton, Comtesse de Gramont, who extended a warm Irish affection not only to Racine and Jean-Baptiste, but also to the outcast community of Port-Royal. It might be thought that some of these cultivated the poet Racine for the wit and charm of his conversation—La Grange-Chancel relates that Conti's son kept a notebook beside him to take down Racine's table-talk—but it is clear that the affection which he inspired in them was more solid than this. He needed neither to fawn nor to sparkle in order to be appreciated, and indeed loved.

He was at home with several different conditions of men. One of his closest friendships was for the Marquis de Cavoie, an important figure in the King's Household who had been his constant companion ever since they had met during the campaign of Gand. In 1698 Cavoie was living "only two steps away" from the Racine home in the Rue des Marais. His wife, a former Maid of Honour of the Queen, was not above accepting homely recipes from Madame Racine.

Other familiar friends were the royal physicians Félix, Dodart, and even Fagon. (Fagon prescribed for little Fanchon Racine after her fit, but she refused to take his remedy until forced to do so by her mother.) He was on excellent terms with such men as Besset de la Chapelle, man of letters and Comptroller of the King's Buildings, with the Abbé Renaudot, grandson of the founder of the *Gazette de France* and its then editor, with Madame de la Sablière's brother, Hessein, with Valincour, his own protégé—another worldly figure—as well as with men of declared piety, such as his sober Jansenist neighbour Willard.

The common denominator of this last group, who seem to have formed his intimate circle, was that all, or nearly all, were professional men, living by medicine, by letters, or by some administrative employment. If they frequented the Court, it was usually by way of business. They were neither of noble blood, nor—although they had attained a certain distinction—were they the most eminent minds of the time. But they were excellent companions, dependable, tolerant, and humorous. The fact that the middle-aged Racine found such pleasure in their company points to a certain mellowing of his character and to a gift for easy friendship which was by no means an inevitable development from his younger days. The man who could describe with innocent glee the unusual billets allotted him during the campaign of Mons, and draw from Boileau the comment: "I am delighted to hear that you are in a convent—and in the same cell as M. de Cavoie. Although you must be rather cramped, I do not imagine that the rules will be kept too strictly", is not a misanthropic or a sanctimonious figure. This is not the Racine of austere Port-Royal, neither is it the acidulous man of letters. It is the Racine who once drank with Poignant and La Fontaine and who, whatever the bitterness of his written attacks on his opponents, rarely seems to have lost a personal friend.

3

Boileau who, together with Cavoie, was Racine's closest companion during the latter part of his life, falls into a special category. Since the two maintained a considerable correspondence, much of which has been preserved, it is easy to determine the nature of the relationship. It extended beyond the two individuals to include the whole Racine family. Whether the younger children are spending a carefree day at Boileau's little house at Auteuil, or Jean-Baptiste is seeking his guidance on literary matters, Despréaux always appears as a trusted and well-liked figure. Racine's own regard for him reveals itself on many occasions, particularly in the summer of 1687 when his friend, having temporarily lost his voice, has gone to Bourbon in the hope of a cure. So concerned is Racine that he transmits conflicting advice from every physician he is able to consult and adds to the confusion by proposing remedies of his own. From this time on, health and medicines figure frequently in their correspondence. One can trace in it the rise and decline of the fashionable cures and their sponsors. For some time the English Doctor Smith and his quinquina hold the field. While respecting the drug, Racine is disappointed in the man. "Chmith [so he writes it] has a red and pimply face and looks more like an innkeeper than a doctor." After this it is Helvetius and ipecacuanha. Before that it was erisymum. But while the experimental nature of these remedies is recognized, the proved old prescriptions of purging and bleeding are always resorted to in dangerous cases and accepted without challenge. "I am not entirely free from my colic," writes Racine in self-reproach, "yet I am still putting off purging myself."

The two poets have a more intellectual bond in their literary compositions. They ask for each other's opinions on the rare verses they write. Racine receives fragments or drafts of the misogynic *Satire des femmes* and of the *Ode sur la prise de Namur*. He shows his practical interest in the first by suggesting that Boileau should interpolate some flattering mention of Madame de Maintenon and so make it clear that he excludes her from his general condemnation of the sex. Having read a draft of the ode, he urges Boileau to omit an uncomplimentary reference to Fontenelle, who —he has discovered—is highly esteemed by the younger Pontchartrain, son of his influential friend the Comptroller-General.

On his side, Racine submits the third of his *Cantiques spirituels* to his friend's criticism. He rejects some of Boileau's suggestions, and adopts others, though not without argument. The four *Cantiques spirituels*, which were published, and probably all composed, in 1694, were the last verses that he is known to have written, with the exception of one or two of his epigrams. They are based on various passages in St. Paul, the Prophets, and the Book of Wisdom. Moreau, who had already performed the same office for the choruses of *Esther* and *Athalie*, set them to music to be sung at Court, no doubt on Madame de Maintenon's suggestion. They are the most limpid and moving of Racine's sacred poems and, together with his earlier *Hymnes du Bréviaire romain*[1] and his isolated *Ode tirée du* * *Psaume XVII*, they complete the body of his religious verse.

[1] The date of composition of the *Hymnes* cannot be determined exactly. Le Tourneux's *Breviary*, a collection of translations by several hands of which Racine's was only one, was published in 1687, but Le Tourneux had obtained a *privilège*, or licence to print, as early as 1675, at which date it would be supposed that the whole contents of the book were already in existence. Or had Racine at that date merely undertaken, but

In the Racine-Boileau partnership, Racine was still the leading member. With maturing years and increasing success, the satirist withdrew further into his shell, influenced in part by his deafness, and his comments on the outside world acquired a sourer and blunter tone than his friend's. Racine was left to carry the main burden of the King's history, of which there is little mention in their correspondence and only one indication—at a relatively early date—that Boileau worked on it at all.[1] In fact, his chief and perhaps only finished contribution was the *Ode sur la prise sur Namur*. It is Racine who, between campaigns, combs Versailles, Marly, and Fontainebleau for informants who can shed new light on his subject, displays a constant interest in current events, and even asks his son, at the time when he is working in de Torcy's office, to keep him posted in the latest news. It is Racine also who pays court to Louis and Madame de Maintenon in Boileau's interest as well as his own, negotiates all their common affairs and even uses his influence on behalf of Boileau's relatives. While the satirist is growing physically isolated and mentally stagnant, Racine is as active, as alert, as nervous as ever. This may explain the tone of slight mockery which sometimes creeps into his style when he writes of Boileau, and which he never uses when speaking of other close friends like Cavoie.

Yet, in spite of an occasional smile at Boileau's eccentricities, Racine never lost his respect for his solidity, or ceased to have a warm personal regard for him. Their point of view was similar enough for them to be agreed on all major issues, while circumstances, as well as choice,

---

not executed, his commission? Should his collaboration in a "sacred" publication while still in his "profane" period be connected in any way with a lingering jealousy of Corneille, whose translation of all the Hymns from the Roman Breviary appeared in 1670?

[1] On 9th August 1687, he writes to Racine from Bourbon: "I have already formed my plan for the year 1667, where I can see a fine field for wit opening up, but, to be quite frank with you, you must not place any great reliance on me so long as I have to drink twelve glasses of spa water every morning."

had given them a common material interest. The blow which befell them in 1692, to which we have referred in an earlier chapter,[1] showed that, as they were associated in their successes, they were also associated in their set-backs. When they were first appointed Historiographers Royal, they had received a basic annual salary of 12,000 *livres*, divided equally between them. The effect of the decision of 1692 was to cut this total by half, Racine receiving 4,000 *livres* while Boileau's share fell to 2,000. This drastic reduction may have had more than one cause. It may have reflected a feeling of the King or of his advisers that the two historians were not producing very much for their money. It may also have been part of the new drive for economy dictated by the declining military fortunes of France. But it is impossible not to connect it primarily with the sudden boom in the fortunes of Donneau de Visé. That persistent wire-puller had prospered greatly as the founder (and, since 1681, the co-editor with Thomas Corneille), of the *Mercure Galant*. Using his monthly miscellany of social and literary information as only a born *rédacteur mondain* crossed with a smart businessman could, de Visé proceeded by shrewd puffs and nicely calculated attacks to an official pension of 6,000 *livres* for his services to literature. But that, granted him in 1684, was only the first stage. Five years later the sum was doubled and soon afterwards he found himself in possession of a free apart-ment in the Louvre and the title of *historiographe du Roi*.

It must have been a bitter blow to Racine and Boileau to share their title with such a man, and no less bitter to see the 6,000 *livres* of which they had been shorn finding their way into his pocket. But they had to bow to the superior force of intrigue. The only hint in their corres-pondence that Racine, at least, did not accept the blow passively, comes in a letter which he wrote, in August 1693, from Marly. To that exclusive little centre of influence, to which only a few chosen courtiers are invited, news has come of the crushing victory won by French

[1] *See* p. 163.

arms at Neerwinden. Having worked far into the night to collect reliable reports of the battle, Racine transmits them to Boileau and to his friend Renaudot for publication in the *Gazette*, and then adds lightly: "This morning I will excite Monsieur de Croissy to prevent, if he can, the miserable *Mercure Galant* from disfiguring our victory."

4

Perhaps the strongest bond between the two men was their common devotion to Jansenism. For many years Boileau had declined to commit himself, and in his published work he always upheld the right of a sincere and reasonable man to pick his friends where he chose, without reference to their theology.[1] But the religious intolerance of the declining century demanded a more exclusive conformism, and Boileau's open admiration of the Great Arnauld was interpreted as a commitment which the spirit of defiance urged him to accept. Three-quarters a Jansenist for the world, in his private correspondence he was even rounder in his preference.

Racine, on the other hand, was considerably more circumspect in his declarations, but more deeply engaged by his acts. There could, of course, be no concealment of his family tie with Port-Royal, and he attempted none. His aunt was the Abbess of the convent and he drove openly in his coach to perform his devotions there, left his daughters in her care, and, in the case of Marie-Catherine, would not have opposed her entering Port-Royal as a nun, had it been a practical possibility. When he was called upon to help the Abbey, he did so equally openly. In particular, he conducted the long-drawn and difficult

---

[1] *See* his *Epître X* (1695):

> . . . *de tant d'écrivains de l'école d'Ignace*
> *Etant, comme je suis, ami si déclaré,*
> *Ce docteur toutefois si craint, si révéré,*
> *Qui contre eux de sa plume épuisa l'énergie,*
> *Arnauld, le grand Arnauld, fit mon apologie.*

negotiations of 1694-6 whose object was to secure the appointment of a new Superior sympathetic to the original aims of the Order. To do this, he had to deal on delicate ground with two successive Archbishops of Paris—first the antagonistic de Harlay, then, after his death, the more sympathetic de Noailles—and it says as much for his courage as for his diplomacy that he dealt with them successfully. For Port-Royal was already doomed, and indeed had been so since the day in 1679 when its protectress, the Duchess of Longueville, had died. Slowly but remorselessly the Jesuits pressed home their advantage. Cut off from its only source of renewal by the prohibition on novices and deprived one by one of its champions and patrons, the convent languished helplessly. The old nuns grew too feeble for the manual work of the community, sickened and died. Finally, by 1709, less than a score of them remained. These were taken out and dispersed among alien convents. In the following year, the Abbey buildings were razed to the ground by royal order, and, as a final act of physical annihilation, the bodies of those who lay there were exhumed and taken elsewhere for re-burial. Among them was Racine's.

A man so sensitive to trends of policy must have realized some years before his death that the Abbey's position was hopeless. But this did not prevent him from following up his negotiations over the new Superior with the drafting of a memorandum for de Noailles in which the rights of the nuns of Port-Royal des Champs were defended against the claims of the renegade Paris house. In all this he acts with the indomitable spirit of his aunt, though with more suppleness than she could ever have shown.

But in his dealings with the Jansenist divines, who were in exile or in nominal hiding, Racine followed a more secretive course. He corresponded regularly both with Arnauld and with Quesnel, who were in the Netherlands, and whom, since the reconciliation, he had treated with affectionate respect. He acted as intermediary in an unsuccessful attempt to negotiate Arnauld's return to

France in 1694, a few months before the old theologian's
death. He encouraged Jean-Baptiste to get into touch with
Quesnel when, four years later, his duties took him to the
Hague. But he was constantly aware of the risks which he
was running, and observed great caution in his communica-
tions with the exiles.[1] He enjoined even greater caution
upon his son, and never mentioned by name the men who
occupied so prominent a place in the minds of both of them.
It was no doubt more dangerous to be suspected of com-
plicity with these great figures living clandestinely than to
be known to visit the Abbey which still existed openly and
which had little power of diffusing heretical ideas. The
theologians, rather than a dwindling community of simple
nuns, were the first target of the Jesuits' hate. While
Racine writes plainly, in letters which he knows may be
intercepted, of his daughter's presence at Port-Royal, he
ciphers Quesnel as "that very saintly and learned ecclesiastic
who is not far from the country where you are".

With Nicole, who had been allowed to remain in Paris
living quietly in his house in the Place du Puits-l'Hermite,
his relationship was closer. He frequently visited the man
whose arguments he had once lacerated in the *Lettres à
l'auteur des Hérésies imaginaires*, and whom he now calls
"one of the best friends I have in the world". His main
concern was, not for Nicole's doctrine, but for his health,
which was precarious for some time before his death in

---

[1] After Arnauld's death, however, he acted more boldly. Either
feeling that secrecy was no longer necessary, or not caring, in his grief,
whether it was or not, he openly attended a memorial service at Port-
Royal. A contemporary rhyme describes how he alone dared to pay
this public homage to the old Jansenist:

> Au service d'Arnauld tout Paris fut prié,
> Aucun n'y fut par politique,
> Comme si le défunt était un hérétique.
> Racine, qui fut convié,
> Assista seul à ce service.
> Lecteur, n'en soyez pas surpris:
> C'est le seul de nos beaux esprits
> Qui connaît le mérite et qui lui rend justice.

1695-6. He quotes to Jean-Baptiste neither Nicole on the Theatre nor Nicole on Grace, but as the author of a country-wise saying on the virtues of economy.

As to the saintly Hamon, he had died in 1687 and no trace remains of any dealings which Racine may have had with him. But it would be strange if the two had not met again in the ten years which had passed since Racine's renunciation of the theatre.

But his admiration for the Jansenist divines did not debar him from appreciating the company of certain Jesuits. The world of letters in which he continued to move was—no less than the world of the Court—full of cultured Jesuits whom only a fanatic or a misanthrope could have avoided altogether. He was on excellent terms with two men who must have been representative of a larger number, Father Bouhours and Father Rapin. These two were sitting one day in Racine's study when a letter arrived from the ailing Boileau at Bourbon.

"I read it to them as soon as I opened it," Racine relates to his friend, "and so gave them very great pleasure. But I looked well ahead while I was reading, to see that there was nothing too Jansenistic in it. Towards the end I saw the name of M. Nicole and I skipped it boldly—or perhaps I should say, weakly. I dared not risk spoiling the great enjoyment and even the bursts of laughter with which they greeted some of the amusing things which you wrote to me . . . . Both of them, I assure you, are your very good friends and, besides this, they are excellent people." (5th September 1687.)

Nine years later, when it might be thought that a more sombre Racine would have adopted a more exclusive Jansenism, he hears that his reputation has been attacked by a teacher in a Jesuit college and expresses his surprise that the Jesuits should have declared war on him. But the same Father Bouhours who had laughed so heartily over Boileau's letter has been able to assure him that the zealous teacher has been reprimanded by his superiors. And Racine easily forgives his detractor "for the sake of so many other

Reverend Fathers whose qualities I esteem, and particularly for the sake of the Reverend Père de la Chaise, who does me a thousand kindnesses every day and in consideration for whom I would overlook many more insults".

To incur the enmity of Louis XIV's confessor would have been as fatal as to incur that of Madame de Maintenon and no man in Racine's position, with his family responsibilities and his ambitions for Jean-Baptiste, would lightly have risked doing so. It is unrealistic and unnecessary to inquire how far policy entered into Racine's apparent respect for the Père de la Chaise. But the fact that he was useful to him is no reason why he should not also have admired him for his character. De la Chaise's goodwill towards Racine continued at least until April 1696—the date of the letter just quoted. After that there was a cooling-off, in which Boileau was included on the grounds of the unorthodoxy of his *Epître sur l'amour de Dieu*.

Looking into the tangle of empirical opinions and shifting interests which compose the intricate problem of Racine's religion, one main conclusion emerges. His respect was for persons rather than for dogma. All Jansenists were likely to be good because they belonged to the world of his boyhood or had a link with him through his family. But some Jesuits might also be good and he was prepared to let them prove themselves so by their attitude towards him and their own integrity. That he was uninterested in the great issues of theology is shown both by his choice of friends and by his religious writings. These latter reveal no search for fundamental causes. God is good, is their theme; the wicked will be punished and the just rewarded. If that is Jansenism, it has become so simplified in Racine's hands that it is indistinguishable from orthodoxy. But the complicated questions of predestination, of grace and of divine justice, which troubled more subtly religious minds, never seem to have preoccupied him. His approach to such questions is humanistic: he looks first, not at the opinion but at the man who holds it. In this, the ageing Racine is consistent with the youthful Racine. If he returns to Arnauld, Nicole, and his aunt it is because he is a Port-Royalist, not because he is a Jansenist.

Racine's most loving service to his old masters was no doubt the *Abrégé de l'histoire de Port-Royal* which he had begun writing by 1693. It is a defence and vindication of the Community written by an intelligent partisan. Its method is to describe persons and events, with frequent use of the relevant anecdote. Theology is expounded in it no further than is necessary to explain the events. The Community is founded, is attacked, triumphs, is attacked again by certain ecclesiastics—so the tale unfolds. But there is no discussion of the deeper issues behind the struggle. Either Racine was not aware of them, or he was disinclined to explore them. His resolutely factual study is as innocent of true theology as the historical books of the Old Testament. Having assumed that God Is and that these are His People he inquires no further.

His humanistic attitude reappears in quite a different context. Towards the end of his life he became friendly with Fénelon—as he was also on terms of friendship with Bossuet and Cardinal de Noailles. The acquaintance may have been made through Madame de Maintenon's circle, through Saint-Cyr or through the Dukes of Chevreuse and Beauvilliers—with all of these Fénelon, like Racine, was linked. What is certain is that by June 1695, Racine was holding up for Jean-Baptiste's guidance and admiration the tutors of the young Duc de Bourgogne, of whom Fénelon was one. Fénelon then fell under the influence of Madame Guyon, embraced the doctrine of Quietism, was disgraced and exiled from Versailles to his diocese of Cambrai. But Racine continued to cherish his friendship. Three months after the appearance of the book with which Fénelon sealed his downfall, Racine was writing to his son: "The friendship which M. de Cambrai had for me does not allow me to be indifferent to matters which concern him, and I could wish with all my heart that a prelate of such virtue and merit had never written a book which has brought so much trouble upon him."

The Quietist teaching which Fénelon's book expounded was as opposed to Jansenism as any doctrine stemming nominally from orthodox Catholicism could be. It was presently to involve its author in a bitter controversy with the remaining Jansenist theologians. But we should never learn this from Racine. He deplores the *Explication des maximes des saints* purely on the grounds that the book has involved his friend in trouble.

From the doctrinal point of view, Racine's religion is inconsistent, or at least inadequate. From the human point of view, it needs no defending. He has chosen or accepted his friends, he remains loyal to them, he tries to help them by every practical means in his power. Had he been more rigid on matters of principle, he would not have been— the word is used in his praise by both Boileau and Arnauld— so *effective*.

CHAPTER XXI

THE LAST PHASE

RACINE'S preoccupation with material questions, together with his personal loyalty to Port-Royal, were jointly responsible for the disfavour which he incurred in the last year of his life. It was not irrevocable; it seems to have passed in a few months; but he was not to end his days without seeing at least the shadow of the royal displeasure.

At the beginning of 1698 Racine found himself in a difficult financial position. The middle years of his married life had been prosperous enough. By 1688 he had accumulated sufficient capital to make a loan of 22,000 *livres* to his patron Chevreuse, followed by loans to Boileau of 10,000 *livres* and 3,000 *livres* in 1689 and 1695 respectively. If his historiographer's salary was reduced in 1692, this loss was compensated by the revenue from his post of *Gentilhomme ordinaire du roi*, which he had acquired at the end of 1690 at the cost of 10,000 *livres*. He then went on to purchase the post of *Conseiller secrétaire du roi* which, although it increased both his income and his social status, was in other ways an unlucky acquisition. It cost him 50,000 *livres* when he obtained it early in 1696, and he had hardly recovered from this considerable disbursement when he was faced with several other heavy calls on his purse. Nanette's entry into the Ursulines, Marie-Catherine's marriage and Jean-Baptiste's promotion to the Embassy at the Hague—all occurring in the winter of 1697-8—cost him in all another forty to fifty thousand *livres*.[1]

---

[1] On entering the convent, Nanette received a 'dowry' of 5,000 *livres* and a life annuity of 200 *livres*. Marie-Catherine's marriage dowry

It was at this date that the officials of the Treasury, casting about for ways of restoring the depleted finances of the country, levied a heavy tax on the office of *Conseiller secrétaire*. Racine was required to find more than 10,000 *livres* at short notice. While it must not be supposed that his resources were exhausted, he did not have the money available in cash and was obliged to borrow it from his lawyer.[1]

Having paid, he took a step which seemed reasonable enough in the circumstances. He petitioned the King, through Madame de Maintenon, to consent to a remittance or a reduction of the tax. There was no reply. He then wrote the letter to Madame de Maintenon which tells the whole story of his 'disgrace' and of his state of mind at the time. Though necessarily obscure on certain points, it nevertheless gives the only reliable indication of what had actually occurred.

"I had taken the liberty of writing to you, Madame, about the tax which has so greatly complicated my small affairs; but not being satisfied with my letter, I drew up [instead] a memorandum, with the idea of begging you to present it to His Majesty. The Maréchal de Noailles generously offered to put it into your hands but, not having found an opportunity of speaking to you, he gave it to the Archbishop (i.e. the Cardinal de Noailles), who can tell you that I had not even mentioned it to him and that for two months before I had not even had the honour of seeing him.

---

amounted to 30,000 *livres*. The expenses of Jean-Baptiste's equipment, journey and allowances in his new post must have totalled several thousand *livres* in a few months.

[1] *See* two of his letters to Jean-Baptiste:

"I will write to you more fully on my return from Marly, since to-day I am overwhelmed with business concerning the money which I have to pay for my tax." (31st January 1698.)

"To-morrow I shall pay the ten thousand francs still owing on my tax; these ten thousand francs have been lent me by M. Galloys." (13th February 1698.)

After a few days, having heard nothing more of this memorandum, I requested the Comtesse de Gramont, who was going to Saint-Germain with you, to ask whether the King had read it, and whether you had had any favourable answer. That, Madame, is the plain truth of my behaviour in this business. But now I find that I have a far more terrible affair on my hands, and that the King has been led to believe that I am a Jansenist. I must confess that, when I caused there to be so much singing in *Esther* about

Rois, chassez la calomnie,

I hardly expected that I should myself be attacked by calumny one day. I realize that, in the King's mind, a Jansenist is at the same time a cabal-man and a rebel against the Church.

"Be so good as to remember, Madame, how often you have said that the best quality that you found in me was a childlike submission to all that the Church believes and commands, even in the smallest things. I have written, on your order, nearly three thousand lines of verse on subjects of piety; can you doubt that I wrote them from the fullness of my heart, or that the feelings which I expressed in them were those which I held most dear? And has it ever been reported to you that a single passage has been found in them which even approaches error and all that is called Jansenism? As for the cabal, who might not be accused of it if they accuse a man as devoted to the King as I am; a man who spends his life thinking of the King, gathering information about the noble actions of the King, and inspiring others with the feelings of love and admiration which he has for the King? I can safely say that the great nobles have sought my company far more than I have sought theirs; but, in whatever company I have found myself, God has given me grace never to be ashamed either of the King or of the Gospel. There are witnesses still living who could tell you with what zeal I have often been heard combating the little grievances which sometimes arise in the minds of those whom the King has loaded the most generously with his favours. Well now, Madame, with what sincerity shall I be able to testify to posterity that this great prince never tolerated false reports against persons who were quite unknown to him, if I must myself suffer so sad an experience of the contrary?

"But I know what may have given rise to so unjust an accusation. I have an aunt who is the Superior of Port-Royal,[1] and towards whom I think I have infinite obligations. It was she who taught me to know God in my childhood, and it was she also whom God used to save me from the disorders and misery in which I was plunged for fifteen years. I learned, about two years ago, that she had been accused of disobedience—as though she had received nuns in the convent in spite of the interdiction which had been placed upon her house. I even learned that there was talk of removing from those poor women the few possessions they had in order to subsidize the wild extravagance of the Abbess of Port-Royal de Paris. Could I, without being the lowest of men, refuse her my poor assistance in that hour of need? But to whom, Madame, did I have recourse in my attempt to help her? I went to the Père de la Chaise and placed before him all that I knew of the state of that house, both in things temporal and spiritual. I cannot venture to believe that I convinced him; but at least he appeared well satisfied with my openness and assured me, as he embraced me, that as long as he lived he would be my servant and friend. Happily, my testimony was confirmed by the Archbishop's Grand Vicar, by two Benedictine monks who were sent to visit the house—one of whom was the Superior of Port-Royal de Paris—and finally by the special confessors who were placed in it—all people as far removed from Jansenism as the heavens are from the earth. They came back saying, some, that they had seen nuns who lived like angels, and others, that they had seen the very sanctuary of the faith. The Archbishop, who [also] desired to see things for himself, did not hesitate to say that he had no nuns in his diocese more orthodox or more submissive to

[1] She was the Abbess or Mother-Superior.

his authority. That is the whole of my Jansenism. I have said the same things as those Doctors of the Sorbonne, as those Benedictines, and finally as my own Archbishop. Moreover, I can swear to you before God that I do not know or frequent any man who might be suspect of the slightest new opinion. I spend my days as quietly as I can in my own home, and practically never go into society except when I am at Marly. I do assure you, Madame, that the condition in which I find myself is most deserving of the compassion which I know you have always had for the unfortunate. I am deprived of the honour of seeing you; I hardly dare to count any longer upon your protection, which yet is the only protection that I have striven to merit. I hoped at least to find my consolation in my work; but I ask you to judge how bitter that work will be made by the thought that this same great prince, with whom my thoughts are continually occupied, perhaps considers me as a man more deserving of his anger than of his kindness.

> I am, with profound respect, your most
> humble and obedient servant,
>
> RACINE.''

The draft of this letter, which alone survives, is dated ''Marly, 4th March.'' It is a revealing and, in some respects, a * bold and ill-advised document. In the situation as he sees it, Racine judges it necessary to clear himself of two charges: first, of having been concerned in a cabal with some of the great nobles, and second, of being a Jansenist beyond the point of his open connection with Port-Royal. He hints at the hostility of the Père de la Chaise, who now appears to have turned against him. He makes it clear that he is temporarily denied access both to the King and to Madame de Maintenon. Finally, it may be deduced from various passages of the letter, and particularly from the opening lines, that he suspects that he has wearied the patience of the King by his earlier *démarches* on behalf of Port-Royal, and finds, now that he wishes to ask something for himself, that his request is arbitrarily related to his championship

[316]

of Port-Royal and the whole built up into an accusation of subversive Jansenism.

All this is consistent and accords with what we know of Racine's character and circumstances. But it does not accord with Louis Racine's more dramatic account of his father's 'disgrace'.

Louis Racine relates, with much circumstantial detail, how his father, acting on the request of Madame de Maintenon, drew up a confidential memorandum on the sufferings of the common people. By an unhappy accident, the memorandum fell into the hands of the King, who was indignant that the poet should presume to have an opinion on such delicate political matters. Racine, advised by Madame de Maintenon to avoid the King for the time being, magnified the disfavour in which he had fallen with the monarch whom he idolized, and fell ill. It was the starting point of the malady which was to kill him some twelve months later.

The question of the remission of the tax on his father's office is now introduced by Louis Racine, but as a subsidiary matter. He quotes a shortened version of the draft letter to Madame de Maintenon, from which he omits each one of Racine's open denials of Jansenism. He then describes a furtive meeting in the Park of Versailles between his father and Madame de Maintenon. "Give the cloud time to pass," she tells him. "I will bring back the fine weather." And, when he refuses to be consoled: "Do you doubt my goodwill or my influence?" "Neither," he tells her in effect, "but I have an aunt who prays continually that I should receive humiliations and undergo penance. Her influence with God is greater." At this moment, the wheels of the King's calèche are heard on the gravel. "Hide, quickly!" cries Madame de Maintenon, and Racine is obliged to conceal himself among the trees.

From then on, his health declines rapidly and, although he is eventually readmitted into the King's presence, he ceases to find any pleasure at Court.

What value can be attached to this colourful story? The

most scrupulous of Racine's biographers, Paul Mesnard, concluded, after a careful summing-up, that it is true in its essentials, including the scene at Versailles. But it is so detailed and so confidently told that if it is incorrect on any one point we are led to distrust it on all. Clearly there has been some tampering with Racine's attitude to Jansenism. The bold allusion to Aunt Agnès, which his son attributes to him in the interview in the park, corresponds to the omission of his denials of Jansenism from the letter. On the dates, his illness might have been provoked by anxiety over the King's reactions, but the evidence—as we shall find when we come to examine it—hardly points to that conclusion. Finally, as has often been pointed out, Racine continued to go to Marly, to which only the inner Court were invited, during the whole time he is supposed to have been in disfavour.

As to the memorandum on the sufferings of the common people, its existence can neither be proved nor disproved. A single hint which might relate to it occurs in a letter which Racine wrote to Boileau from Fontainebleau on 8th October 1697:

"I have not made much progress on the memorandum which you mention. I am even afraid that I have entered into details which would make it much longer than I thought. Besides, you know how distracting it is to work in this place."

If we look at Racine's letters to Jean-Baptiste during the crucial period, we find a strong preoccupation with financial matters coupled with injunctions to economy, and we can also detect a certain shortness of temper in January and February which dies away in the succeeding months. A sort of diary can be compiled by extracting from the letters those items which have a particular bearing on the question.

27th February. I have been rather unwell the last few days, but nothing came of it.

4th March. Letter to Madame de Maintenon.

10th March. [Apropos of Jansenists.] Letters may be seen and you must write with great caution on certain subjects.

16th March. Am going to-morrow to see Marie-Catherine at Port-Royal. Will sleep that night at Versailles and go on Wednesday to Marly.

14th April. Have been (again) at Marly—left on the 12th.

[Racine tentatively suggests that Jean-Baptiste might enter into contact with certain "very virtuous ecclesiastics" in Holland.]

25th April. Have been very indisposed since I last wrote. Heavy cold, rheumatism in back, slight erysipelas on the stomach.

You will not be sorry to hear that Rousseau, the usher of the King's chamber, has been put in the Bastille. He had given up saluting me and always wanted to shut the door in my face when I went to see the King.

There has been an outcry over the nomination of the new Bishop of Poitiers. Deplorable, not only for the two-day Bishop, but much more for his protector, the Père de la Chaise, who has had the chagrin of seeing his work undone in conditions of such public scandal.

3rd May. Still at home with erysipelas. Am enjoying the rest and wish I could go on living this quiet life.

16th May. Better. Have been out to visit personal friends.

[This is a cheerful letter. Racine shakes his head over the impenitence of the dying Champmeslé, but recounts a "strange affair" at Versailles, in which two gentlemen kicked each other in the back " by mistake".]

5th June. Am at Versailles.

16th June. Have been at Marly. Left on the 14th.

24th July. My health is fairly good but the heat exhausts me. The time is coming when I shall have to think of retiring. I take more and more pleasure in home life. I do not think I will go to Compiègne [to witness a review of troops], but will reserve myself for Fontainebleau.

1st August. Have definitely decided not to go to Compiègne, where I should have little opportunity to pay my court. The King would always be on horseback, and I should never be.

These letters deflate the romanticism of Louis Racine's version. They show Racine going openly to Port-Royal but maintaining his cautious attitude towards the exiled Jansenists, in entire consistence with his letter to Madame de Maintenon. They betray a certain spite against the Père de la Chaise and the royal usher. They record an illness and a growing disinclination for the fatigues of the Court. But they contain no hint of such a blow as Louis Racine suggests. If Racine had been heartbroken by the attitude of the King, it is true that he would not have written of it openly, but some trace of his disappointment would surely have appeared in the tone of these intimate letters. Neither here nor elsewhere in the familiar correspondence of his fifties is there any sign of a personal affection for Louis XIV. The conventional admiration of his public utterances is a different matter.

No. Racine's 'disgrace' seems to have consisted of a temporary financial setback, of a temporary and relative loss of the royal favour engineered by the faction of the Père de la Chaise and—concurrent with this but independent in its causes—an illness which makes his thoughts turn to a quieter life in the peace of his own home. His reference to Compiègne at the end of July shows that by this date at latest he has access again to the King if he wishes for it. But, for the sake of a few brief meetings he is disinclined to make the effort; he will reserve himself for the visit of the Court to Fontainebleau in October.

2

Racine did not go to Fontainebleau. A more serious illness in the autumn left him much weakened and with a recurring pain in his right side. The journey to Melun in

November for Nanette's taking of the veil tired him greatly, and he rested uneasily at home, nominally convalescent but growing more and more conscious of what he had come to call the tumour in his side. Jean-Baptiste, for whom the friendly Ambassador had arranged a special mission to Versailles, remained at home or at Court and was not pressed to return to the Hague.

On the 30th January 1699, Racine wrote to him:

"I went for a walk this afternoon in the Tuileries with your mother, thinking that the air would do me good. But I had hardly been there half an hour when I was seized by an unbearable pain in my back, which obliged me to return home. I can see that I shall have to be patient about this and wait until the weather is warmer."

It was the last letter that Racine has left. Towards the beginning of March, going into his study to drink tea, as was his custom in the morning, he had a sudden realization that he was desperately ill and knew that this time there would be no reprieve. He went down to his bedroom where Louis and Madelon were playing. "I remember", writes Louis, "that he said to us, so as not to frighten us, 'My children, I think I have a slight fever, but it is nothing. I am going to bed for a little while'."

Weeks of suffering were still to be faced, but he, who had always shrunk from pain, bore it with wonderful fortitude and accepted his moments of agony as an expiation for his past sins. He had put his affairs in order and had done what he could to make his peace with God; in a codicil which he had added to his will in October he had requested that his body should be laid at Port-Royal at the foot of Hamon. A priest of his old parish, whom he had taken as his confessor, was at hand to give him spiritual consolation. The Court doctors came to visit the man whom they had come to regard with such affection. To Dodart, who had also been the physician of the *solitaires*, he entrusted in his last days his *Abrégé de l'histoire de Port-Royal*.

Other friends were round him, as well as his family. Boileau, ailing himself, deserted his beloved Auteuil in order to be at his bedside. Valincour, the Abbé Renaudot, Elizabeth Hamilton, and the Jansenist Willard were constantly in the sickroom.

The news that Racine was dying brought anxious inquiries from Versailles. The King sent to ask news of him. In person or by messenger the great lords expressed their sympathy and their concern. Liselotte, Duchess of Orleans, wrote to her friend the Electress of Hanover:

"A man is passing from life to death, whose loss will be felt deeply indeed. It is Racine, the one who wrote such great comedies. He is dying of an ulcer."

The physicians, convinced at last that their remedies were not proving effective, decided to resort to surgery. An incision was made in the patient's side in order to drain the abscess on the liver—for such was the final diagnosis of his complaint. There was a temporary improvement, but it was deceptive. During the next month Racine grew steadily weaker. He died in the early morning of 21st April 1699.

Port-Royal buried him at the head of Hamon's grave since there was no space at the foot. The obituary which they wrote was no doubt the one which in his last days he would have wished for:

"On this day there died in Paris Jean Racine, Treasurer of France, Secretary of the King, and Gentleman-in-Ordinary of his Bedchamber. He had been brought up in this Monastery with other persons who were pursuing their studies here and, having been obliged to depart from hence, he followed for some time the ways of the world. But God at last showed him His grace by renewing in his spirit the light of truth which had been darkened there and by awakening the sentiment of piety in his heart. He had much affection for this Monastery; and he has given us testimony of his zeal, using his influence to protect us. His body has been brought here and buried in the outer cemetery as he directed. He left us eight hundred *livres* in his will."

But Port-Royal saw with a single eye and Racine, who

had followed the ways of the world, deserved also to reap the world's praises. In the *Gazette*, his friend Renaudot recorded his death in different terms:

"The Sieur Jean Racine, Secretary of the King, Gentleman-in-Ordinary of the Household of His Majesty, one of the Forty of the French Academy, died in this town on the twenty-first of this month, aged fifty-nine. He was as commendable for his piety as for his wit, his learning and his marvellous talent, which will transmit his works and his name to posterity, as one of the rarest spirits of this age."

CHAPTER XXII

THE ORIGINALITY OF RACINE

HOW great was Racine? What was his achievement as an artist? The temptation which lies across every assessment of his work is to consider him primarily as a poet and to base his preeminence on that aspect of his talent alone. That Racine was a great poet is now hardly disputed; that he was a great poet because of, rather than in spite of, his limitations, is widely recognized; that he was of necessity a unique poet is less often pointed out.

There are no disciples of Racine, no competent minor poets writing pleasantly in the Racinian vein. His imitators, who supplied a large proportion of the French tragedies of the eighteenth century, are without exception flat and artificial. Between the master's success and their failure the contrast is complete: it is all or nothing. In the same way, Racine has proved untranslatable. He comes limping into English in so pitiable a plight that it is kinder not to recognize him. Yet men of some discernment have attempted the task because, it must be supposed, they admired the qualities of the original and wanted to display them to their compatriots. One and all—from Philips and Thomas Brereton to R. B. Boswell and Lacy Lockert—have failed to produce a rendering which evokes the poetry of Racine or * which has much independent merit as English verse. While the task of translation has been competently performed for such far more 'difficult' authors as Villon, Rabelais, Rimbaud, and Mallarmé, the English student must accept the fact that Racine can only be read satisfactorily in French, and that even then the full flavour of his verse will not become apparent for a considerable time.

Approached from one angle, the verse of the plays is jargon raised to the level of great poetry. The conventional figures of speech which disconcert some English readers were hardly intended to be other than conventional, though they were a little fresher when Racine used them than they have become since. Racine was in any case forced to use them by his close-packed method of construction. Since he never stops to contemplate the subject, but is continually moving on to a new facet of character and of situation, his language must be clear enough to register immediately on the audience. There is no time for repetition or for gradually expanding circles of meaning. A point missed has gone for ever, inevitably with some detraction from the total effect.

Now a poet who aims at the same time at speed and clarity, and who wishes to remain in full control of his material because he knows better than anyone else what its value is, will resort of necessity to the cliché: it is the most effective device that exists for immediately meeting the hearer's understanding. The familiar metaphor evokes from him a response a little keener than the plain unimaged word, but does not distract him with the more beguiling associations suggested by original imagery. In this Racine is the considerate author, seeking to make things easy for his audience. He has too much regard for their breeding to bludgeon them with rhetoric, too little respect for their imaginations to tempt them into dreaming their own dreams. He communicates with them in a kind of shorthand. Those familiar with it can read it at sight, without making a transcription. They accept it for its convenience, as they accept other more technical jargons for the sake of rapid intelligibility. They do not examine the literal sense of such lines as:

> Je prétends qu'à mon tour l'inhumaine me craigne,
> Et que ses yeux cruels, à pleurer condamnés,
> Me rendent tous les noms que je leur ai donnés.

A reader less familiar with Racine's language may at first have to transcribe some of his abbreviations, but he can perform the operation quickly and will never hesitate between two possible meanings. When, as happens more frequently in the later plays, Racine uses an image a little out of the conventional, the effect is memorable by contrast. But on the whole he did not seek such effects and used them very sparingly.

In shunning the striking metaphor, it may well be that Racine was reflecting not only the prejudice of his century but also a certain mistrust of his own taste. The border-line between the bold and convincing image and the absurd and extravagant one is exceedingly elusive. It tends to alter with the period and point of view of the reader. When Phèdre, recalling how she has sacrificed animals on the altar of Venus in a vain effort to placate the goddess, says:

Je cherchais dans leurs flancs ma raison égarée,

this breath-taking metaphor seems to us entirely successful. Yet it is very near a conceit, and to some readers might appear no less manufactured than Théramène's much-criticized line describing the arrival of the sea-monster on the shore:

Le flot qui l'apporta recule épouvanté.

There is no doubt that, by his cautious use of imagery, Racine minimized both the immediate risk of appearing extravagant and the long-term risk of being read for his quaintness—an accidental quality which, more than most critics will admit, enters into the modern appreciation of seventeenth-century poetry.

To those who are accustomed to look upon imagery as the heart of poetry, Racine's verse may thus seem to lack an essential element. But before we examine the compensating qualities which it possesses, it is worth considering the value of this plainness, or rather leanness, as a poetic virtue in itself. The demonstration is easy if Racine is compared to some of his compatriots, as has been done in a remarkable essay by Giraudoux. He contrasts Racine with such inflated poets as Hardy, Rotrou, Corneille, and points to the gain in vigour and in truth which Racine achieves by his skin-tight language.

"[In Racine's plays] the hero is never being prompted in his words by the author. There is never that impression of sublime ventriloquism which before him and since him we are continually given by all the French tragic dramatists. When images or metaphors occur, their effect is prodigious, for they are not the poetic deposits of an inspired mind, but the very words of the hero—the gleam, the sudden flash, the crackling produced when the Fable rubs its divine skin against our atmosphere. The metaphor is no longer, as with his predecessors, a flourish, a poetic challenge, a slight attack of forgetfulness of reality, or the swelling and syncope of those singing birds which hear nothing while they are singing . . . but the moment at which human language is transubstantiated, because of the acoustic elevation and the poetic tension, into the language of poetry itself."[1]

This is true enough when Racine is compared to the earlier poets of his own century and even to most of those of the sixteenth century. It holds good equally when he is compared to the Romantics, but does not give him any superiority over Baudelaire, or over the Symbolists who thought directly in original images—as does Giraudoux himself—and whose best verse succeeds in being as concise as Racine's, but much richer in evocative content. But these latter poets were not dramatists and, as far as the theatre is concerned, Giraudoux is entirely right. On the French stage, terseness and rapidity have only been achieved by discipline of style. The Shakespearian formula of packing original images so closely that they merge does not seem feasible in French dramatic literature. So Racine's un-pretentious imagery remains a supreme virtue in a drama-tist, if only a relative virtue in a poet.

[1] Jean Giraudoux: *Racine* (Paris, 1930).
Quoted by permission of MM. B. Grasset et Cie, Paris.

The main richness of his verse lies in another feature which hardly recommends it to-day: its melodious qualities. While all Racine is easy to speak, many passages are delightful, both to the tongue and to the ear. The factors which produce this 'music' are not difficult to find in the repetitions and combinations of consonants and vowel sounds which become apparent if an examination is made of any of the more famous passages, particularly in *Bérénice*, *Iphigénie*, and *Phèdre*. It is then seen that the musical design occurs not only in isolated phrases but may run through a whole speech and constitute something comparable to a passage in a movement. Such verse has overtones, as we suggested when discussing the poetry of *Phèdre*,[1] but they are less the overtones of mental association which imagery produces, than the overtones which result from a perfect merging of sense and sound. Such a line as

> *Tous les jours se levaient clairs et sereins pour eux*

is a simple statement, not attempting to be anything more than Phèdre's spontaneous reflexion at that particular moment of despair. Yet, long after it has been spoken, it haunts the imagination as strongly as Mallarmé's association-packed

> *Le vierge, le vivace et le bel aujourd'hui.*

When Racine writes

> *Ariane, ma sœur, de quel amour blessée,*
> *Vous mourûtes aux bords où vous fûtes laissée.*

he has produced something more than a sequence of echoing vowels yet nothing which resembles the intellectually contrived overtones of

> *Mon âme vers ton front où rêve, ô calme sœur,*
> *Un automne jonché de taches de rousseur*
> *Et vers le ciel errant de ton œil angélique*
> *Monte, comme dans un jardin mélancolique,*
> *Fidèle, un blanc jet d'eau soupire vers l'Azur!*

[1] See p. 233.

[328]

If we could define what it is that Racine omits and that Mallarmé spent his whole poetic career in seeking, we should then possess the secret of Racine's greater immediacy. But it eludes definition. The name of Ariadne, apart from Racine's line, is not a name to conjure with, except perhaps among a relatively small number of classical scholars. A tenuous booming of vowels would not, by itself, detain the mind for long. Yet the two brought together constitute, in Giraudoux's uncritical but entirely appropriate phrase, "le langage de la poésie même".

The music which any practised ear can detect in the Racinian line goes a long way—for his contemporaries no doubt it went the whole way—to compensate the perfunctoriness of his metaphors. But his verse is not merely melodious. The alexandrine which can give out these notes of tenderness or melancholy can also render irony, bitterness, despair, anger, or ferocity with no apparent effort in the transition. It can lend itself without incongruity to rapid, almost colloquial dialogue. In certain scenes it can be as direct as prose, and in isolated lines indistinguishable from it. The following dialogue from *Bajazet* is composed for the most part of lines which could occur unchanged in a modern French conversation:

ROXANE: *Madame, j'ai reçu des lettres de l'armée.*
De tout ce qui s'y passe êtes-vous informée?
ATALIDE: *On m'a dit que du camp un esclave est venu:*
Le reste est un secret qui ne m'est pas connu.
ROXANE: *Amurat est heureux: la fortune est changée,*
Madame, et sous ses lois Babylone est rangée.
ATALIDE: *Hé quoi, madame? Osmin . . .*
ROXANE: *Etait mal averti,*
Et depuis son départ cet esclave est parti.
C'en est fait.
ATALIDE: *Quel revers!*
ROXANE: *Pour comble de disgrâces,*
Le Sultan, qui l'envoie, est parti sur ses traces.
ATALIDE: *Quoi? les Persans armés ne l'arrêtent donc pas?*

ROXANE: *Non, madame: vers nous il revient à grands pas.*

ATALIDE: *Que je vous plains, madame! et qu'il est nécessaire*
D'achever promptement ce que vous vouliez faire!

ROXANE: *Il est tard de vouloir s'opposer au vainqueur.*

ATALIDE: *O ciel!*

ROXANE: *Le temps n'a point adouci sa rigueur.*
Vous voyez dans mes mains sa volonté suprême.

ATALIDE: *Et que vous mande-t-il?*

ROXANE: (handing her the letter) *Voyez: lisez vous-même.*

Between such a scene and one of the monumental tirades such as Oreste's last speech or Phèdre's last dialogue with Oenone (Act IV, Sc. vi) lie a great variety of tones and modulations, yet it is always the same poet using the same instrument, whose most striking characteristic when it is closely examined proves to be not harmony, but flexibility. It responds to the voice and mood as a pliant stick responds to the hands. It can be curved into various shapes and, released from a rhythmic movement, made to spring up with sudden brutality. Yet it does not cease to be the same verse, tough, whippy, consistent at the core.

Racine was the perfect executant on this instrument, but since he found the alexandrine already created, it might be said that he invented nothing but the Racinian manner of using the alexandrine. While that in itself would be a considerable achievement, it can be claimed further that he made his own instrument. Every great French poet has shaped the alexandrine anew. In the hands of some it is stiff and pompous, with some it waves and wanders in intricate sound-patterns, with others it suddenly throws out blossoms like an enchanted rod. But none of these other alexandrines would have stood the strain that Racine put on his. Corneille's would have snapped for lack of resilience, Hugo's would have exploded into technicoloured fireworks, Verlaine's have sagged for want of strength. Only Racine's could do everything that he required of it and, after the most varied exercises, remain as springy and responsive as ever.

2

Yet, whatever Racine's achievement in creating a unique variety of the alexandrine, he can hardly have thought of his verse as more than a means to an end. Except in his two first plays and, in a lesser degree, in *Britannicus*, where he is emulating the dignified sonority of Corneille, his language is always the servant of his dramatic plan. The excellence of his dramatic craftsmanship can be put to the test by making a scene-by-scene analysis of any of his great plays and at the same time plotting the emotional fluctuations of the chief characters. Or it can be tested more pleasurably, if less consciously, by going to the theatre and experiencing the steady rise in emotional tension up to the middle of Act V, the tightening of suspense up to breaking point, the swift and competent clearing away of the fragments in the last one or two scenes. This progressive growth of suspense —which is expected, though not often achieved so smooth-ly, in any modern play—is attained at the cost of a weakness which a modern dramatist would avoid. Whereas most later dramatists have preferred to open with some startling effect and to place the explanatory scenes—which they cannot avoid—later, Racine opens quietly. The whole of his first act is usually given over to the exposition. His characters are introduced and, in conversation with each other, explain their circumstances in scenes which, if not lifeless, are at least low-keyed. But, having once established his play, Racine has a clear course during the remaining four acts and need never halt or retrace his steps to give additional explanations. If the audience will be patient for the first twenty minutes they will afterwards find themselves com-pletely caught up in the ever-quickening march of emotion and plot.

In the preparation and placing of the climax in such a way that it gave the maximum effect, the pioneer work had been done by Corneille; but Racine perfected, if he did not invent, this important aspect of dramatic technique. While Corneille's experiments might have been overlooked, in

Racine the lesson is so plain that no French dramatist after him could blunder through ignorance of the objective.

Nor could he ask for a more masterly demonstration of the way in which the much-discussed rule of the three Unities should be applied. That these rules became a fetish, forcing other writers with less disciplined talents to use a mould which cramped them, was not Racine's fault. He never preached their infallibility. "The first rule is to please," he wrote in one of his few printed references to them. "All the others are but means to that end." But it happened that the guiding principles of One Plot, One Place, One Day, accorded perfectly with his conception of play-construction. He could follow them without violation of probability—without, in short, it being apparent to the audience that any rules were being observed. Modern productions of Racine usually give variety to the single décor by changes of lighting, or by altering the position of the background curtains from act to act. Such devices, if not exaggerated, usefully mark the passage of time or a change in the dramatic atmosphere. But they are only embellishments to a play which is complete and intelligible without them.

To watch a Racinian tragedy with the attention fixed on its construction is to experience a pleasure comparable to watching a game of chess played by a master. But those wonderful sequences of correct moves which constitute *Andromaque*, *Bajazet*, or *Phèdre*, perhaps amount to virtuosity rather than art? If challenged on the point, most lovers of Racine will reply that the name does not matter; if further pressed, that they find virtuosity the more fascinating.

3

This, then, is the Racine whom generations of Frenchmen and a smaller number of Englishmen have grown to appreciate and love: a skilled constructor of smoothly-functioning tragedies and a supremely intelligent maker of supple, nervous verse. In no other writer are the same virtues found so highly developed and so perfectly co-ordinated, and the true Racinophil, being fully satisfied by them, is disinclined to look for anything beyond. But if this were all, Racine would hardly be more than a highly accomplished secondary author. Limited by his perfection, he would rank a long way below the Greeks, or Shake-speare, or Goethe. To praise him only for his technical excellence is to misrepresent his genius and to ignore his true significance in the evolution of French literature. Without Racine, neither it nor that large part of European literature which has been affected by it would have followed the same course.

The greatest of Racine's innovations was to regard the passion of love as a disease and to write of it in that light. His attitude is that of a physician observing the course of an illness, noting—with understanding certainly, but with detachment—the symptoms of the patient, the alternations of calm and crisis, the deceptive improvement followed by the relapse, the sick fancies, all the vicissitudes which the victims of Eros must endure. Though he knows that the patient will die, his attitude is impeccably professional. His interest is nowhere morbid, nor—in a different order of ideas—is it ever prurient. He is a trained observer and not a Peeping Tom. His attention is fixed, not on the person, but on the symptoms.

In minds of inferior quality, this same approach has degenerated in two ways. The insufficiently detached observer grows excited, identifying the illness with himself, allowing sympathy and irrelevant curiosity to contaminate his objectivity. From this source have come innumerable works of vulgarization on the subject of love, chiefly by ill-equipped novelists. Second-rate French literature and its foreign derivatives too often assume this pseudo-scientific guise, concealing beneath an appearance of profundity their lack of accurate observation and of co-ordinated thought.

The opposite development is in the direction of over-dryness. Here the writer's imagination is deficient, not his faculties of observation. He sheds even the appearance of sympathy and, being genuinely interested neither in the patient nor in the course of the disease, attaches a disproportionate significance to isolated symptoms. This meticulous cynicism is the second typical vice of indifferent French writers. It was what the generation of 1820 detested in their neo-classics. It was the horror which Marie Bashkirtseff felt when she remarked that "un Français m'a toujours l'air de disséquer les choses avec un long instrument qu'il tient délicatement entre ses doigts, un lorgnon sur le nez".

But the great French writers have followed Racine worthily in their intense and competent studies of the disease. The Abbé Prévost, Stendhal, Balzac—paying lip-service to his period by exalting the person, but in reality fascinated by the thing—Baudelaire (making experiments on himself), Proust, Mauriac, and many humbler yet sincere practitioners have gone on from the point at which Racine began with such skill and conviction that it is sometimes startling to recall that love can be written about in any other way. But it may, of course, be treated even in French literature as a quest, a pursuit, a struggle, an ordeal, an impediment, and even a sin. In European and American literature as a whole, these are commoner than the physician's approach. Before Racine, experiments were made with all of them in France. After him, his method predominated and proved so compatible with the native genius that it might be said that he simply found the thing that was waiting to be discovered.

His title to be the first can hardly be disputed. If Madame de La Fayette hit upon it at approximately the same time, her treatment was too tenuous and experimental to mark an epoch. No doubt Racine was led to his discovery, as she was, by the pastoral novels and their ancestors in Italian literature. But there the malady was of a benign and agreeable type, of little more gravity than an attack of the vapours when compared to the plague which rages through
* Racine's tragedies. To diagnose it as a mortal sickness, he

first had to learn seriousness from the Greeks. They taught him, as his Italianate models could not, that to be alive and subject to the passions of humanity was no frivolous matter. Beyond that, they did not instruct him, but left him to make the application for himself and for his century. There, Port-Royal stepped in and, by implanting in him a habit of mind according to which the passion of love was considered as an abnormality (*égarement*), almost completed his formation. The last stage was accomplished by his own idiosyncracy which led him, not to shun the abnormal, as Port-Royal had intended, but to contemplate it with a fascinated attention.

It has often been observed that Racine's characters are monsters. They stand out in shocking contrast to the orderly lines of his play-construction and his verse. The regularity of these performs the necessary function of framing their horror, on the same principle by which a single shot in a drawing-room shocks more than a shell on a battle-field. But they are monsters of a particular kind— of the terrible kind into which any man or woman can be converted in an hour by a small grain of dust on the brain, by accidentally touching a leper. Their sickness has suddenly become their world and their sole awareness is of their own suffering and of the means by which they hope to relieve it. Their case is too desperate for them to be able to consider the welfare of any other person, not excluding the object of their desire. Indeed, desire is too weak a word for Hermione's thirst for Pyrrhus, or Phèdre's for Hippolyte.

So far, this is realistic. The sufferer isolated in his agony fills hospitals and psychiatrists' consulting-rooms. But nature nearly always provides an anaesthetic. The living patient becomes partly insensible to his suffering. His lucidity becomes blurred.

The dramatist cannot copy this. Unlike the novelist, he must allow his characters to make their own analysis, and is therefore forced to combine in one fictitious person both the victim and the observer of the disease. The unblunted sensitivity of the Racinian character, his clarity of vision in the midst of what would otherwise be blind passion, is the second of Racine's innovations, and has been hardly less full of consequences than the first, from which it necessarily derives.

Here, however, there had been strong precedents. Not only the pastoral novels and the cult of self-analysis which reigned in *précieuse* literature and conversation, but the tragic stage itself had used—had been obliged to use—the character who comments on his own grief. Racine's achievement was to weave the analysis into the action so closely that the two became one, and in order to do this he developed a type of character new to French literature—a *persona* living by its emotions yet at the same time sensitively intelligent. Such characters—more remote from reality than any Cornelian giantess or Shakespearian virgin—he presents with so masterly an illusion of life that they have become an essential factor in West European literature, which to-day would be crippled without them.

Racine's finest emotional machines are female. It was partly a concession to his period, partly a result of his artistic integrity. As a man, he was psychologically incapable of violating verisimilitude to the extent of presenting this elaborately idealized personage under the appearance of his own sex. Yet, considered objectively and apart from the immediate requirements of the theatre, the machine might equally well have been male. That it was not is the reason why a modern American critic can write of Hermione—and be typical in doing so: "She is one quivering compound of intense emotions, veering impulses, unreason and vicious spite—*utterly feminine and eternally real.*" (Italics ours.)

While it is clear that outside literature these qualities occur with equal frequency in men—except insofar as conduct may be patterned on reading—the compliment is so great and the interest of the feminine psyche so intensified by such attributions that the adoption of Racine's invention was inevitable. A West European of to-day, unless deeply read in pre-Racinian literature, accepts it without question and, if he is a writer or an artist, continues to propagate it.

The Greek houselady, the medieval Griselda, the Elizabethan consort-and-equal, the ever-recurrent doxy, all have a pallid appeal beside Racine's vibrant creation. Into her can go the keenest emotions, the subtlest perceptions, the most carnal longings ever possessed or divined by a highly-civilized man. Embodied in the form of a seductive woman, spirit and flesh seem to meet in a perfect synthesis such as only an artist of genius could have achieved.

If there had been no Racine, the formula would no doubt have been found by another, for it corresponded to an insistent need of the post-Renaissance age. But who that other would have been it is not easy to see. The conception which might have been laboriously built up by several hands, bungling here, exaggerating there, was defined with certainty and completeness by Racine in a creative period of some thirteen years.

A final word on Racine the man. Some have been struck by an incompatibility between the *Racine embourgeoisé* of his later years and the brilliantly original artist of his prime. Yet this was clearly the same man, turning at a critical moment of his life from a major to a secondary field of action. The decision, it is possible to say now, was mistaken. But it was inevitable that Racine should make it. A fatal respect for opportunities impelled him to seize this one.

But the artist was never entirely extinguished in him. *Esther* and *Athalie*, his malicious epigrams, his pungent comments on his old enemies, were all proofs that the spark was still alight. And was there not an irreducible element of pride in the self-condemnation with which he finally came to speak of his tragedies? It was no mean sin that he had committed in presuming to construct a new world and to design a new variant of humanity.

[337]

APPENDIX

LA VOISIN'S TESTIMONY

GIVEN before the Chambre Ardente on 21st November 1679. This transcription from the Archives de la Bastille in the Bibliothèque de l'Arsenal (MS. 10, 356 verso and 357 recto) is exact except that we have modernized the punctuation and spelling. Thus, *Racine* is spelt *Rassyne* and *Rassine* in the original.

Qui lui avait donné la connaissance de la Du Parc, comédienne?

A dit qu'elle l'a connue il y a quatorze ans, étaient très bonnes amies ensemble, et qu'elle a su toutes ses affaires pendant ce temps, qu'elle avait eu intention de nous déclarer, il y a déjà du temps, que la Du Parc devait avoir été empoisonnée, et que l'on en a soupçonné Jean Racine, que le bruit en a été assez grand, ce qu'elle, respondante, a d'autant plus lieu de présumer que ce Racine a toujours empêché qu'elle, respondante, qui était la bonne amie de la Du Parc, ne l'ait vue pendant tout le cours de la maladie dont elle est décédée, quoique la Du Parc la demandât toujours, mais quoiqu'elle, respondante, allât chez la Du Parc pour la voir, on ne l'a jamais voulu laisser entrer, et ce par l'ordre dudit Racine, ce qu'elle, respondante, a su par la belle-mère de la Du Parc, appelée la Demoiselle de Gorle, et par les filles de la Du Parc, qui sont à l'Hôtel de Soissons, lesquelles lui ont marqué que ce Racine était cause de leur malheur.

S'il n'a jamais été fait de proposition à elle, respondante, pour se défaire de ladite Du Parc par poison ?

A dit que l'on y aurait été bien mal reçu.

Si elle ne sait pas que l'on s'est adressé pour cela à la Demoiselle de La Grange ?

A dit qu'elle ne sait point cela.

Si elle ne connaît pas un comédien boîteux ?

A dit que oui, et que c'est le nommé Béjart, qu'elle n'a vu que deux fois.

Si ledit Béjart n'avait pas quelque mauvaise volonté contre la Du Parc ?

A dit que non, et que ce qu'elle a su touchant ledit Racine a été premièrement par ladite Demoiselle de Gorle.

Ce que la de Gorle lui a dit, et interpellée de nous le déclarer précisément ?

A dit que la de Gorle lui dit que ce Racine, ayant épousé secrètement la Du Parc, il était jaloux de tout le monde et particulièrement d'elle, respondante, dont il avait beaucoup d'ombrage, et qu'il s'en était défait par poison et à cause de son extrême jalousie, et pendant la maladie de la Du Parc ce Racine ne partait point du chevet du lit de la Du Parc, à laquelle il tira de son doigt un diamant de prix, et avait aussi détourné les bijoux et principaux effets de la Du Parc, qui en avait pour beaucoup d'argent, que même on n'avait pas voulu la laisser parler à la nommée Nanon, sa femme de çhambre, qui est sage-femme, quoiqu'elle demandât la Nanon et qu'elle lui fît écrire pour venir à Paris la voir, aussi bien qu'elle, respondante.

Si la de Gorle ne lui a point dit de quelle manière l'empoisonnement avait été fait, et de qui l'on s'était servi pour cela ?

Non. .

NOTES

p.4   This paragraph now requires modification. An article published almost simultaneously with the original edition of this book (J. Orcibal, *L'Enfance de Racine* in *Rev. d'Hist. Litt. de la France*, Jan-March 1951) virtually proved that Racine's grandmother did take him with her to Port-Royal in 1649-50. He was thus a pupil of the *solitaires* from the age of about ten, not fifteen, and his revolt, when it came, was all the more striking (see Chap. 6 below). His stay at the Collège de Beauvais was an interlude, probably lasting two years (October 1653-55) and due to a partial dispersal of the *petites écoles* then under heavy hostile pressure. He *returned* to Port-Royal in 1655. (See R. Picard, *La Carrière de Jean Racine*, pp. 25-6.)

His aunt Agnès became a postulant at Port-Royal in 1642, some three years after the arrival there of the Vitarts. In the interval she is believed to have looked after her motherless infant nephew, which would link the two of them still closer.

p.5, l.2   For 'fifteen' read 'twelve'.

l.32   For 'seventeen' read 'eleven'.

p.10   For 'arrived at' read 'returned to' and see note to p.4.

p.21, l.17   It now appears quite possible that *la déhanchée*, 'the hip-swayer', was Marquise Du Parc. See note to p.66.

l.22   For 'forties' read 'fifties'. Birthdate unknown, but probably between 1600 and 1610. She retired on a pension in 1676, "après avoir servi le théâtre pendant plus de quarante ans ou peut-être même une cinquantaine d'années," and died 6 January 1683. (See W. Deierkauf-Holsboer, *Le Théâtre de l'Hotel de Bourgogne*, I, p.149 and II, p.158.)

p.50 For '1643' read '1647'. Mme Deierkauf-Holsboer argues convincingly that Floridor was forced to change by royal order (See *Le Théâtre du Marais*, I.)

p.63 See, however, the note to p.66 below.

p.66 This version has been rehabilitated in recent years. It is supported by a new interpretation of Racine's remark in a letter to Le Vasseur ("On promet depuis hier *La Thébaïde* à l'Hotel, mais ils ne la promettent qu'après trois autres pièces"), according to which Racine was referring here to a *Thébaïde* by Boyer. Racine would be working on a play of the same name commissioned initially by Molière to compete with the rival theatre. When the Hôtel postponed Boyer's play, Molière did the same with Racine's. The main weakness of this theory is the absence of any definite trace of such a play by Boyer.

In a previous letter Racine says that his "young princess" (the Antigone of *La Thébaïde*) is to be played by "la déhanchée". "Vous savez bien, je crois, qui est cette déhanchée" . . . Rather than the Beauchâteau it could have been Marquise Du Parc, then in Molière's company. Her mincing walk and manner are mentioned in *La Critique de l'Ecole des Femmes* (Sc. 2) and *L'Impromptu de Versailles* (Sc. 4): "Prenez bien garde, vous, à vous déhancher comme il faut et à faire bien des façons." (See J. Pommier, *Aspects de Racine*, p.43.) If this were entirely conclusive it would show the early relationship of Molière and Racine in a slightly different light from that described in these pages.

p.104 On 12 May 1668 Racine stood as godparent with his mistress's daughter by her earlier marriage, Anne-Marie Du Parc, to a certain Jeanne-Thérèse Olivier. This infant has been hypothetically identified with a supposed daughter of Racine's who died at the age of eight and may have existed, though the assumption rests on hearsay retailed in the eighteenth century. (See B. Dussane, *Du nouveau sur Racine*, Divan, 1941).

p.113 More than twenty years after writing this page and the next I feel it necessary to modify some of the judge-

ments and facts they contain. It is now established that
Corneille left the Marais for the first time in 1647, trans-
ferring to the Hôtel with the actor-manager Floridor.
Rodogune was therefore produced by the Marais, as was
his next tragedy, *Théodore*. Though different from the
great Roman tragedies, *Rodogune* was a success and did
not show declining power. Corneille's later plays met
with mixed receptions from contemporaries, but were by
no means all failures. When they were, the fault was in
the age more than in the author. Out of touch, certainly,
with contemporary taste as time went on, Corneille continued to experiment boldly on his own lines and to
produce plays whose inherent merits have been undeserv-
edly neglected for too long. Readers who may be
interested are referred to the chapters on Corneille in my
French Tragic Drama in the Sixteenth and Seventeenth Centuries
(Methuen, 1973) and to the bibliography of that book.

p.136   The criticisms expressed here are also too severe.
Compared to Racine's tragedy, *Tite et Bérénice* indeed
appears an over-loaded and over-complicated play, too
dependent on melodramatic twists and surprises. The
dialogue matches the situations and is not always aimed at
'high seriousness'. But these features were typical of later
Cornelian drama, which had special qualities of its own.
Tite et Bérénice should be judged in this context.

p.144   Reproduced opposite p.132.

p.145   Since these lines were written, the importance of
the Versailles portrait has diminished. It now seems
doubtful whether its subject was in fact Racine. The
sketch reproduced opposite p.261 was apparently drawn
by Jean-Baptiste from memory some time after his
father's death.

p.162   This open defence of Racine (Boileau's famous
Epître VII) may have been written as early as February
1677. If so, it would be premature to say that the appointment of the two poets as Royal Historians had then been
settled, though it may already have been under consideration at court. (See below, pp.215-6 and R. Picard,

Carrière, pp.283-4 particularly). None of this affects our general assessment of the Racine-Boileau relationship, though it would modify one detail.

p.174 Four years later, however, he wrote a much longer preface, which took account of some of the criticisms of *Bajazet*. See p.204 below.

p.217 M. Picard (*Carrière*, p.282) has pointed out that these eminent people did not attend the wedding in person. The register was taken to their houses to be signed there.

p.228 After Euripides (and Seneca) several French dramatists used the Hippolytus-Phaedra story before Racine. There were tragedies of *Hippolyte* by Garnier (1573), La Pinelière (1635), Gilbert (1647) and Bidar (1675). Like Racine, Bidar has a young princess. Tristan l'Hermite in *La Mort de Chrispe* (1645) dramatised a similar situation drawn from Roman history. His hero is also in love with a young "princess", but she bears little resemblance to Aricie. Though these dead and half-dead plays should be recorded, they in no sense account for the creation of Racine's Phèdre and her surrounding group, even on the most superficial level.

p.250 They now appear to have been rather later, which would destroy the hypothesis linking them with the poisoning trials. Though the Montespan's eclipse began in 1680-81, she remained powerful, or apparently so, for several years and Racine seems to have performed various literary tasks for her and her family until 1683-4, though the exact dates are uncertain.

p.253 Such deductions can no longer be drawn from the Ode, which has been proved conclusively not to have been written by Racine. Louis Racine is exculpated. (See J. Vanuxem in *Rev. d'Hist. Litt.*, April-June, 1957 and Compte-rendu by J.D. in *Bulletin de Liaison Racinienne*, Uzès, 1958). It might be added that La Fontaine had paraphrased the same Psalm in his *Recueil de poésies chrétiennes et diverses* (1671).

p.269 One should perhaps add the general influence of the Senecan dream of foreboding, common in French sixteenth-century tragedy and continued in the seventeenth century by T. l'Hermite (*La Mariane*, 1636) and Corneille (*Polyeucte*, 1642). But it had disappeared from French drama several decades before *Esther* and *Athalie*.

p.277   An ingenious theory developed by J. Orcibal in *La Genèse d'Esther et d'Athalie* (1950) has proved unsustainable. According to this *Athalie* was a Jacobite play inspired by the recent overthrow of James II of England and his attempt to recover the throne with French support. Athalie would represent William of Orange, Joas, James II's son, the infant Prince of Wales, and so on. M. Orcibal's "key" to *Esther* connected the oppressed Jews with the Congregation of the *Filles de l'Enfance* at Toulouse, dissolved after Jesuit pressure in 1686. This seems equally untenable.

p.291 and footnote.   To-day (1973) the figure of £8000 should be at least doubled. Equivalent money-values are notoriously difficult to establish because of class-variations in living-standards, but the *livre* or franc would now represent £1 or more.

Last paragraph of footnote: The man of letters pension was raised to 2000 francs in 1679. Between 1680-90 the special grants, with other probable ex gratia payments, have been estimated at an annual average of 6-7000 *livres*. Meanwhile Racine's income from private investments also grew. M. Picard (*Carrière*, pp. 333-5) reasonably estimates his total average yearly income over this period at 20-25,000 *livres*. This had to cover the expenses of court representation and campaigns, plus the cost of an increasing family.

p.302   For the *Ode tirée du Psaume XVII*, see note to p.253.

p.312   This requires emendation. Nanette's entry into the Ursulines occurred the following winter (November 1698), as did Marie-Catherine's marriage (7 January 1699), leaving only Jean-baptiste's expenses of the items mentioned here to account for Racine's financial difficulties at the date in question. But these difficulties were real and seem to have been mainly connected with the post of *conseiller secrétaire*. The full tax on this was 20,000 *livres*, part of which Racine had evidently paid before borrowing from Galloys. In addition, only ten days earlier he had repaid a loan of 15,000 *livres* contracted to finance his original purchase of the post (See R. Picard, *Carrière*, p.545).

p.316   M. Picard doubts, on the grounds of this letter's unsuitability, whether Racine ever sent it to Mme de Maintenon. My own hypothesis would be that he did so after re-writing it, since he seems to have made *some* request or protest. But there are no certainties on the point.

p.324   Since this was written there have been several more nearly successful attempts to translate Racine. But the basic problem—to find an idiom which is neither pastiche nor "period", yet is still "poetic" and not too discordantly "modern"—still eludes complete solution. The most interesting experiment has been Robert Lowell's *Phaedra* (Faber, 1963), a free adaptation rather than a translation.

p.334   The conception of love as a disease—even a fatal disease—was not new, as is partly conceded in these pages. To limit the question to French literature since the sixteenth century, this idea of passionate love had become a commonplace of poetry and of such drama as the plays of Racine's contemporary Quinault. Racine's unique achievement was to rescue it from the commonplace and the cliché and endow it with tragic significance by attaching it to seriously credible characters whose malady also disastrously affected the characters around them. This in *Andromaque*, *Bajazet* and *Phèdre*, though more doubtfully in *Bérénice*, whence the reservations on the tragic depth of that play.

BIBLIOGRAPHICAL NOTE

THE following lists are selective and mainly composed of works having a direct biographical significance or dealing with the social and theatrical background of Racine's life. A few studies dealing predominantly with his work in critical or interpretive terms are listed in Section (5). Critical editions of separate plays are not listed.

I. RACINE'S WORKS.
   With related texts and documents in:
   Oeuvres, ed. P. Mesnard, 8 vols. and 2 albums (Grands Écrivains Français, Hachette, 1865-73).
   This edition contains almost everything that Racine wrote, including his correspondence. Also other relevant correspondence, Louis Racine's *Mémoires*, *pièces justificatives*, etc., etc.
   Oeuvres complètes, ed. R. Picard, 2 vols. (Pléiade, 1951-52).
   The modern successor to Mesnard (containing some material not available to him), when taken together with the information, texts and documents in:
   R. Picard, *La Carrière de Jean Racine* (Gallimard, 1956) and *Corpus Racinianum* (Les Belles Lettres, 1956) and *Suppléments* (1961, 1963, 1966).
   Also:
   Oeuvres complètes, ed. P. Clarac (Ed. du Seuil, 1962).
   Théâtre complet, ed. M. Rat (Garnier, 1960).
   For views of modern producers on staging:
   Phèdre, commented by J.-L. Barrault ('Mises en Scène', Ed. du Seuil, 1946).
   Bajazet, commented by X. de Courville (id., 1947).
   Athalie, commented by G. Le Roy (id., 1952).

II. GENERAL.

Much general information, with references to other source and background material, will be found in:

H. C. Lancaster, *A History of French Dramatic Literature in the Seventeenth Century*, 9 vols. (Johns Hopkins Press, 1929-42).

P. Mélèse, *Le Théâtre et le public à Paris sous Louis XIV* (Droz, 1934) and *Répertoire analytique des documents contemporains d'information et de critique concernant le théâtre à Paris sous Louis XIV* (Droz, 1934).

III. SOME PRIMARY SOURCES.

Significant quotations from most of these can be found in the works by Mesnard, Picard, Mélèse and Lancaster listed above. Substantial bibliographies in the first three.

Boileau-Despréaux, *Satires*, ed. C. Boudhors (Les Belles Lettres, 1934); *Épîtres, Art poétique, etc* (id., 1939); *Dialogues, Réflexions critiques, Oeuvres diverses* (id., 1942); *Lettres à Racine et à divers* (id., 1943).

(His correspondence with Racine is also in Mesnard and Picard. See Section I above).

Brossette, C., *Correspondance entre Boileau et Brossette* and *Mémoires sur Boileau-Despréaux*, ed. A. Laverdet (Techener, 1858).

Boursault, E., *Artémise et Poliante* (Guignard, 1670).

Bussy-Rabutin, R. de, *Correspondance* (1666-93), ed. Lalanne, 6 vols. (Charpentier, 1858-59); *Mémoires*, ed. Lalanne, 2 vols., (Marpon et Flammarion, 1882).

Caylus, Mme de, *Souvenirs*, ed. Lescure (Paris, n.d.).

Corneille, P., *Oeuvres complètes*, ed. C. Marty-Laveaux, 12 vols. and album (Grands Écrivains Français, Hachette, 1862-68).

Dangeau, Marquis de, *Journal*, ed. E. Soulié et al., 19 vols. (Didot, 1854-60).

Granet, F., *Recueil de dissertations sur plusieurs tragédies de Corneille et de Racine*, 2 vols. (Gissey, 1740).

(Contains much contemporary criticism).

Hébert, F., *Mémoires du curé de Versailles*, ed. G. Girard (Editions de France, 1927).

La Fayette, Mme de, *Mémoires de la Cour de France pour les années* 1688 *et* 1689, ed. E. Asse (Librairie des Bibliophiles, 1890).

La Grange, *Registre* (1659-85), ed. B.E. and G.P. Young, 2 vols. (Droz, 1947).

La Grange-Chancel, J., *Oeuvres* (Paris, 1758).

Le Mercure Galant, (years 1672-4 and 1677).

Molière, *Oeuvres*, ed. E. Despois and P. Mesnard, 13 vols. (Grands Écrivains Français, Hachette, 1873-1900).

Olivet, *Histoire de l'Académie française*, ed. Livet, 2 vols. (Didier, 1858).

Orléans, Duchess of, Princess Palatine, *Correspondance*, ed. Jaeglé, 3 vols. (Paris, 1890).

Parfaict frères, *Histoire du théâtre français*, 15 vols., (Le Mercier, 1745-49).

Pradon, J., *Nouvelles Remarques* (Jean Strik, La Haye, 1685); *Phèdre et Hippolyte* (Ribou, Paris, 1677).

Ravaisson, F., *Archives de la Bastille*, années 1678-81 (Durand, 1871).

Robinet, *Lettres en vers* in J. de Rothschild, *Les Continuateurs de Loret*, 3 vols. (Morgand et Fatout, 1881-99).

Saint-Évremond, C. de, *Oeuvres mêlées*, ed. Des Maizeaux, 5 vols. (Amsterdam, 1739); *Oeuvres*, ed. Planhol, 3 vols. (Cité des Livres, 1927).

Saint-Simon, L. de Rouvroy, duc de, *Mémoires*, ed. Boislisle, 41 vols., (Grands Écrivains Français, Hachette, 1879-1928).

Sévigné, Mme de, *Lettres*, ed. E. Gérard-Gailly, 3 vols. (Pléiade, 1953-57).

Subligny, G. P. de, *La folle querelle* (1668) and *Dissertation sur les tragédies de Phèdre et d'Hippolyte* (1677) in Granet, *Recueil* (above).

Valincour, Du Trousset de, in Olivet, *Histoire de l'Académie* (above).

Visconti, Primi, *Mémoires sur la Cour de Louis XIV* (1673-81), ed. J. Lemoine (Paris, 1908).

IV. SOME MODERN BACKGROUND STUDIES.

Literary history, theatre, social history and ideology, Port-Royal, contemporaries of Racine.

A. Adam, *Histoire de la littérature française au XVIIe siècle* (Domat, 1949-56). Vols. 4 and 5 particularly.

G. Brereton, *French Tragic Drama in The Sixteenth and Seventeenth Centuries* (Methuen, 1973).

S.W. Deierkauf-Holsboer, *Le Théâtre du Marais*, 2 vols. (Nizet, 1954-58); *Le Théâtre de l'Hotel de Bourgogne*, 2 vols. (Nizet, 1968-70).

H. Lyonnet, *Les 'premières' de Racine* (Delagrave, 1924).

E. Mas, *La Champmeslé* (Alcan, 1927).

G. Michaut, *La 'Bérénice' de Racine* (Société Française d'Imprimerie, 1907).

F. Funck-Brentano, *Le Drame des poisons* (Hachette, 1878).

Urbain and Levesque, *L'Église et le théâtre* (Grasset, 1930).

C.-A. Sainte-Beuve, *Histoire de Port-Royal*, 3 vols. (Pléiade 1961-65).

L. Cognet, *Claude Lancelot, solitaire de Port-Royal* (Flammarion, 1950).

P. Bénichou, *Morales du Grand Siècle* (Gallimard, 1948).

L. Goldmann, *Le Dieu caché* (Gallimard, 1955).

D. Mornet, *Boileau* (Boivin, 1942).

G. Couton, *Corneille* (Hatier, 1958).

R. Bray, *Molière, homme de théâtre* (Mercure de France, 1954).

E. Gros, *Philippe Quinault, sa vie, son oeuvre* (Champion, 1926).

V. SOME WORKS ON RACINE SINCE 1925.

P. Butler, *Classicisme et baroque dans l'oeuvre de Racine* (Nizet, 1959).

J. Giraudoux, *Jean Racine* (Grasset, 1930).

L. Goldmann, *Racine* (L'Arche, 1956).

R. Jasinski, *Vers le vrai Racine*, 2 vols. (A. Colin, 1958).

R.C. Knight, *Racine et la Grèce* (Boivin, 1950); Editor, *Racine, Modern Judgements* (Macmillan, 1969).

J.C. Lapp, *Aspects of Racinian Tragedy* (University of Toronto and Oxford University Press, 1955).

T. Maulnier, *Racine* (Gallimard, 1936).

F. Mauriac, *La Vie de Jean Racine* (Plon, 1928).

C. Mauron, *L'Inconscient dans l'oeuvre et la vie de Racine* (Annales de la Faculté des Lettres, Aix-en-Provence, 1957).

P. Moreau, *Racine, l'homme et l'oeuvre* (Hatier, 1952).

D. Mornet, *Jean Racine* (Aux Armes de France, 1944).

J. Pommier, *Aspects de Racine* (Nizet, 1954).

M. Turnell, *Jean Racine, Dramatist* (Hamish Hamilton, 1972).

E. Vinaver, *Racine and Poetic Tragedy* (Manchester University Press, 1955).

VI. SOME RECENT TRANSLATIONS.

J. Cairncross, *Phaedra and Other Plays* (Penguin, 1963); *Andromache and Other Plays* (Penguin, 1967).

R.C. Knight, *Phèdre* (Edinburgh University Press, 1971). Bilingual text.

Robert Lowell, *Phaedra* (Faber, 1963).

Kenneth Muir, *Five Plays* (MacGibbon and Kee, 1960).

Samuel Solomon, *Complete Plays*, 2 vols. (Random House, 1967).

INDEX

Molière, his players, 20—*see also*
Palais-Royal; popularity of, 54;
and patronage of Louis XIV,
55, 60, 61; moves to Palais-
Royal, 55; and the Comic War,
55–60; his marriage to Armande
Béjart, 58, 62; his view of
tragic acting, 58–59, 152;
acquaintance with R., 61–62;
produces *La Thébaïde*, 65–66;
produces *Alexandre*, 69, 71, 99;
later relations with R., 72–73;
supposedly rebuffed by the Du
Parc, 97; at Versailles fête,
98; befriended by Henrietta of
England, 132; and Corneille's
Tite et Bérénice, 136; his aim in
comedy, 140; supposed coterie
with R., Boileau and La
Fontaine, 166–167; and *turquerie* fashion, 170; death of,
191; mentioned, 31, 95, 98,
100, 108, 114, 130, 190
Mondory (actor), 50
Monime (in *Mithridate*), character
of, 128; compared with Aricie
(*Phèdre*), 229
Monmouth, Duke of, 185
Montespan, Marquise de, relations
with sorcerers, 146, 147n,
250; replaces La Vallière, 147;
befriends R., 147–148, 216,
250; eclipse of, 250, 255;
mentioned, 195, 218, 265n.
Montfleury (actor-manager), and
Molière's expulsion from Petit-
Bourbon, 54; his acting mim-
icked by Molière, 59–60; petition against Molière, 61–62;
produces *Alexandre*, 72; acts in
Andromaque and dies, 93, 111,
130; his type of acting, 152;
mentioned, 57, 58, 100, 117
Monvoisin, Catherine (La Voisin),
and R.'s supposed poisoning of

Du Parc, 104, 106, 246–254;
and Marquise de Montespan,
146, 250; trial and death of,
245–251; testimony of, 338–
339
Morambert, Colin de, 296
Moreau, Jean Baptiste, 302
Mort de Pompée, La (Corneille), 113
Moulins, R. appointed *Trésorier
de France* in, 190 and n.

Namur, R. at siege of, 244
Nevers, Philippe Mancini, Duc de,
and the *Phèdre* quarrel, 212–
213; mentioned, 136, 208, 246
*New Method of Learning Italian
Easily and Rapidly* (Lancelot), 6
Nicandres, Les (Boursault), 69
Nicole, Pierre, his condemnation
of playwrights, 75–76; R.'s
controversy with, 78–83; R.'s
reconciliation with, 219, 307–
308; mentioned, 6, 23
Nîmes, R. at, 32
Noailles, Anne Jules, Duc de, 258,
299, 306, 310, 313
Nymphe de la Seine, La, 18–19, 23,
31, 43

Ode on the King's Convalescence,
47, 63
Ode sur la prise de Namur (Boileau),
302, 303
Ode tirée du Psaume XVII, 253, 302
Oedipe (Corneille), 113
Oenone (in *Phèdre*), example of
"low and servile" mind, 226–
227
Oreste (in *Andromaque*), R.'s treat-
ment of, 223–224
Oreste et Pylade (La Grange-
Chancel), 285
Orléans, Philippe Duc d' (Mon-
sieur), protector of Molière,
54; suspected in death of